Illegitimate power

In Renaissance drama, the bastard is an extraordinarily powerful and disruptive figure. We have only to think of Caliban or of Edmund to realise the challenge presented by the illegitimate child.

Drawing on a wide range of play texts, Alison Findlay shows how illegitimacy encoded and threatened to deconstruct some of the basic tenets of patriarchal rule. She considers bastards as indicators and instigators of crisis in early modern England, reading them in relation to witchcraft, spiritual insecurities and social unrest in family and State.

The characters discussed range from demi-devils, unnatural villains and clowns to outstandingly heroic or virtuous types who challenge officially sanctioned ideas of illegitimacy. The final chapter of the book considers bastards in performance; their relationship with theatre spaces and audiences. Illegitimate voices, Findlay argues, can bring about the death of the author/father and open the text as a piece of theatre, challenging accepted notions of authority.

Alison Findlay is Lecturer in English at Bretton Hall College, University of Leeds.

For David

Illegitimate power
BASTARDS IN RENAISSANCE DRAMA

Alison Findlay

Manchester University Press
Manchester and New York

Published by Manchester University Press
Oxford Road, Manchester M13 9NR, UK
and Room 400, 175 Fifth Avenue, New York, NY 10010, USA
www.manchesteruniversitypress.co.uk

Distributed exclusively in the USA by
Palgrave, 175 Fifth Avenue, New York NY 10010, USA

Distributed exclusively in Canada by
UBC Press, University of British Columbia, 2029 West Mall,
Vancouver, BC, Canada V6T 1Z2

British Library Cataloguing-in-Publication Data
A catalogue record for this book is available from the British Library

Library of Congress Cataloging-in-Publication Data
A catalog record for this book is available from the Library of Congress

ISBN 13: 978 0 7190 8085 2

First published in hardback 1994 by Manchester University Press
This paperback edition first published 2009

Printed by Lightning Source

Contents

Preface and acknowledgements

At the end of his first soliloquy in *King Lear*, Edmund asks the gods to 'stand up for bastards'. This book cannot claim to have god-like insight but it does try to respond to Edmund's appeal. It aims to read bastardy from a positive perspective as a subversive presence in Renaissance drama. Standing up for bastards does not mean denying the villainy of characters like Edmund. Instead, it focuses on their power to challenge the dominant patriarchal culture. My work on the topic has grown alongside my interest in feminist approaches to literature and has led me to research a fascinating number of plays, some at the heart of the Renaissance canon and others, like the bastards, marginalised. For convenience, all references to plays by Shakespeare are to *The Riverside Shakespeare*, edited by G. Blakemore Evans. In the case of *King Lear*, I accept the theory that F1 represents a version of the play in revised form and I have pointed out where lines quoted from the conflated text (as it appears in this edition) are unique to quarto or folio versions of the play. For other plays, I have tried to use an easily available 'modern' edition where possible or I have quoted from original printed texts. References therefore range from act, scene and line divisions (5.1.54) to page numbers (57), line numbers (2,995) and page signatures (K2v). Spellings and punctuation are reproduced from the editions used. In each chapter, I have referred to a play's authorship on the first occasion it is mentioned. For the reader's convenience, a list of plays with bastard characters, giving details of authorship and date (so far as it can be established), is included as an appendix. The dating of these plays is necessarily speculative in many cases; it is based on the third edition of Alfred Harbage's *Annals of English Drama 975–1700*, revised by Samuel Schoenbaum and Sylvia Wagonheim, London, Routledge, 1989.

I owe thanks to many people for helping my ideas on bastardy to grow and prosper. My interest developed as part of my postgraduate research and I thank Robert Smallwood for his help in the early stages of the project. I also thank my parents for supporting me during my studies. While I have been writing the book, my Head of Department, Linden Peach, has given me considerable encouragement, for which I am grateful. I am endebted to Bretton Hall College for granting me four weeks' study leave in spring 1993 which helped me to complete the manuscript. I would like to express my thanks to Inga-Stina Ewbank for the encouragement she has given me and for reading a draft of Chapter 3 of the text. Martin Butler, Michael Hattaway, Stanley Wells and Gweno Williams very kindly read early versions of the other chapters. I am grateful to them for their comments and suggestions which have helped me to make alterations to improve the book. Its remaining errors, ommissions and other things of darkness, I acknowledge mine. Finally, and most of all, I thank my husband David, whose help has been invaluable. His love has sustained me through the whole endeavour.

'A great kindred in the kingdome': illegitimacy in Renaissance England

In Shakesepeare's Troilus and Cressida (1602), Margarelon introduces himself as 'a bastard son of Priam's' (5.7.15). Not to be outdone, Thersites proclaims his illegitimacy as a form of self-definition: 'I am bastard begot, bastard instructed, bastard in mind, bastard in valour, in every thing illegitimate' (5.7.16). His words indicate the negative status of the bastard in Renaissance culture: without a name or a place in the social structure, outside its values and norms, deviant. Illicit conception leads to illegitimate education, consciousness, actions, to an alternative life 'in every thing illegitimate'. Bastardy makes Thersites a personification of a distinct 'other', an existence which is governed by other values, codes of behaviour, activities.

The image of the bastard as outsider is typical. This is hardly surprising in a society organised round paternal authority. The family structure was a fundamental basis for political and social order in Renaissance England. The kingdom was ruled by a series of father figures and analogies between family and State drew attention to the interrelationship of domestic and national politics. The family was a 'little common-wealth' where father ruled over wife and children (Gouge 1622: 18). The Church fathers and lords held paternal control in the community and were commanded by the prince, 'a naturall Father to all his Lieges' as James I observed in *The Trew Law of Free Monarchies* (1598). James explained that the monarch was bound by 'his fatherly duty' to rule his nation like a family and 'to care for the nourishing, education, and vertuous government of his children' (James I 1918: 55). The supreme authority of the Heavenly Father formed the pattern and justification for this patriarchal model on earth. In *Bethel; or a forme for families* (1633),

Matthew Griffith describes the king and his civil authorities as
'our Fathers but as they represent unto us the image of God's
paternity' (45).

To validate its constitution from an earthly perspective,
Renaissance hegemony cultivated an interest in genealogy,
explaining historical and social processes in relation to a male
ancestoral line. Inheritance of property, civil office, membership
of trade and professional guilds, all conventionally followed this
pattern where the transfer of power was justified with reference
to a line of masculine forebears which stretched back into the
mists of time. Elizabeth I's claim to the thone as a Tudor
monarch via her grandfather, Henry VII, depended on the
same genealogical propaganda. Tudor historians produced
myths of ancient descent from legendary figures like King
Arthur in order to validate the Tudor dynasty's claim to the
English throne (Rackin 1990: 158–9).

The presence of illegitimacy deconstructs a social and political
structure based on paternal authority. It threatened to undermine the genealogical myths on which Renaissance power relied.
King Arthur, the founding father of the Tudor family tree, was
of dubious paternity and was cited as illegitimate in many
Renaissance texts. Henry VII's claim to the throne was through
his mother and the illegitimate Beaufort line, and was therefore
tenuous at best. Queen Elizabeth had been declared a bastard by
the 1536 Succession Act and was still technically illegitimate
when she ascended the throne. Catholic supporters even suggested that she was the child of one of Anne Boleyn's lovers and
not the King's daughter at all (Ridley 1987: 25). Elizabeth's
bastardy was an open secret; to mention it was to challenge
her authority and was therefore treasonable. In 1576, Mary
Cleere of Ingatestone in Essex was burned at the stake for
saying that Elizabeth was 'baseborn and not born to the
crown, but that another lady was the right inheritor' (Sharpe
1987: 108). Even when Elizabeth and the Tudor line died, the
spectre of illegitimacy remained. It was rumoured that James I
was the bastard of his mother's secretary, Rizzio, rather than the
son of Darnley, Mary Queen of Scots's husband (Willson 1959:
50).

Beyond the realms of earthly power, illegitimacy could even

threaten the supreme authority of heaven. Marlowe's attack on religion as a power created only 'to keepe man in awe' included the declaration 'Christ was a bastard and his mother dishonest' according to the Baines note (Kocher 1962: 28). This view was not unique to Marlowe (or Baines). Sir George Buck (1614: 18v) and Thomas Milles both cite Christ in their defences of illegitimacy; Milles refers to Matthew's Gospel to show that Christ was willing to acknowledge bastardy 'in the ranke of his holie Genealogie' (Milles 1613: 725). The Puritan divine William Ames (1576–1633) considers Christ's identity as the son of God in his book *The Substance of Christian Religion*, and emphasises that 'the perfections onely of the analogie are to be understood to agree; and all the imperfections and defects are to be removed in our thoughts' (Ames 1659: 91). The idea of Christ's corporal body, leading to thoughts of a corporal conception and illegitimate identity, is too dangerous to consider as the substance of Christian religion. The view of Christ as a bastard deconstructs from the top the whole Renaissance edifice of power based on a divinely inspired paternal pattern.

The bastard, with no father, represented something 'other', something outside this divinely ordered pattern. Born of a female sexuality unsanctioned by patriarchal authority, its birth created an extraneous social unit – a family which was not one since it had no paternal governor to nourish and educate the child according to social norms. Thersites is 'bastard instructed'. The 'non-family' created and headed by a woman was outside fatherly authority and cut off, ultimately, from God. Thersites, who is 'bastard in mind' prays only to the 'devil Envy' (2.3.21). As the Poor Law of 1576 remarked, the bastard was 'An Offence against Gods Lawe and Mans Lawe' (Pinchbeck and Hewitt 1969: 206). Contemporary colloquial expressions for bastard birth, 'to come in at the window', 'at the wicket' or 'at the hatch', describe the bastard's irregular entry into society.

Because domestic and political authority were mutually dependent, an illegitimate birth was not simply a private matter. The absence of a father in the little commonwealth of the family was an implicit challenge to Renaissance authority, to gender and class distinctions. The bastard is 'an element which does not fit into the social order, having no clear identity, no

name' and as such it 'presents a threat to the hermetic household
for it is a free-floating agent held in check by no clear anterior
model of paternal authority' (Docherty 1987: 110). Bastardy
drew attention to the artifical nature of order in Renaissance
England by confronting society with another world of 'every
thing illegitimate'. The existing hierarchy was suddenly not as
natural as those who promoted it suggested. A gap opened up
between the ideal and the real, between what was sanctioned and
what was possible. Fletcher and Stevenson (1985) have pointed
out that while Renaissance society was not fundamentally
unstable it became increasingly aware of the fragility of the
means of control, aware that 'neither patriarchalism nor the
ideology of the rule of law rested in the end on anything more
than persuasion and propaganda' (38).

Concern with illegitimacy in Renaissance England represents
an important element of people's increased sense of insecurity.
When a St Paul's Cross preacher claimed that, without the
punishment of sexual incontince by the authorities, over half
the children in a parish would be bastards, he was giving voice
to a common phobia (Ingram 1987: 371). The high proportion
of bastardy cases in parish registers and court presentments
indicates that this phobia was not altogether unfounded. Civic
and clerical records suggest a growing interest in bastardy as a
cultural phenomenon and a rise in the illegitimacy rate itself,
peaking at the the turn of the century and falling again only in
the 1620s. Peter Laslett's findings on the national illegitimacy
ratio (Laslett *et al.* 1980: 1–64) are supported by Martin Ingram's
later work on parish records from Wiltshire. He identifies population size and density and the scale of local poverty as the most
important reasons for the increase of illegitimate births (Ingram
1987: 275).

The actual incidence of bastardy seems to have been a
symptom of economic problems in the late sixteenth and early
seventeenth centuries. The writers of the Norwich Census certainly perceived it as a crime related to poverty and complained
that 'when their bellies were filled' the poor 'fell to lust and
concupiscence . . . and brought forth bastardes in such quantitie
that it passed belief' (Hudson and Tingey 1910: 344). Levine and
Wrightson (1980) argue that the bastardy peak was the result of

changing social habits resulting from the economic circumstances which followed the bad harvests of the years 1594–98. Margaret Spufford (1985) has shown that there was a strong link between poverty, the inability to raise marriage portions, and bastardy prosecutions. Illegitimacy is therefore intimately connected to social problems resulting from the economic base, something which will be more fully investigated in Chapter 3.

Coinciding with the increased concern over bastardy in socio-historical documents is an interest in illegitimacy in the drama. The subject features in nearly a hundred extant plays of the period which fall into two main categories: plays with bastard characters (or characters who believe they are illegitimate) and texts dramatising situations where characters are pregnant with or give birth to illegitimate children. Some plays, such as Middleton's *Women Beware Women* (1621), cover both areas (Scragg 1964). My examination of illegitimacy as a phenomenon related to notions of crisis and subversion will look primarily at the presentation of bastard characters. Since the plays are all written by men, the 'women' and the 'bastards' are all apparently male-constructed (even more literally so in the case of women presented on the stage). Over ninety per cent of bastards in the plays are male – probably because legal illegitimacy affected one's rights to inheritance, succession and the exercise of authority, advantages usually enjoyed by men. Under patriarchal law, women were normally excluded from the inheritance of estate, position or power so bastardy merely reinforced their already marginal status. For men it had a much more radical effect. It is therefore not surprising that dramatists thought of it primarily as a male condition; in discussing the type generally, I shall use the masculine form.

While recognising a distinction between the depiction of illegitimacy in these fictional dramas and in other Renaissance literature such as parish records and pamphlets, I wish to show that they can be usefully examined concurrently. I don't want to imply that the plays reflect 'factual' history since each type of writing is constructed by historically conditioned subjects and each is active in the production of Renaissance ideas about bastardy. My selection and reading of the material is subject to my own socio-historical identity of course and so cannot hope to

recreate a 'factual' view of illegitimacy in Renaissance England –
and the range of contradictory ideas suggests that no single view
existed anyway. I am not attempting a fully interdisciplinary
analysis in this book but I believe that, by seeing these writings
as subject to the intertextual influences of one another, the
production of illegitimacy as a cultural phenomenon can be
studied. My exploration abandons a strictly chronological
approach to the material (and the historical continuity this
offers). Instead, the following chapters will look at a range of
ideas associated with illegitimacy which informed the creation of
bastard characters. To illustrate these ideas I will draw on texts
from throughout the period whose bastards exhibit strikingly
similar qualities in spite of the historical distance between their
'conceptions'.

The representation of illegitimacy in both fictional and non-
fictional literature locates the bastard as a centre of subversive
energies: uncontrolled speech or sexual activity, witchcraft, disobedience in the family, rebellion against Church or State. Many
of these are associated with transgressing women, and the
bastard can be seen as a powerful sub-group of the 'other',
expressing ideas which are linked with feminism. As such, illegitimates needed to be publicly persecuted to persuade society that
what was possible but unsanctioned was not desirable. The ways
in which the literature of the period engages with this task of
propaganda reveal a variety of attitudes towards such disruptive
forces. It shows insecurity in the characterisation of bastards as
figures infused with a dark, natural energy; fear in the use of the
bastard as a force of evil and rebellion; curiosity in the depiction
of the type as a mysterious 'other'. Since the bastard's origins are
in the sexually transgressive female, I will begin by examining the
threat she posed to society before moving on to consider the
bastard's own position: his role as a subversive which is produced
by society and which interacts with the legitimate structure,
threatening and supporting it.

'Ye fillers of the world with bastardy': female sexuality and illegitimacy

The idealisation of married chastity in Protestant England was accompanied by a celebration of woman as the bearer of offspring to immortalise the patriarch. A panegyric of motherhood formed the basis of many defences of women in the rhetorical debate on the nature of woman (Woodbridge 1984: 34–5). Fertility was celebrated in a Renaissance idea of the feminine which was firmly rooted in the pastoral, a cult of primavera which focused on 'the embodiment of the growing-principle itself, the mystery of childbirth and the annual recurrence of the colour green' (Davies 1986: 8). Woman's creative power within this cult was severely limited, subordinated to male desires and economic management. The patriarch begot, via the woman, a son to whom he bequeathed property, public office, power. Maternity remained an essentially passive function in which the mother received, carried and gave forth to the paternal family a child stamped with its name (Segal 1990: 136). To preserve this orderly state of affairs, the territory of women's bodies had to be strictly enclosed by the cult of chastity (Stallybrass 1986). Female fertility, whose regenerative power was advertised in the cult of primavera, needed to be fenced in. Penetration into the secret garden by another man would make the land worthless. As Varchi's *The Blazon of Jealousie* put it, 'When this our high pric'd Commoditie chanceth to light into some other merchants hands, and that our private Inclosure proveth to be a common for Others we care no more for it' (Varchi 1615: 20).

The familiarity of the enclosure image as part of the rhetoric of chastity (applicable to unmarried as well as married women) is shown by its casual use in Field's play *A Woman is a Weathercock* (1609), where pregnant Mistress Wagtail is advised to find a father 'in the scroll of beasts, horses and assess that have fed upon this common of yours' (44). The metaphor is found again in *The Birth of Merlin* (1608) by William Rowley. The Clown, whose sister Joan is pregnant, tells Nicodemus 'There's one of your Courtiers Hunting Nags has made a Gap through another mans Inclosure. Now sir, here's the question, who should be at

charge of a Fur-bush to stop it?' (97). Joan's lack of chastity is
shown through the metaphorical enclosure whose hedges have
been broken and in the play's physical setting. She searches for
the child's father through the wild forest where it was conceived
and the Clown suggests that, had she been brought up in the
city, she would have found a father before having a baby (79).
The metaphor of enclosed or common land identifies the woman
as a passive object of male protection, violation or exploitation.
The example from *The Birth of Merlin* defines Joan's body as the
property of her brother since she has no husband or father in the
play. Mistress Wagtail in *A Woman is a Weathercock* has more
autonomy. Although her flesh is 'common', and used by a large
number of men or 'beasts', it appears to belong to her in some
sense. She uses her pregnancy to trick Sir Abraham Ninny into
marrying her even though he is not the baby's father.

In cases of illegitimate conception female fertility becomes
threatening. Natural fruitfulness is the controlling male's enemy
rather than his resource and its abundance seems abhorrent. In
Middleton's *Women Beware Women* (1621), Leantio praises
female sexuality as the beautiful walled garden of 'spring's
chaste flowers' surrounding a banqueting house of wedlock
(3.2.8–11), but the Ward is disgusted at Isabella's fertility
(which has resulted in the conception of a bastard):

> *Sord.*   Here's a sweet plum-tree of your guardiner's graffing!
>
> *Ward.*   Nay, there's a worse name belongs to this fruit yet, and you
>   could hit on't; a more open one. For he that marries a
>   whore looks like a fellow bound all his lifetime to a
>   medlar-tree; and that's good stuff, 'tis no sooner ripe
>   but it looks rotten – and so do some queans at nineteen.
>   (4.2.95)

The medlar tree, found in the unenclosed wilderness of hedges
and woods, is the unchaste wife who yields bastard fruit.

The insecurity which produced and was furthered by such
rigorous enclosure of the female body was founded on a knowledge that female fertility could never be absolutely controlled,
that its containment relied solely on women's acceptance of the
dominant ideology. The power of official discourse on chastity
cannot be underestimated; no woman would have been unaware

of the shame and ill-treatment suffered by unmarried mothers or female adulterers. Susan Amussen's study *An Ordered Society* (1988) points out that few women would have risked becoming pregnant even to secure a marriage settlement because the stigma associated with illegitimacy was so strong (117). It needed to be forceful because the virtue of chastity had been accorded a significance beyond the sexual, becoming the key-note for female submission to patriarchy as a whole. The status of chaste wife/daughter automatically implied obedience to husband and father and State. To bear a bastard, the most public form of unchastity, was not just a matter of disrupting inheritance lines or burdening the parish with another charge. Male insecurity about female fertility was part of a more general unease about woman's place in society. Catherine Belsey (1985) has shown that conflicting ideologies about gender gave woman no fixed subject position (150). The roles assigned to her by liberal humanism as helpmeet, spiritual equal to her husband and learned educator of her children could not easily be recon-ciled with the subservience demanded by the paternal hierarchy, which placed her as inferior to husband or father in the family. The potential danger of this contradiction was its revelation that woman was not naturally fixed to a patriarchal world picture but, like her supposedly wandering womb, was a free-floating agent.

It is not surprising that threats associated with this freedom should be focused in the bastard fruit of a womb which really did wander out of the husband or father's control. The problems raised by the birth of illegitimate babies are 'a perfect illustration of the indirect nature of challenges to the gender order' (Amussen 1988: 111). Again and again pregnancy out of wed-lock is linked with other forms of transgression. The bastard-bearer is pigeon-holed with the scold and the witch. Elizabeth Busher of Henton was presented at the Somerset quarter sessions, where she was accused of living in 'woods and obscure places without obedience to the laws of God and this land', and of being

> of lewd life and conversation, as, namely the mother of divers base children, the suspected maintainer of incontinency in her own house, the continual disturber of her neighbours' quietness and

threatening mischief against them, and lastly, both reputed and
feared to be a dangerous witch through the untimely death of
men, women and children.

(Bates 1907: 96)

Elizabeth's choice of habitation in 'woods and obscure places'
outside the realm of civil law results in a loss of chastity. Giving
birth to bastards leads to a rejection of other social laws:
encouraging more illicit sex, making a noise and allying herself
with devilish instead of heavenly powers to harm members of
the community. Like Elizabeth Busher, the witch Sycorax in
Shakespeare's *Tempest* (1611) is described as a promulgator of
'mischiefs manifold, and sorceries terrible' against the human
community (1.2.264), transgressions which are linked with her
pregnancy. She is banished from Algiers 'with child' as though
the bastard foetus is a sign of rebellions yet unborn that society
wishes to expel.

The unchaste woman's threat to the whole realm is implied in
the body–territory metaphor. Chastity, which made a single lord
master of a woman's body, supported an autocratic rather than
democratic regime. Wye Saltonstall's picture of an ideal maid
carried the motto 'Let Maids then give to one their loves and
selfe / To be a Monarchy, no Commonwealth', equating female
sexuality and Renaissance government (Saltonstall 1946: 8). To
make one's land common and bear a bastard was to give birth to
potential revolution. In *The Advancement of Learning* (1605),
Francis Bacon uses imagery of the female body and illegitimate
birth to describe verbal criticism of State power:

> when princes and monarchs have suppressed actual and open rebels,
> then the malignity of the people (which is the mother of rebellion)
> doth bring forth libels and slanders, and taxations of the states,
> which is of the same kind with rebellion, but more feminine.
>
> (Bacon 1974: 82)

The mother figure of the aggrieved commonwealth gives birth
to an illegitimate verbal attack on patriarchal structures, conceived by the feminine populace without reference to any
masculine authority.

Court presentment records for scolding show a common
association between 'more feminine' verbal rebellion and

uncontrolled sexuality. In 1583, Barbara Driver was 'suspected of living incontinently by common report with divers persons . . . and it is noised that she hath had a bastard and never punished for it; also a maker of debate between neighbour and neighbour and a common scold and brawler' (Emmison 1973: 24). Within marriage, the woman who dared to speak out against her husband was presumed to be an adulterer as well. In extreme cases of female shrewishness, the supposed cuckold and his termagent, promiscuous wife were mocked in skimmington rides which often featured the display of animal horns. These rituals helped to ease the whole community's fears about female subversion (Ingram 1985: 177). The drama makes similar connections between overbearing female behaviour and sexual transgression. In Ford's *Love's Sacrifice* (1632), for example, the label of bastard-bearer gives the Duchess Bianca a voice to reveal her true feelings about her husband with an unflattering honesty which he sees as 'impudence above all history'. To the Duke, her 'immodest language' confirms her identity as 'shameless harlot' and bearer of Fernando's child (91–2).

Illegitimacy functions as a metaphor for Leonora's unseemly conduct in Webster's *The Devil's Law Case* (1617). Her attempt to take control of the paternal inheritance line, confound her son of his fortunes and make her daughter heir is expressed in a confession of adultery. Her declaration that Romelio is a bastard is proved false, but the play links it with other types of insubordination. In 3.1 Ariosto tells Crispiano of the 'mad tricks' which have 'been played of late by ladies': their management of their husbands' estates, ambitions to rule the Viceroy's court and even the council of war (3.1.9–25). Crispiano vows that he will only sit on the court bench again to 'curb the insolencies / Of these women' (3.1.27). His next appearance in the play is in judging Leonora's case against Romelio. To Crispiano, Leonora's confession of bastard-bearing is devilish practice (4.2.254), a view shared by Romelio (4.2.292) who sees in his mother's supposed adultery a demonic quality characteristic of the grotesque female body itself:

> Oh the violencies of women!
> Why, they are creatures made up and compounded

Of all monsters, poisoned minerals,
And sorcerous herbs that grow.

(4.2.289)

Whether Leonora has literally given birth to a bastard or not
does not matter. She has committed the same offence in trying
to disinherit Romelio and take the law into her own hands.
Crispiano disproves her confession of guilt only to condemn
her non-sexual transgression. He reveals her story as a falsehood, declares Romelio legitimate and re-asserts male control
over property. The law which decrees that the unscrupulous
Romelio should inherit all and his comparatively virtuous sister
nothing is scrutinised here. Although Leonora's own motivation
is not morally sound, her outlawed woman's voice, using illegitimacy as an entrance into the discourse of power, questions the
justice of its gender divisions.

The bastard's mother, who steps outside the boundary of
chaste marriage or unmarried virginity, interrupts male control
of property in a very concrete way. Lisa Jardine (1983) has
argued the importance of female sexuality as a force which
'regularly represents woman's uncontrollable interference with
inheritance' (92) and discusses women who subvert the patrilinear system from within as subsidiary heirs or in marriage
settlements. Illegitimacy disrupted property transactions in two
distinct ways depending upon the marital status of the mother.
Unmarried women and publicly acknowledged mistresses who
bore bastard children diverted finances in the form of maintenance. The Poor Law of 1531 had placed financial responsibility
for the upbringing of fatherless children on the local parish,
making them 'children of the people' or 'children of the
parish'. Sir John Fortescue's discussion of civil laws about
bastardy quotes a jingle about the labels:

> To whom the father people is,
>   to him is father none & all:
> To whom the people father is,
>   wel fatherles we may him cal

(Fortescue 1573: 93v)

Fulfilling this paternal role placed a considerable burden on the
people as records from St Botolph's Church, Aldgate, show.

Payments had to cover the cost of shelter, food and clothing. In the case of Susan Olliver, 'a poore fatherles chyld', St Botolph's paid 10s in 1588, 26s 8d in 1590, 14s 8d in 1591 and 3s in 1592 (Forbes 1971: 192–9). Poor Laws of 1563, 1576, 1579 and 1601 gave the municipalities power to collect poor rates to pay for maintenance, undoubtedly increasing the prejudice against bastard children as 'an economic problem, likely to be a drain on communal resources' (Macfarlane 1980: 75).

The 1576 Poor Law complained of the large number of bastards 'being now lefte to bee kepte at the charge of the Parishe where They bee borne, to the greate Burden of the same Parishe'. It recognised the impracticability of the present system and enabled parishes to charge parents a sum to contribute to the cost of maintaining their bastard child (Pinchbeck and Hewitt 1969: 206–7). Henry Swinburne, author of *A Brief Treatise of Testaments and Last Willes* (1590), approved of this law since it achieved a double purpose: 'as well for the convenient reliefe and keeping of the poore and miserable children . . . at the charges of the reputed father or mother . . . as for the punishment of the mother and reputed father of such unlawfull issue' (200v). In addition to being fined, the offending parents could be whipped, put in the stocks or forced to stand outside the church wearing a white sheet (the same penalty imposed on Eleanor for her involvement with witchcraft in *2 Henry VI*). An act of 1609 allowed the parish to send the mother of a fatherless child to work in the House of Correction to raise maintenance money.

The parents were not the only ones held responsible for bringing trouble to the parish. Innkeepers who harboured unmarried women about to give birth could also be fined. Financial motives reinforced the moral concern of the Church courts in cases such as the presentment of John Pike of Little Bedwyn who was charged in 1610 'for harbouring a stranger in his house that came to him from Gloucester great with childe . . . We desire that the said Pike and the woman may be cited to court that the father be known and the parish discharged' (Ingram 1987: 286). In spite of the various fines and punishments, the 1609 Parliamentary Statute still made a special point of noting in its introduction that 'great charge ariseth upon many places within the Realm by reason of Bastardie' (Pinchbeck and Hewitt 1969: 207). In Brome and Heywood's play *The Late Lancashire Witches* (1634), the bastard Whetstone says that illegitimacy 'is growne a great kindred in the Kingdome' (2,175). His comment carries extra resonance in the light of such complaints.

To a large extent, plays featuring bastard babies or illicit pregnancies follow the conventional line of public disapproval. Variants of the title 'son of the people' are used as insults in plays like Shirley's *The Ball* (1632) reflecting the unpopularity of the poor rate payment. In *Coriolanus* (1608), the servants outside Aufidius's tent agree that, since peace is a begetter of bastards, they would rather put their money behind the wars (4.5.223–32). Bastardy appears as a national problem in Robert Wilson's play *The Cobbler's Prophecy* (1590), in which the ruin of a realm is embodied in Ruina, the base daughter of Venus and Contempt. Ruina's case history is given in detail:

> Ruina, otherwise caled Ruine the child
> Contempt the father, Venus alias lust the mother
> Ru and Ina the godmothers
> Ingratitude the godfather and grandfather
> And securitie the nurse
> Heere's a brood that all Boetia shall curse.
>
> (1,258)

Wilson (1969) and Cameron (1982) read the play as an allegory on the Elizabethan court and religious politics but the reason for national 'ruin' may be apparent in the surface meaning. Certainly the details about Ruina could be modelled on the current dissatisfaction with poor rate charges: a contempt for (chaste) love degenerates into lust and the parents produce a brood that will be nursed by the social 'securitie' of the poor rate provision. Warnings that the State must be defended, 'Else you, they, it will soon be *ruinate*' (1,378), imply the extent of the financial problem of bastardy. The birth of Ruina is described very specifically; Venus is confined in a stinking 'Spittle . . . Where foule Lazars and loathed Lepers lie' (833). The details give a clear warning about the consequences of illicit conception to any potential bastard-bearer in the audience. Whatever else it may

have meant in terms of the need for reformation of the English
Church or court, the play is unequivocal in its condemnation of
illegitimacy and the trouble it caused for the community.

Apart from plaguing the parish with the burden of an
unwanted child, an unmarried woman who became pregnant
could disrupt financial transactions within the family. A pre-
nuptial pregnancy could thwart her father's plans to give her
(and her dowry) to a suitor of his choice and he might have to
raise her marriage portion to marry her off quickly. If she was
also his heir, his estate would eventually pass into the hands of
the bastard of another man if she did not marry its father. This
idea is taken up in *The Bastard*, probably written by Cosmo
Manuche and published in 1652. The play begins by assuming
a common knowledge of the maintenance problem, introducing
the bastard, Gaspar, with the words *'He's born, and must be
kept!'* (A4v). Another source of financial trouble is the clandestine relationship between Alonzo's unmarried daughter,
Mariana, and her lover Chaves. Alonzo is outraged by the
disruption of his plans to marry her to Balthazar and the
thought of bastard children inheriting his wealth:

> Insatiate Strumpet! Was not
> The man I destin'd for your husband, good:
> (Too good for thee) but that thy wanton eyes
> Must choose another? Must the Patrimony
> I sought to leave thee, the estate I purchas'd
> With such a care become a salary
> To your hot sin: your Bastards shortly will
> Call Grandfather, and look for portions
> Out of my wealth.
>
> (G1)

Potentially more disturbing than the conscious redirection of
finances to an acknowledged or parish-dependent bastard was
the case of a child born out of adultery. Here the mother could
corrupt property transactions covertly by producing bastard
children within the family. A married woman's lack of chaste
constancy could not be seen since there was no ocular proof for
paternity. Failure to detect the spurious bastard had serious
consequences for the patriarchal family: woman's infidelity
could transfer estate and title to the son of another family

altogether. Henry Bullinger, author of *The Christian State of
Matrimony* (1575), sees this as reason to condemn the adulteress
more than her male counterpart:

> For oft times it fortuneth, that an adulteress hath children by an
> adulterer, and then must the sayde children inherit all the substance
> of their pretended father as lawfull children which are yet unlawfull,
> whereby the father loseth his honour, his kinred, his body and
> goodes . . . Therefore though adultery be horrible both in men
> and women, yet in women it is most hurtfull and detestable.
>
> (43)

The nightmare of spurious bastardy is a commonly repeated
theme in the plays. In Ford's *Love's Sacrifice*, D'Avolos provokes the Duke by telling him 'you shall be sure to have a
bastard – of whom you did not so much as beget a little toe, a
left ear, or half the further side of an upper lip – inherit both your
throne and name: this would kill the very soul of patience itself'
(75). We see an example of nobility stained with bastardy and
land falsely possessed in Field's *A Woman is a Weathercock*,
where Wagtail's marriage to Sir Abraham Ninny will redirect
an aristocratic fortune to the son of a man who is 'not worth
the estate of an apple wife' (45). She tells the unborn baby
'When thou inherit'st land, strange both to thy father and
grandfather, and rid'st in a coach, it may be thy father, an old
footman, will be running by thy side' (69). Wagtail's very
obvious pregnancy is undeniable physical evidence of female
subversion. It reminds the audience of disobedience, actual and
potential, sexual and non-sexual, on the parts of Bellafront,
Katherine and Lucida, the other female characters in the play.
Scudamore, believing he has been betrayed by Bellafront,
declares

> Women! women!
> Hee's mad by heaven, that thinks you anything
> But sensual monsters. . . .
> Ye fillers of the world with bastardy.
>
> (37)

His views seem to be confirmed when Wagtail enters and plots
to find a 'better' man – a knight or a gentleman – to father her
child.

Chastity could only be achieved through active consent so the child born to a married woman and carrying the paternal family's name could never be proven to be entitled to that name. This gap in male control was the cause of widespread unease in Renaissance England. The popular medical guide *The Problemes of Aristotle, with other Philosophers and Phisitions* (1597) described conception in the following way:

> The seede [male seed] is the efficient beginning of the childe, as the builder is the efficient cause of the house, and therefore is not the materiall cause of the childe . . . The seedes [male and female] are shut and kept in the wombe: but the seede of the man doth dispose and prepare the seed of the woman to receive the forme, perfection, or soule, the which being done, it is converted into humiditie, and is fumed and breathed out by the pores of the matrix, which is manifest, bicause onely the flowers [i.e. menses] of the woman are the materiall cause of the yoong one.
>
> (E3v)

As well as showing woman once again as a passive mediator, a mass of amorphous 'materiall' to be shaped by the male, the extract reveals the insubstantial nature of the male 'seed' and thus the basis for doubts about paternity. Superficially the theory asserts male superiority – the male seed endows 'forme' and gives significance to the undefined 'materiall' provided by the woman, as a builder actively arranges the materials to make a house. The 'materiall' projects another, contradictory, message. Only the woman is the 'materiall cause of the childe', and it is only through her that the 'perfection' and 'soule' of the male seed are embodied. The seed could be that of any man. The identity of the builder is not within the direct control of the man who will own the house. The architect of any building which she finally produces is therefore not necessarily male.

The insubstantial nature of biological paternity and its wider implications preoccupies many male characters. For Posthumus in Shakespeare's *Cymbeline* (1610), the supposed infidelity of Imogen raises doubts about his mother's chastity and his own identity as the son of a nameable father:

> Is there no way for men to be, but women
> Must be half-workers? We are all bastards,
> And that most venerable man which I

Did call my father, was I know not where
When I was stamp'd. Some coiner with his tools
Made me a counterfeit; yet my mother seem'd
The Dian of that time. So doth my wife
The nonpareil of this.

(2.5.1)

The metaphor of counterfeit coin reminds us that only the
mother has a visible connection to her child. The father's stamp
is no more than an artificial (and unreliable) attempt to authen-
ticate the relationship between father and son. Posthumus's
doubts about his paternity are reflected in his name. He is called
Posthumus rather than Leonatus, as though the certainty of his
link to his father (the name they share) has died in the present
age where women are 'not constant but . . . changing still'
(2.5.30). Posthumus's lack of paternal name is highlighted in
the opening moments of the play where, in response to the
question 'What's his name and birth?', the second gentleman
admits 'I cannot delve him to the root'. He then gives an
elaborate account of Leonatus's titles and describes his three
sons without naming any of them until he recounts how
Posthumus was given a name – not by his father but by the
King (1.1.27–41).

The Renaissance theatregoer was often included in recogni-
tions of doubt about paternity, particularly when these took the
form of a soliloquy. The Prologue of *The Bastard* directly
challenges the audience's legitimacy with the words:

> *My Faith assures me, many of you have known*
> *To make some* Bastards *that you durst not own*
> *For shame or fear; and some of you may be*
> *Mistaken in your* Fathers Pedigree.

(A4)

Such speeches reminded listeners that authenticity as the child of
a particular father was something given rather than inherent,
something signalled only by a verbal tag – the name of the
father. Texts exploring women's potential to produce illegitimate children expose patrilinear genealogy as a fragile cultural
construct. If legitimacy was something created through
language, then so was bastardy. To consider the importance of

naming and defining the illegitimate 'other' we must turn our
attention from the transgressing mother to examine the position
of the bastard child.

'What title shall I set to this base coin? He has no name': the cultural definition of bastardy

While the mother was the 'materiall cause' of the bastard, its
social identity as 'other' was constructed by the patriarchal order
she had disobeyed, an order whose authority relied on language.
In *The Triall of Bastardie* (1594), an important treatise on
marriage legislation and legitimacy, William Clerke remarked
on the restrictive nature of a law which 'bridles now the parent
to be father of Legitimation' instead of allowing the subject to
form his or her own identity by making independent relationships with the formally constituted order (A1v). By 'parent' he
means father; woman's role as a parent is negligible in legal
terms. A bastard's bond to the community reversed the binary
opposition, privileging the bodily link between mother and child
instead of the father's name. This was dangerous in a society
which relied on persuasion as a means of control, and was
increasingly insecure about the effectiveness of those means.
Plays exploring situations where illegitimacy is suspected adver-
tise an awareness of the false consciousness which creates
legitimacy and upholds the patriarchal State.

In the trial scene of Webster's *The Devil's Law Case* (1617),
Crispiano gives two opposing views of illegitimacy. He begins by
judging it very strange that Leonora should attempt to injure her
son Romelio by testifying that he is a bastard. Locating her as a
representative of natural law in respect of the maternal affection
she should show, Crispiano reminds her that 'compassionate
nature' makes no difference between so called 'base' and 'legitimate' offspring (4.2.244–5). Nevertheless, he sits in judgement
while the trial to prove Romelio's bastardy proceeds. He speaks
as a representative of phallocratic law, declaring the justice of a
precept which would disinherit both Leonora's children if they
are base-born. The scene seems to reinforce conservative values
but Crispiano's inconsistent behaviour, recognising the equality

of and then the difference between bastard and legitimate child, is subversive. It shows that the Law of the Father is unnatural rather than natural, an instrument of power to control and dominate the 'other'.

Crispiano must identify Romelio as different because the distinction of base from legitimate is essential to a society founded on binary oppositions of culture/nature; father/ mother; lawful/unlawful; where the first term is privileged. The fatherless child must be labelled with the name of the mother, as a negative reflection of the legitimate subject. As such, he has no positive signifier. In *The Two Gentlemen of Verona* (1590), Launce lists woman and bastard as variations of the same negative opposite. He refers to his mistress's 'nameless virtues' as '"Bastard virtues", that indeed know not their fathers, and therefore have no names' (3.1.317–18). The legal anonymity of bastard characters sometimes makes it difficult to fix their names in plays. In Shakespeare's *King John*, for example, the names Sir Richard, Falconbridge and Philip are all used of the bastard but none seems to ring quite true since each eclipses one side of his oxymoronic shifting identity. In such cases, the editor or critic is faced with a problem when writing about bastard characters or deciding how to prefix their speeches. 'Bastard' may seem the only appropriate name but obviously in a discussion like mine this is hardly practicable. In the case of *King John*, I have had to resort to the name 'Sir Richard', which the bastard is given when he chooses illegitimate identity (Braunmuller 1989: 67).

Two plays, *The Revenger's Tragedy* (1606) (probably by Middleton), and Thomas Nabbes's *The Unfortunate Mother* (1639), solve the problem by using 'Spurio' and 'Notho' as names. These generic terms for bastardy are explained by William Clerke, who distinguishes between '*Notho*' (the child of an adulteress), '*Spurio*' (the bastard of a concubine) and '*Manser*' (the offspring of a whore) (Clerke 1594: 26). In each case a negative term signifies lack of legal paternity. By a careful use of the name Spurio, *The Revenger's Tragedy* maintains the anonymity of its bastard character throughout. Spurio is referred to as 'the bastard' by both noble and servant characters except on two occasions. Supervacuo and Vindice use the word

'Spurio', but combine it with a definite article: Vindice remarks 'here comes the Spurio' (2.2.114), and Supervacuo asks Ambitioso 'Not'st thou that Spurio, brother?' (5.1.169). Even though the other characters' names define their qualities, they do not function in this way. Spurio's title reflects his mysterious origins; he admits that he is 'an uncertain man / Of more uncertain woman' (1.2.133), following Agrippa's view that a bastard had no fixed social identity because 'he hath an uncertayne father and a naughty mother' (Agrippa 1545: B8). The relative anonymity of bastards marks them off as essentially 'other' rather than socially integrated.

Labelling the bastard as a negative is dangerous. In *The Devil's Law Case*, Crispiano experiences considerable difficulty when trying to impose his authority on the illegitimate Romelio because he cannot address him: 'What title shall I set to this base coin? / He has no name' (4.2.127). The bastard, with no paternal stamp – no verbal connection to society – is outside official discourse and thus ultimately uncontrollable. Like woman, he is 'beyond nomenclatures and ideologies' (Kristeva 1974: 137). Rowley's *The Birth of Merlin* explores how freedom from patriarchal language (and specifically names) leads to illicit sexual practices and illegitimacy. In Act 2, the pregnant Joan cannot remember the name of her lover, the Clown protests that he won't be able to call the bastard by a name when it is born, or address Joan's lover by name. He even says that he is now ashamed 'to call thee Sister' (79). Noble characters seem to be affected by the same illicit desires as Joan when denunded of their titles. The Clown invites 'any man that wants a name' to come and be called a whore master, and Prince Uter enters lamenting that he does not know the name of his beloved (81). She is, in fact, his brother's wife so the potential for incest and adultery is linked to anonymity. The Clown believes Uter is talking about Joan and comments 'he knows not thy name neither a couple of wise fools yfaith, to get children and know not one another' (81). Two types of 'knowing' are opposed here: freed from social knowledge (names and the proper relations which these mark out), the characters pursue sexual impulses and acquire carnal knowledge of each other with complete disregard for conventional morality. The quest to find the

bastard child a father and give it a name is a means to restore
order as well as legitimacy.

The male bastard's own relationship to the official language
which denies him a name is problematic. This is apparent if we
consider him in the light of Lacan's theory of language acquisition and sexual difference. Lacan proposes that the Symbolic
Order – the system of signs governing social exchanges – is
masculine in nature. Its language is constructed by the *nom-
du-père*, the Name (or Law) of the Father which privileges the
phallus as a positive signifier. When a child speaks and enters the
Symbolic Order, his or her identity is defined in relation to this
transcendental signifer, its presence in herself or himself, and in
the mother and father. Boys define themselves in positive terms.
They identify with the father, confirm their privileged gender
identity and align themselves with authority in the Symbolic
Order. Girls, whose relation to the phallic master-signifier is
one of lack, define themselves with their mothers and confirm
their gendering in negative terms (Kaplan 1986: 59–63). Following Lacan's theory, fatherless children must relate somewhat
differently to the Symbolic Order. Female bastards presumably
do not sense the lack of a phallus in the mother until they enter
wider society and may identify themselves with her more
positively.

The male bastard fits into neither of the conventional gendering patterns offered by Lacan. His point of access to the
language of authority, through contact with the father, is miss-
ing. Male bastards experience particular problems in relating to
the Symbolic, which labels them as negatives (because they are
illegitimate) and yet establishes the phallus as positive signifier.
They are faced with a contradiction of positive and negative self-
definitions. Their eccentric gendering has significant implications. Many characters strive to suppress or escape from their
strong maternal inheritance and identify themselves with the
Symbolic culture which defines them in terms of lack. This
inevitably causes serious crises of identity. Their alienation
means that their voices remain outside the play's most prestigious linguistic registers which affects their position on stage.
Their unusual relationship with the language and structures of

authority in their plays will be investigated in subsequent chapters.

Legal definitions of bastardy

Localised marriage practices and confusion as to what actually constituted a marriage complicated the supposedly absolute distinction between legitimate and illegitimate. Definitions of bastardy were particularly inconsistent in cases of pre-nuptial pregnancy and pre-contracted marriage. The Miseries of Enforced Marriage by George Wilkins (1606) explores the confusion in such a situation. Scarborow, previously contracted to Clare and believing that his second marriage to Katherine is adulterous, regards their children as bastards. The exchange

> Scar. Harlot.
> Kath. Husband.
> Scar. Bastardes.
> Chil. Father.
>
> (2,479)

makes the differentiating labels look artificial. A public re-contract at the end of the play brings relegitimation and a happy resolution. The same situation causes tragedy in the anonymous A Yorkshire Tragedy (1606), based on a true story. The double contract causes the father to murder two of his children whom he calls 'bastards'. Dramatic situations focusing on the legality of marriage contracts and the legitimacy of the children may have been influenced by a contemporary legal case surrounding the clandestine marriage of Penelope Devereux and Charles Blount and the unsuccessful attempts to legitimate their children (Bradbrook 1980: 62–5). Two plays by Dekker, The Noble Spanish Soldier (1622) and The Welsh Ambassador (1623) (a revised version of the former text), again present situations involving double contracts to problematise the labelling of children as 'bastards'.

Inconsistency in the laws highlighted the cultural production of bastardy. In Elizabethan Church law a distinction was made between cases of 'general bastardy' where the parents of the child never married and cases of 'special bastardy' where the parents did marry after the birth of the child (Macfarlane 1980: 173). In the first instance the children were always regarded as illegitimate by both Church and civil law but in cases of 'special bastardy' a further inconsistency arose: 'special' bastards, often blessed under a mantle at the time of their parents' marriage, were legitimate in the eyes of the Church but were judged illegitimate by the State. William Clerke, in his *Triall of Bastardie* (1594), points out that, owing to this contradiction, the 'bastard' could be awarded dignitaries by the Church but be excluded from inheritance. The ludicrousness of the situation is indicated in his comment 'the ordinarie may certifie both right and wrong in diverse respects, for hee may certifie *Mulier*, that is to say him, legitimate, and rightly to orders and dignitaries: but of the land *Bastardus*, that is, To inheritance, a bastard' (D3).

In addition to these complications, children who were quite obviously illegitimate often had their legal legitimacy maintained. Under English civil law it was extremely difficult to establish the paternity of a bastard born within marriage and disinherit him. The child of an adulteress was regarded as legitimate and its maintenance the responsibility of the mother's husband unless either impotence or non-access of the husband could be proved. Sir Edward Coke's *First Part of the Institutes of the Lawes of England* (1629), the foremost authority on the subject, explains the position:

> By the Common Law, if the Husband be within the foure Seas, that is, within the Jurisdiction of the King of England, if the Wife hath Issue, no proofe is to be admitted to prove the Child a Bastard (for in that case, Filiato non potest probari) unlesse the Husband hath an apparent impossibilitie of procreation ... if the Issue be borne within a moneth or a day after marriage, between parties of full lawful age, the childe is legitimate.
>
> (244)

That this principle was accepted as the basis of English civil law gives some indication of the need to maintain a rigid appearance of legitimacy for economic and ideological reasons. The law relieved the parish and its community of even higher poor rate payments and refused to acknowledge the existence of wifely disobedience whenever possible. In *The Anatomy of Melancholy*

(1621), Robert Burton observes, somewhat sarcastically, that under this law 'married women are all honest' (Burton 1964: 138). However expedient it may have been in the short term, its protection of legitimacy exposed the operations of power to critical scrutiny. References to it in the drama present it as politic rather than just. In Shakespeare's *King John*, the bastard's appearance proclaims his identity as Coeur de Lion's son and makes a mockery of the law expounded by King John. Robert Falconbridge argues the case of non-access to prove his brother's bastardy, claiming that Sir Robert was beyond the distance of the four seas at the time of his brother's conception. Because this was not for the whole nine months of the pregnancy, John disregards Robert's claim as invalid:

> Sirrah, your brother is legitimate,
> Your father's wife did after wedlock bear him;
> And if she did play false, the fault was hers . . .
> In sooth, good friend, your father might have kept
> This calf, bred from his cow, from all the world.
>
> (1.1.116)

To an audience already informed that John's claim is based on 'strong possession' rather than right (1.1.40), this judgement proves that the King's law relies on a type of justice which ignores immediate evidence. The illegitimate body and the word of law confront and contradict each other. While the bastard's evidence is physically present and obvious to to all in the court, the word remains detached, relying on a lack of evidence – the same kind of paternal 'absence' found in human reproduction.

A deconstruction of verbal power is dramatised in the scene. Hélène Cixous theorises this process as an opposition of positive pleasure (the apple) and restrictive masculine law:

> The law . . . is absolute, verbal, invisible, negative, it is a symbolic *coup de force* and its force is its invisibility, its non-existence, its force of denial, its 'not'. And facing the law there is the apple which is, is, is. It is the struggle between presence and absence, between an undesirable, unverifiable, indecisive absence and a presence, a presence which is not only a presence: the apple is visible and it can be held up to the mouth, it is full, it has an *inside*.
>
> (Cixous 1988: 16)

The bastard fruit of sexual pleasure is able to demonstrate the emptiness of the laws shaping the world of *King John*, laws whose power lies in their inscrutability rather than their relation to the world around them. Like the semen or stamp of the father, the law is immaterial, absent, in spite of its power. The bastard, by contrast, is undeniably there: full of the qualities which liken him to Coeur de Lion, just as the connection between mother and child is physically evident. The bastard privileges the body over language and rejects an identity constructed by patriarchal law based on absence (which will make him an owner of land), in favour of a more maternally structured self as a bastard who is 'Lord of [his] presence' (1.1.137). His power of presence as a son of Coeur de Lion undermines John's position as ruler. The scene demonstrates how 'the body is with the King, but the King is not with the body' (*Hamlet* 4.2.27). John holds the name of king, but this is a thing of nothing since he holds it without right. The nameless bastard, who embodies the kingly qualities of Richard I, cannot inherit the crown since he has not inherited the father's name, even though he is re-titled Sir Richard. The third candidate for the throne, Arthur, has what both John and the bastard lack – right – but he does not have full presence which is fragmented between the other two in the form of *de facto* kingship and direct blood link to Richard I and his kingly qualities.

The fragmentation of full royal legitimacy between these characters is magnified in the disintegration of absolute values in their world. Bastardy is a powerful metaphor for such decay in *King John*. John's and Arthur's claims to the crown are disputed by Elinor and Constance in terms of the chastity of the claimants' mothers, and thus their sons' legitimacy:

> *Elinor.*   Out insolent, thy bastard shall be king
> That thou may'st be a queen and check the world:
> *Constance.* My bed was ever to thy son as true
> As thine was to thy husband, and this boy
> Liker in feature to his father Geffrey
> Than thou and John in manners, being as like
> As rain to water, or devil to his dam.
> My boy a bastard! By my soul I think
> His father never was so true begot –
> It cannot be, and if thou wert his mother.

Elinor.   There's a good mother, boy, that blots thy father.
Constance. There's a good grandame, boy, that would blot thee.

(2.1.122)

The Queens' insults are not intended to declare either John or
Arthur illegitimate – as Elinor remarks, if Constance did mean
her accusation to be taken seriously, it would cast serious doubts
on the legitimacy of Elinor's other son, Geffrey, and Arthur's
own claim to the throne. Neither are the Queens' words meant
simply as insults to wound each other's honour. The slanders
work more insidiously, casting doubts on whether either John or
Arthur have inherited the royal blood and inherent kingly qualities which would characterise God's deputy. Shakespeare associates Arthur and John with bastardy, in the form of insults, to
suggest the lack of absolute right in either candidate for the
throne. The suspected rebellion against the divine right of husbands mirrors the disappearance of divine right of kingship in the
play. The exchange ceases in deadlock, leaving the audience with
the impression that John's and Arthur's claims are neither fully
legitimate nor actually illegitimate. The metaphor of covert
bastardy in marriage, because of the inability to prove unique
biological paternity, effectively suggests an intermediary state
where no absolute (including that of a binary opposition
between legitimate/illegitimate) is possible.

In practice, then, the desire to distinguish and dominate the
bastard 'other' highlighted the mythical nature of the values
which were needed to perpetuate an ordered Renaissance
society. The difference between legitimacy and its unnameable
opposite became hard to distinguish when marriage practices,
betrothal customs and the laws of the land themselves were full
of contradictions. Dramatic presentations of cases where a character's legal legitimacy was brought into question showed that
one is not born a bastard; one becomes one. Society's attempts
to relegate illegitimates to a negative category, outside naming,
also placed them outside the controlling discourse. Since 'naming is the means whereby we attempt to order and structure the
chaos and flux of existence which would otherwise be an undif-
ferentiated mass' (Spender 1980: 107), the unnamed is a menace
to the constituted order. The bastard's existence 'in every thing

illegitimate' inevitably decentred the legitimate world which outlawed him and confronted society with a dilemma: how to deal with what it had produced? Even though it had been instrumental in the 'conception, formation, gestation and labour' of the bastard (to borrow from Derrida), would it attempt to ignore the loss of centre suddenly evident by turning away 'when faced by the as yet unnamable which is proclaiming itself and which can do so, as is necessary whenever a birth is in the offing, only under the species of the nonspecies, in the formless, mute, infant, and terrifying form of monstrosity' (Derrida 1966: 135).

The number of writings which give the bastard a voice to proclaim itself show that dramatists and pamphlet writers did not turn away but engaged with the problems raised by the illegitimate 'other'. For those members of society with a bastard in their own family or immediate community, turning away was hardly an option anyway. Their problem was more likely to be reconciling private feelings with the public view which was anxious to condemn illegitimacy. The final sections of this chapter will outline in general terms some of the ways in which society reacted to bastardy, how it tried to contain, restructure or celebrate this subversive element.

'A wretch exposed to want, to scorne or paines': the bastard as object lesson

By defining an illegitimate 'other', Renaissance patriarchy admitted the existence of subversion and was committed to publicly exercising a dominant authority over bastards to reassure everyone of the power of the controlling discourse. Bastards had to be seen to suffer at the hands of the absolute subject group. Jenny Teichman remarks that 'because outsiders hold groups together by being object lessons, it is ideologically necessary that they should be, or at least appear to be, unhappy, and this is part of the reason why outsiders have to be persecuted' (Teichman 1982: 12). The public reaction to illegitimacy was to persecute children born out of wedlock and to stress their disadvantaged state. The title character in Sir

William Alexander's play *Croesus* (1604) outlines the image which such persecution aimed to promote: 'A wretch exposed to want, to scorne or paines / The bastard childe of Fortune, barr'd from blisse / Whom heavens do hate and all the world disdaines' (2.1.371).

The most immediate form of persecution was the murder of the bastard baby. A sense of shame and a fear of punishment, combined with the financial problems a bastard baby raised, led many unmarried women to terminate their pregnancies or murder their offspring. A Renaissance obstetrician, Percival Willoughby, associated the crime of infanticide with 'the looser sort' of women (by which he meant bastard-bearers) and research shows that illegitimates were its main victims (Wrightson 1975: 11–12). In Essex between 1558 and 1603, twenty-seven of the thirty recorded cases involved bastards. The forms of murder included drowning in wells and ponds; suffocation by pillow, in a haystack, in an oven, in a chest; the cutting of the babies' throats, strangulation, beating to death with a bedpost; live burial, abandonment in ditches and open places exposed to the elements (Emmison 1970: 157). The extent of infanticides was such that, ironically, an Act had to be passed in 1624 to 'prevent the murthering of Bastard children'. It noted that 'many lewd Women that have been delivered of Bastard Children, to avoyd their shame and to escape Punishment, doe secretlie bury or conceale the Death of their Children'. Under the Act, a mother was presumed guilty of murder unless she could prove by the oath of one witness that the child had been born dead (Wrightson 1975: 11).

Public condemnation of murder (even before 1624) encouraged parents to find more subtle ways of disposing of bastard babies. Infanticidal nursing was one such method, where the child was delivered to the 'care' of a woman who would kill it with neglect. Some nurses specialised in taking base children and there is evidence to support the existence of a virtually institutionalised means of bastard-disposal in areas with a high incidence of illegitimate births, particularly the north-west and London (Wrightson 1975: 17–18). Records of 1621 for St Botolph's Church, London, include details of 'Paludia Foord a Base-borne Child nursed in the house of Thomas Overlin, a

Tyncker of Rosemarie lane (where it was base-lie used, and
Starved)'. Marie Sedway, another bastard who had been put
out to nurse with Edith Jones, died in 1623 and the record
noted, somewhat ominously, 'there are very few Children
prosper Long in our Parish, that are Nursed in such Places'
(Forbes 1971: 199).

The disadvantages suffered by bastards who survived as object
lessons were similar to those endured by women, their fellow
representatives of the 'other'. The protest made by French
feminists in *Questions féministes* outlines the social position of
women but could equally well apply to that of bastards in
Renaissance England: 'We – living beings – are treated like
objects because a society based on violence, exploitation and
oppression assumes that our lot is dispossession (no name, no
identity, no rights, no body)' (Marks and Courtivron 1981: 230).
Bastards were dispossessed of legal identity and lack of family
name excluded them from any right to inherit. Although
apparently a less violent form of persecution than the murder
of babies, it was keenly felt and had many ramifications. To
begin with, it affected bastards' rights to property; like
women, they could not normally be heirs to an estate. Land-
lords' fear of the 'alienation' of property directed inheritance
laws to favour patriarchal primogeniture rather than allowing a
woman or her family to be heirs (Jardine 1983: 79–80). Since a
bastard heir would also alienate property, mothers' sons were
reduced to the status of women when it came to inheritance.
The shock of seeing a male character in this position helps to
explain why male bastards predominate in the drama. Their
dispossession (invariably a source of dramatic action) could be
used to alert audiences to the arbitrary nature of English inheritance laws which also excluded women and younger brothers.

In Ireland an alternative system existed. Under the principle
of gavelkind or 'give-all-kind' bastards, women and younger
sons could inherit. Gavelkind was adopted in parts of England
(notably Kent and north Wales) but, according to Sir Edward
Coke, 'as to Bastards that custome was abolished' (Coke 1629:
175–6). A memorandum attached to the manuscript of the play
Tom a Lincoln, in the hand of Morgan Evans, includes details of
the case of Wynifreed Ednevett, who 'was borne in adultery' and

therefore disinherited 'although the lawe would allow her to be the daughter of Richard Ednevet' (*Tom a Lincoln* 1992: 88). The strict line on bastard inheritance is probably explained by the fact that a bastard heir would disrupt class distinctions based on genealogy. Sir John Davies gives voice to common apprehensions about gavelkind in his *Discoverie of the True Causes why Ireland was never entirely Subdued* (1612) in which he complains that 'that Irish Custom of Gavel-kinde, did breede another mischiefe; for thereby, every man being borne to Land, as well Bastard, as Legitimate, they al held themselves to be *Gentlemen*' (171).

Nevertheless, some bastards did inherit from their parents' wills. Under ecclesiastical law they could inherit money to cover maintainance costs or dowries (Swinburne 1590: 200). Essex records show that people bequeathed money and possessions to their own bastard children and even, in one case, to another man's bastard (Emmison 1976: 216). In *The Triall of Bastardie* (1594), William Clerke implied that the civil law barring inheritance should be changed, saying that he did not call the present law unjust 'but yet it is temporall, and within the libertie of Princes justly to be altered by the time' (Aiv). The Elizabethans had seen a most public alteration of the law in the case of their Queen who had inherited the crown in spite of being, as Cardinal Allen remarked, 'most justly declared illegitimate and uncapable of succession to the croune of England . . . by Henry him self' (Allen 1588: viii). Elizabeth never repealed the 1536 Sucession Act which bastardised her, but saw the urgent need to proclaim herself 'rightly, lineally and lawfully descended' from the blood royal by means of an Act of Recognition in 1559 (Prothero 1913: 21). Although the Act exposed the Elizabeth's embarrassing position, it was important ideologically as well as in establishing her right to the throne. To allow a bastard to stand as a public figurehead, wielding such power as Elizabeth did, flatly contradicted the image of the bastard as disadvantaged.

For most base-born men, loss of inheritance rights had consequences beyond the realm of property. Membership of trade guilds was normally hereditary so a bastard was unable to take over his father's position here. In effect, he was also unable to obtain any municipal office as guild membership was the route

by which men usually achieved such positions. These were
major disabilities, often underestimated in the present day
(Given-Wilson and Curteis 1984: 49). Women were similarly
disadvantaged. Citizens' wives could not be members of trade
guilds and, even if they worked in their husbands' shops, they
were not entitled to any of the profit. Like bastards, they were
unable to hold public office, plead a case at law or be guardians
or tutors. As Linda Woodbridge (1984) points out, 'the middle
class could boast no lady mayor of London' (55). The exclusion
of bastards from positions of power within the polity was
justified with reference to the Bible. Luther's lecture on
Deuteronomy set out the common reasons why bastards were
denied access to worldly inheritance, following their prohibition
from the Church assembly:

> [Base birth] renders a man unfit for upright administration, and it is
> proverbial that bastards are seldom good men and always harbour
> some outstanding fault. This law is observed also among Gentiles,
> especially in some cities. They do not admit them to trades, perhaps
> because they have previously experienced their worthlessness.
>
> (Luther 1960: 230)

Having no automatic entry into the job market and no self-
sufficiency, bastards were left utterly dependent upon the
absolute subject group for survival, relying on private charity
or parish maintenance. The nursing of many bastard children
under the Poor Law took place at 'hospitals', institutions such as
Christ's Hospital in London, where a home was set up specifically for the care of bastards abandoned in the city. Stow's *Survey
of London* (1603) describes the reburbishment of Christ's
Hospital in 1552 and records that almost four hundred 'poor
fatherless children' were taken in when it opened (Stow 1956:
286). In the folio version of *Every Man in his Humour* (1616),
Kitely recounts the upbringing of the bastard Cash at a hospital
(2.1.15). To relieve the parish of maintenance costs, the 'children
of the parish' were then 'bound' as apprentices between the ages
of nine and fourteen to earn their own keep. Records for St
Botolph's Church show that on 18 December 1594 John
Williams, who had been nursed and cared for at the parish's
charge since 1587, was summoned 'to the masters of this parishe

at christmas next for that the masters weare to put the said chyld to service'. After one final maintenance payment on 22 December, John disappears from the records (Forbes 1971: 197).

In the position of apprentice or servant, the bastard was again structured as a powerless victim, to be controlled by the will of the legitimate subject. Like women who were treated by their husbands 'not as wives but as servauntes' (Vives 1550: K8), bastards were a cheap form of labour. There are several examples of bastard apprentices or servants in the drama. In Middleton's *A Chaste Maid in Cheapside* (1613), Sir Walter plans to bind his bastards Wat and Nick as apprentices to a goldsmith and a vintner (1.2.131), and in Brome's play *The English Moor* (1637), Quicksands's base son is apprenticed to the spinning trade in Norfolk. Edricus, the bastard in *Edmund Ironside* (1595), relies on an awareness of this custom when he tells the audience that his villainy would make anyone suppose he 'had been bound apprentice to deceit' (305). Curio in Chapman's *All Fools* (1601) and Gaspar in *The Bastard* occupy the position of servant in their households.

The visibility of the bastard's disadvantage was of paramount importance to the State. It exhibited publicly the dominant authority of the subject group over the disadvantaged 'other' and displayed its supposedly natural power of control. Publicly persecuting the bastard was a way of perpetuating the myth of Renaissance patriarchy. For this reason, illegitimacy could not be eliminated or disappear (the 1624 Act outlawing the murder of bastard babies may have been partly designed to protect their survival as object lessons). John Donne, considering the problem 'Why have Bastards best Fortune?', identifies illegitimacy as a necessary 'other'. One of his answers is 'because the two greatest powers in the world the Divell and Princes concurre to theyr greatnesse, the one giving Bastardy, the other Legitimation, as Nature frames and conserves greate Bodyes of Contraryes' (Donne 1980: 32). Donne's choice of opposites is telling. Both princes and the devil create the greatness of bastards; bastardy is as necessary to legitimation as evil is to the myth of sovereignty based on divine right. The comparison points to the bastard's role in the maintenance of State power. Because illegitimacy was useful, the State was able to tolerate the more sympathetic attitudes held privately in Renaissance England. The contradiction between the public persecution of bastards and their nurturing in the family therefore remained. The condition of this toleration was, of course, that it remained private - in families who would maintain their base-born children as discreetly as possible.

The discussion of illegitimacy in published writings or on the stage was more problematic to the authorities. A play presenting the bastard as naturally inferior to the legitimate world could be very useful in reinforcing the official position. On the other hand, a dramatist offering a sympathetic view would be bringing into the public realm that which should be reserved for the unfortunate family's hearth or for the private contemplation of individuals. Plays which showed the bastard's power to overturn the legitimate world order could threaten the whole power structure. Francis Bacon remarked 'the stage is capable of no small influence both of discipline and corruption' and noted that the latter was more prevalent in current drama (1857–61, 4: 316). The particular danger of 'bastard' literature may have inspired his definition of poesy as 'a luxuriant plant, that comes of the lust of the earth, without any formal seed' (1857–61, 4: 444). Dramatic literature, a bastard form of writing without any obligation to historical accuracy (no formal seed), was notoriously difficult to confine to a single meaning. This inherent freedom and ambiguity allowed dramatists to draw on both public and private views when creating illegitimate characters.

Bastards as object lessons in the drama

Respresentations of the bastard on stage exhibit contradictions between the authorised image of illegitimacy and opinions held privately. While images of disadvantaged characters appear to conform to the official view, their comments question the justice of laws which discriminate against them. In many plays the bastard character slides in and out of a variety of relationships with the legitimate hierarchy, allowing the dramatists to raise questions about that world and, by implication, about the power structures in Renaissance England.

On the surface, texts showing bastards as object lessons seem to demonstrate the legitimate hegemony's controlling power. Numerous plays include details of infanticides which publicise the persecution of illegitimacy. The witches in *Macbeth* (1606) refer to a 'birth strangled babe / Ditch delivered by a drab' (4.1.30) and in *A Chaste Maid in Cheapside*, Touchwood hastily advises the whore to get rid of her bastard baby 'anon i' th' evening by one of twenty devices' (2.1.97). In another London play, Heywood's *The Wise Woman of Hogsden* (1604), the title character keeps a very dubious nursery where unmarried women can be delivered of their children. She explains that the babies are quietly disposed of: 'at night we send them abroad and lay one at this man's doore, and another at that . . . and what after becomes of them, we inquire not' (1964, 5: 306). A blatant form of infanticide is seen in Shakespeare's *Titus Andronicus* (1591) where Tamora sends Aaron their child and bids him 'Christen it with thy dagger's point' (4.2.70). The baby's colour declares its illegitimate identity; as an embodiment of Tamora's transgression in sexual and State affairs it deserves destruction. At the same time, it is proof of her disobedience and would promote the restoration of patriarchal order. A wish to preserve the bastard and an awareness of its potential danger provokes an ambiguous response from the audience which reflects the wider ideological problem of containing the bastard as a useful 'other'.

In Heywood's *The Silver Age* (1611) and *The Brazen Age* (1611) another complex picture emerges in the treatment of bastard infanticides. Both plays show Juno's attempts to destroy her husband's bastards in defence of the power structure of which she is part. In *The Silver Age*, she casts a charm to imprison Hercules in Alcumena's womb (121–2) and wants to kill 'the adulteresse' (123). She does not succeed in this case but when Semele also becomes pregnant by Jove, Juno disguises herself as Semele's nurse and, knowing that Semele will be burned to death, tricks her into making Jove promise to appear like a god before her (149–53). In both cases Juno attacks fellow victims of Jove's abuse. Heywood is careful to portray the women as divided, aiming their criticisms at each other rather than at Jove, whose lust is responsible for the suffering of all.

Within this conventional framework, Heywood criticises the

persecuting power and the legitimate hierarchy as a whole.
Juno's sadistic pleasure hardly encourages sympathy from the
audience. She rejoices in the expectation of seeing Semele 'with
her bastard, blowne / And hang'd upon the high hornes of the
moone' (153). She appears increasingly manic in her attempts to
destroy Hercules. As he overcomes more of her traps, she tells
Euristeus

> If neither tyrants, monsters, savages,
> Giants nor hell-hounds, can the bastard quell;
> Let him be pasht, stab'd, strangled, poisoned,
> Or murdered sleeping.
>
> (126)

More significant than the alienating effect is the message that
Juno, in upholding the legitimate hierarchy, is disobeying the
wishes of her husband and, what is more, the supreme heavenly
deity. Jove stands up for bastards and their preservation (each
time Juno plots against his bastards he intervenes to save them).
Juno, the hysterical villain of the piece, persecutes them.
Heywood encourages criticism of the sadistic behaviour of a
woman in a mythical story to suggest that the powers persecuting bastards in Renaissance England may be misdirected, the
result of hysteria.

Older bastard characters who are victims of official persecution provoke an even more complex response since they have
articulate voices to express their individuality and ideas. Sometimes sympathy for a character could, paradoxically, be twisted
round to rally support for the harsh official response to bastardy.
For example, the opening of *The Bastard* tricks the audience into
showing an interest in the villain's affairs. The Prologue points
out that Gaspar is laid at the doors of the audience in the hopes
that their '*milder* Genius' might bestow favour on him, adopt
him, and allow his play to begin. His utter dependency, '*by your
hand / Our Brat must dye or live, must fall or stand*' (A4),
appeals to their sense of power, and the moral obligation to
protect him is stressed in the lines

> *Your favour cannot shame you; may h'invite*
> *Your bounty, though but in a smile or mite.*
> *Some Childless Signor, take him to his feet;*

'Twere Cruelty *to let him lie i' th'* street:
A sin! alas! a shame! a sin! that He
Should beg *upon the* Parish-Charity.

(A4)

Because Gaspar gradually emerges as a powerful villain, the audience is invited to condemn the charitable view which allowed him to develop as a character. They are shown just how dangerous such sympathy can be when Gaspar, newly committed to wickedness, plays the role of helpless victim again to win the trust of Roderigo, whom he plans to use in the furtherance of his plots. He dupes Roderigo into believing he is 'honest' with the pathetic lines 'I am a man whom stepdame *Fortune* made / To eat my bread in servitude' (D2). The audience recognise their own experience in that of the gullible Roderigo, whose response mirrors their earlier sympathy for Gaspar. Criticism appears to be directed at the indulgent view of illegitimacy, but further investigation proves that the audience themselves are deeply implicated in the play's censure. Their vanity in accepting the invitation of the flattering Prologue is ultimately responsible for the creation of a character who must act villainously to achieve his goal. Their wish to construct the bastard as an utterly dependent figure – reassuring them of their own power to control – is arrogant and dangerous.

A more conventional appeal to the audience is found in Richard Brome's play *The Damoiselle* (1638). Phillis is one of the few female bastards in the drama and broadens the scope of Brome's criticism by drawing a link between the dispossession of women and bastards. She offers a pathetic picture as a beggar amongst the rogues and paupers of the streets:

I have allowance here, as well as any
Brokers, Projectors, Common Bail, or Bankrupts,
Pandars and Cheaters of all sorts that mix here
Mongst men of honour, worship, lands and money.

(406)

Phillis lists her fellow supplicants: 'Brokers, Projectors, Common Bail, or Bankrupts / Pandars and Cheaters', beside the 'Men of honour' with wealth and property. All are part of the oppressive system of homosocial exchange, whether victims or oppressors.

She alone suffers by virtue of her identity (as female and illegitimate), rather than by participation in the system. She appeals to
the audience to recognise the injustice of her situation. Such
characters must have elicited a very mixed reaction from an
audience whose laws persecuted the bastard. Dramatists rely
on popular ideas about illegitimacy – its immorality, its expense
and threat to society – to complicate feelings of pity.

More dangerous and dramatically exciting is the resentment
of a character like Edmund in *King Lear* (1605). His aggressive
questions carry energy and and drive which may not elicit the
sympathy of the audience but makes them question

> Why bastard? Wherefore base?
> When my dimensions are as well compact,
> My mind as generous, and my shape as true,
> As honest madam's issue?
>
> (1.2.6)

They are forced to see the implications of being labelled 'base'
and recognise that the individual so persecuted was unlikely to
accept his position as object lesson willingly. Voices like
Edmund's alterted the audience to the dangerous idea that,
instead of remaining within his assigned role as victim, the
bastard might structure his own identity to create a world 'in
every thing illegitimate' outside the control of the legitimate
hierarchy.

*'What a largeness in your will and liberty': subversive power and
containment*

Illegitimate status, which defined base-born children as outsiders, could give them considerable freedom of movement. In
the late sixteenth and early seventeenth centuries, bastards who
did not die in childhood were 'a highly mobile group in the
population' (Oosterveen and Smith 1980: 103). Plays with
bastards sometimes indicate their freedom of movement explicitly. In *The Late Lancashire Witches* (1634), for example,
Whetstone's words 'Where do I lye? why, sometimes in one
place, and then againe in another, I love to shift lodgings'
(100) suggests the physical mobility of the type. More important,

bastardy and its accompanying social isolation allows a character freedom to observe, criticise and rebel not generally enjoyed by woman as legitimate 'other'. In most cases, woman's negative status is linked to the positive controlling presence of her husband or father, but the bastard, who is cut off from the name of the father, enjoys more independence from patriarchal influence. In Middleton's *Women Beware Women* (1621), Isabella's belief that she is illegitimate frees her from her father's authority. Livia points out

> How weak his commands now, whom you call father?
> How vain all his enforcements, your obedience?
> And what a largeness in your will and liberty,
> To take, or to reject, or to do both?
>
> (2.1.158)

Female subservience is replaced by an illegitimate autonomy which allows Isabella to choose to commit adultery with Hippolito. In becoming a bastard, she has assumed the independence usually accorded to men in the drama.

The bastard's freedom of movement is dramatically exciting and unnerving. It gives a natural unpredictability to characters which makes them ideal figures to introduce dramatic action. At the same time, independence renders them difficult to contain within the boundaries of the play's official discourses. Their difference threatens to erupt beyond the confines of the social world of the play. Dramatists who chose not to characterise bastards as helpless object lessons were faced with the problem of how to present the type's subversive power – or 'otherness' – in a way that could be reconciled with official attitudes to illegitimacy. They responded to the challenge in a range of ways, many of which seem to vindicate the letter of the orthodox view while subverting its spirit.

The most obvious was to present the character's difference as villainous. As a product of female transgression, illegitimacy was a terrifying unknown, a dark continent of dangers to Renaissance patriarchy. This encouraged the presentation of bastards as evil, deformed, ugly and terrifying. The majority of adult bastards are villains. Sometimes they are part of a demonic environment, related to witches or devils or to the Vice of the morality

tradition. In plays with a secular focus, they are shown acting
'unnaturally' in society's eyes, involved in incest, adultery, parricide, fratricide, regicide and rebellion. Such negative characterisations appear to reinforce the worst social prejudices but, at the
same time, they attribute a sense of power to a group which the
authorities wished to display as victimised. Bastard villains are
disturbing; their ruthless destruction of family, community and
State hierarchies exposes the fragility of the legitimate world
order. If they have an opportunity to explain their alternative
point of view, their actions can acquire a perverse logic.

The danger of the unsocialised bastard comes from his origins
in a feminine, uncivilised world of nature. A second way to retain
his distinct identity, while still conforming to the authorised
image of bastardy, was to present him as a 'natural' or clown.
Plays such as Heywood's *Love's Mistress* (1634) or Brome's *The
English Moor* (1637) make fun of the bastard to exorcise fears of
the 'other', though these grotesque figures have an unnerving
way of dislodging typically held beliefs. In some plays, such as
Brome's *A Jovial Crew* (1641), the bastard's closeness to nature
is perceived as an asset. The condition of such positive images
was that the bastard should, ultimately, service legitimate society
as a force of renewal rather than remaining independent.

Reintegrating bastards into the legitimate community was
another way of containing their subversive power, but one
which involved many risks. The ruling power could not relin-
quish its authority so the inclusion of a bastard relied on a
restructuring of the 'other' at the expense of the bastard's
alternative world view. By getting him to accept the very laws
which persecuted him, society would force the bastard to accept
his role as victim. A figure thus brainwashed would consolidate
the legitimate hegemony. Texts which speak out in favour of
illegitimacy do so with a consciousness of how useful it could be,
and with the imposition of clear conditions so as to channel its
energy in support of the status quo. William Clerke (1594) and
Thomas Milles (1613) both write with these ideas in mind. Milles
argues that the bastard cannot be blamed for the sins of his
parents, that 'what Bastard soever he bee; in a well disposed,
holy, and vertuous life, he may bury the name and impudicity of
his parents and all the rememberence of their unchast act'

(Milles 1613: 725). To be regarded as virtuous, the bastard had to forget the subversive elements of his conception and birth; only if he adopted the ideology of those in power, living 'well disposed' to their notions of what was holy and lawful, could room be made to include him. An example of reintegration according to this model can be seen in Jonson's *Every Man in his Humour* where Cash is adopted, educated and employed by Kiteley. He is given the name 'Cash' which matches his job as cashier and reduces his identity to his legitimate function within the system (2.1.18).

Further up the social scale, bastards who were publicly acknowledged by kings or aristocrats could be admitted into the legitimate family as long as it was on the family's terms. They were not allowed to share the family name but many had names invented for them or were named after places. Sir George Buck says 'The bastards of sundry kings were called Fitzroy Oxenford, Fitzherbert Clarendon, Fitzhenry Longuespee Cornwall' (Buck 1982: 76). They were allowed to bear the family arms, provided it was distinguished with a mark to indicate illegitimacy – the band azure or band sinister. Henry Peacham's *The Compleat Gentleman* says that bastards were granted a form of nobility 'by giving them sometimes their Fathers proper Coate, with a bend Sinister, as *Reginald Earle of Cornewall*, base sonne to the Conqueror, bare his Fathers two Leopards passant gardant, Or, in a field *Gules*, with a bend Sinister Azure' (Peacham 1634: 9). Such bastards could achieve high status positions in society. In *The Devil's Law Case*, Crispiano reminds the court of the respect generally paid to the bastards of kings or noblemen by asking 'When do we name Don John of Austria, / The emperor's son, but with reverence?' (4.2.327). In Renaissance England, Henry Fitzroy, a base son of Henry VIII, had been made Duke of Buckingham and Lord High Admiral of England (Given-Wilson and Curteis: 174–5). Through special dispensations, procured for a certain sum, noble bastards were also permitted to enter the Church. Wolsey's illegitimate son was appointed Dean of Wells.

The advantages such figures enjoyed seems to contradict the image society wanted to promote, but the public exhibition of noble bastards was extremely useful for the governing powers. In

adopting a position of status, the bastard embraces those very
laws which persecute him, reduce him to nothing. He becomes
attached to the ruling order which denies him inheritance and
equality with his legitimate brothers. He appears to accept the
fact that he has no rights and relies absolutely on their charity. In
court, he is displayed as evidence of male sexual prowess and the
kindly authority of patriarchal rule which grants him a place,
albeit an inferior one. A public proclamation of difference and
disadvantage – through the mark of the bar sinister – relays the
message that acceptance of the dominant power's values and
one's own inferior position can bring qualified rewards. This
consolidates the State's authority. Bastards who appear to be
wholly complicit with the legitimate world can provide even
more powerful object lessons than victims like babies and
children since their acceptance of an inferior position seems to
be based on conscious choice.

At the same time, the re-absorption of the aristocratic bastard
was extremely dangerous since its usefulness depended on a very
fragile means of control, enforced only through abstract symbols
(the bar sinister and the differentiating lack of family name). The
power of these symbols to mark out the bastard was totally
reliant on the meaning attached to them by the community
and by the bastard himself. Was he likely to accept his position
as inferior without question? Would others continue to distinguish between the bastard and his legitimate siblings? The
instability of a process where the negative term was absorbed
back into the positive one was that it could easily break down the
opposition betweeen the two. The discourse which permitted
the acknowledgement and civilisation of the illegitimate aristocrat also revealed the possibility of an opposite movement, a
devolvement of power into the hands of the bastard and the
disintegration of legitimate hierarchy.

Dramatists were obviously interested in noble or royal
bastards because there are a large number in the drama. These
characters show the difficulty of reconciling the bastard's difference and the legitimate world's values. In more orthodox
presentations the noble bastard's 'otherness' is a tragic flaw.
His heroic support of the legitimate structure is praised throughout the play but his birth dooms him to commit an anti-social

action which causes his downfall. The fault is perceived as endemic, in his blood rather than in the system which labels him illegitimate. The majority of plays take a more controversial line and explore the dangerousness of re-absorbing the illegitimate other. They focus on the bastard's paradoxical attitude to the system which persecutes him, showing that his integration into the court has led him to accept and admire its values but that his disadvantage inevitably makes him want to change it. His wish to destroy the legitimate world is combined with a desire to be part of it. Self-contradictions in the bastard character offer the opportunity to dramatise a conflict of ideologies and question the relative merits of each, airing heterodox ideas about the ordering of society.

Even more radical are dramatic presentations of illegitimacy which take as their starting point the idea proposed by William Clerke that, in certain circumstances, the bastard might prove more virtuous than the legitimate child, that 'vertue sometimes springes from lawlesse knowledge, and vice from lawfull' (Clerke 1594: *4v). Defining bastardy as a positive (virtue) and legitimacy in essentially negative terms (vice) reverses the conventional binary opposition. Several writers adopt this approach, presenting the isolated bastard character as virtuous in contrast to a society where 'the life, the right, and truth' of the whole realm are demonstrably absent (*King John*, 4.3.144). In such cases, the bastard's detachment is an asset, allowing him to uphold principles normally associated with legitimacy in a world which is evil. Teichman (1982) notes the development of this type in nineteenth-century literature where 'the illegitimate child or love child is quite often used by novelists as a symbol of natural goodness as opposed to worldly vanity or family greed' (123). Its inception in isolated cases in Renaissance drama indicates a daring attempt to challenge the established order on the part of a few writers.

The title of Milles's treatise, 'A Paradoxe, in the Defence of Bastardie' (1613) reminds us that a positive view of illegitimacy contrasted with a much more prevalent prejudice. Bastardy was usually defined as an immoral, cumbersome and potentially threatening 'other'. The bastard was perceived – in public at least – as an economic problem, a type essentially alone, disadvantaged and often discontented with this; an individual non-socialised and thus inherently dangerous to society; a figure barred from heavenly bliss and morally tainted from birth. From an initial survey of the plays it seems that the dramatic depiction of bastardy is part of the pattern of prejudice, producing and produced by current insecurity in the legitimate world. This overview is deceptive, however. Bastard characters, both villainous and virtuous, reveal a complex repsonse to the challenge of illegitimacy. In Renaissance drama, the bastard is an amazing crossroads for social and dramatic influences, conservative and radical. He is a site of struggle for conventional views which would uphold the dominant ideology and attempts to criticise it. The following chapters will examine in detail a variety of ways in which this theatrically versatile type is constructed to frame ideas about authority and its subversion.

2

Bastardy and evil

In *The Revenger's Tragedy* (1606), Vindice introduces Spurio as 'true-begot in evil' (1.1.3). The other courtly characters are defined in relation to their sins but Spurio is essentially wicked. Because he is born out of wedlock, he is a true son of evil. The Duchess elaborates this idea in the following scene, telling him that he was cursed in the womb, 'Begot against the seventh commandment, / Half damned in the conception by the justice / Of that unbribed, everlasting law' (1.2.160). Bastardy is condemned by the highest moral authority, divine law, which is incorruptible. Spurio's evil nature seems to be confirmed by the reference to Scripture. By placing the text in the mouth of the Duchess, though, the scene problematises religious authority. Her own moral position is immediately suspect since she wants to break the seventh commandment herself. It is she rather than Spurio who is the figure of vice, tempting him to accept the incestuous kisses which will pluck open hell. Even more disturbing, she uses Scripture to further her devious ends. Its law is hardly 'unbribed' or disinterested as it is cited to encourage Spurio's feelings of resentment and diminish his moral sensiblities. The dramatic context shows that religious authority is not stable or absolute at all. It is connected to worldly concerns and, as such, can be manipulated, corrupted. Labelling the bastard as evil was not as simple as it appeared.

It was further complicated by the wider spiritual context in post-Reformation England where 'fundamental questions were being asked about the grounds on which religious authority was justified' (Hill 1986: 37). Even if the Church could distinguish between legitimate and base, and unequivocally condemned illegitimacy, there was no absolute agreement on who 'the

Church' was. Distrust of the State ecclesiastical and its ministers
reflected and produced a variety of faiths in organised non-
conforming groups and in a more vaguely folklorised Christianity, a syncretism of pagan and Christian beliefs (Reay 1985: 112).
Thomas Cooper's *Admonition to the People of England* (1589)
claimed 'the whole state ecclesiastical . . . is grown into hatred
and contempt, and all inferior subjects disdain in any point to be
ruled by them'. The people had 'conceived an heathenish contempt of religion and a disdainful loathing of the ministers
thereof' (Hill 1986: 52–3). Dissenting voices denounced the
official Church as reproducing the hierarchy of the Roman
model. John Penry complained that since the Reformation
there had been 'no alteration at all' in the offices of the priest,
the deacon, the bishops or archbishops and 'very little' in the
form of service (Hill 1971: 55). Presbyterians demanded reform
of ecclesiastical government from within while separating con-
gregations made up an underground movement of radical sects.
In 1593 a new law decreed that all non-conformists would be
treated in the same harsh way as Catholic recusants. The Reformation was a centrifugal force, producing a fragmentation of
religious belief which proliferated right up to the outbreak of
civil war and beyond. As part of this environment, the presentation of evil bastard characters was more than a conservative
judgement on fornication; it could be an active engagement
with the religious controversy of the time, a projection of
spiritual insecurities.

Religious authority formed the backbone of patriarchal order
in Renaissance England so the spiritual condemnation of bastardy had important economic and social dimensions. The
Church legitimated the activities of the ruling hierarchy by
demonising forces alien to it. The most obvious example is the
witch, a figure whose close relationship with the evil bastard will
be discussed below. Like female non-conformity, illegitimacy
was inevitably perceived as an alien element. A child born outside wedlock was a dangerous supplement to the legitimate
family, a product of unsanctioned female fertility. As we have
seen, it was a surplus which disrupted economic, social and
moral order by redirecting finances, disturbing property transactions and transgressing the laws set up to maintain patriarchal

control. It was therefore damned so that it could be disempowered in social and material terms. The bastard can be seen as a human example of *la part maudite*, Georges Bataille's economic category of the accursed surplus. *La part maudite* is that excess which society produces and then identifies for sacrifice: 'The victim is a surplus taken from the means of useful wealth . . . Once chosen, he is the accursed share, destined for violent consumption' (Bataille 1988: 59). In Renaissance England, bastardy was constructed as the accursed share. It was chosen for sacrifice to preserve the legitimate order.

Biblical authority figures prominently in texts dealing with the legal position of bastards. Writers wishing to justify the civil laws which discriminated against illegitimacy pointed out that children conceived in sin (against the seventh commandment) were essentially evil and could only escape this inheritance by means of God's special grace. Sir John Fortescue (1573) remarks 'it is a common sayeinge: If a bastard be good, that commeth to him by chance, that is to witte by special grace, but if hee bee evill, that commethe to hym by nature. For it is thought that the base childe draweth a certaine corruption and staine from the sinne of his parentes, without his owne fault' (95v). Fortescue goes on to argue that illegitimacy categorises one as 'the chylde of synne' (96v), that bastards are born 'wyth a certeyn privye marke in their soules' (97v). The idea that inbred corruption led to evil behaviour was elaborated by Henry Swinburne, whose *Treatise of Testaments and Last Willes* (1590) was the standard work on ecclesiastical law. Swinburne concluded it was only right that bastards should not inherit above legitimate children because 'the brood of bastardes are commonly infected with the leprosie of the Sires disease: and being encouraged with the example and patterne of their fathers filthiness, they are not onely prone to follow their sinfull steppes, but do sometimes exceede both them and others in all kinde of wickednesse' (Swinburne 1590: 200).

Other useful biblical references to bastardy were found in Hebrews and Deuteronomy. Hebrews 12: 5–8 stated that those born out of wedlock were not the children of God, defining them in opposition to God's dutiful sons who endure and accept his chastening punishments. This effectively criminalised bastards. There was no Scripture saying that the faithful should not suffer a bastard to live (unlike Exodus 22: 18 which licensed the murder of witches), but Deuteronomy unequivocally excluded them from God's kingdom: 'A bastard shall not enter into the congregation of the Lord: even unto his tenth generation shall he not enter into the congregation of the Lord' (Deuteronomy 28: 2). This text was used to legitimate the exclusion of bastards from trade guilds, and from civil as well as ecclesiastical office. Children who were born in defiance of divine law were damned by that law. Renaissance plays include numerous incidental references to the curse of illegitimacy. In Sir William Alexander's *Croesus* (1604), the King describes a bastard as one 'barrd from blisse / Whom heavens doe hate' (2.1.371). Scarborow in *The Miseries of Enforced Marriage* (1606) believes that his children are 'accurst of heaven' even in the cradle (2,484). In Davenant's *The Just Italian* (1629), Florello tells Dandolo 'y'are illegitimate, begot / By the motion of an evil spirit' (249).

However absolute these condemnations appear, they were, of course, open to question in a society where contradictory readings of the Bible by different religious groups co-existed and there was no ultimate authority to decide between rival interpretations. Bastard plays, which are part of this culture, often undermine the religious authorities they quote, as in the case of *The Revenger's Tragedy*. What was more, constructing bastardy as evil did not relegate it to a totally negative category. The bastard acquires a new life of his own as the accursed share. Damnation transforms him from an object in protocapitalist society to an autonomous subject. As Georges Bataille puts it: 'The curse tears him away from the *order of things*, it gives him a recognizeable figure, which now radiates intimacy, anguish and the profundity of living beings' (59). The bastard gains a sovereignty of self not shared by the legitimate world which is obsessed with acquisition and self-preservation. In this, he is like the witch; he gives life to alien energies. His independence endows him with a dangerous charisma which raises questions about the values of the order which condemns him. Dramatists use the bastard character to present a complex picture of evil appropriate to their own spiritual environment, to make critical interventions into a social structure which appealed to the Bible for support.

'Got by the devil himself'

The most obvious way for a dramatist to legitimate his portrayal of evil was to give the bastard character satanic parentage. As the son of a devil or a witch, he was undeniably born *ex damnato coitu* since one or both of his parents had already consecrated themselves to the powers of darkness. Most demonic bastards are the offspring of a witch and a devil or incubus. They are often monstrous, following popular myths about devil-children such as Tom Thumb, Sir Growther and Robert the Devil. In Drayton's poem *The Moone Calfe* (1627), for example, the earth admits that the father of the child she is about to bear is not an elephant or a sea monster but Satan. The baby to which she gives birth is a monstrous siamese twin, 'The most abhorrid, the most fearfull sight / That ever eye beheld' (1931–41, 3: 166). The moon-calf's appearance is a visual sign of the demonic sexual liaison from which it was conceived. Merlin in *The Birth of Merlin* (1608) and Caliban in *The Tempest* (1611) are both moon-calves with satanic parentage. The pain surrounding the birth of a monstrous devil-child is described in detail in the anonymous prose romance *Robert the Devyl* (c. 1500). Robert takes a month to be born and when he enters the world, amidst darkness and thunder, he is already the size of a one-year-old and has teeth (Thoms 1858: 7–8). Thomas Nashe parodies the tradition in his account of Gabriel Harvey's birth in *Have With You To Saffron Waldon* (1596). Gabriel's mother dreams that her womb harbours devils like a 'hollow vessell full of disquiet fiends', and that she will give birth to a hand gun, a garden full of weeds and a kestrel. When the child is born, he immediately starts to write so people conclude 'an *Incubus*, in the likenes of an inke-bottle, had carnall copulation with his mother when hee was begotten' (1966, 3: 61–2).

Rowley's play *The Birth of Merlin* appropriates many of the details common to devil-child myths to characterise Merlin, the son of Joan Go-Too't and an incubus. The devil tells Joan 'The fatal fruit thou bear'st within thy womb / Shall here be famous till the day of doom' (100) and orchestrates Merlin's birth amidst thunder and lightning: 'Mix light and darkness, earth and heaven dissolve, be of one piece agen and turn to Chaos, break all your works you powers, and spoil the world' (104). The spectacular birth scene builds up expectations of a pagan Antichrist who will overthrow the Christian king, Aurelius. Merlin is a 'mixture of infernal seed' (105) and like other devil-children he is monstrous. When Joan asks her brother to welcome the baby, the Clown replies 'Make much of a Moncky? This is worse then Tom Thumb, that let a fart in his mother's belly' (108). Merlin's appearance – fully grown, with teeth and a long beard – goes some way to justify the Clown's reaction and his protest 'some Baboon begot thee' (108). The first part of the play leads the audience to fear the worst of this 'fien'd begotten childe' (118). Merlin's heroic actions reverse the process. He becomes a figure of Christian salvation who defeats the pagan magician Proximus (121) and imprisons the devil in the underworld, thereby redeeming Joan and the kingdom (134-5). As a 'traitor to hell' (134), he confounds the audience's expectations and throws conventional moral categories (including those related to bastardy) into confusion.

Merlin's parentage as the son of a supernatural father and a relatively virtuous mother is unique in the drama; all the other demonic bastards are the sons of witches (although Joan is referred to as a 'witch' by her brother, the insult is related to her illicit pregnancy rather than to any involvement with black magic). The witch shares the bastard's role as the accursed surplus because, like him, she is a figure of excess. As Sandra Gilbert remarks, witchcraft is a culturally stylised channel 'into which *excess* demonically flows – excess desire, excess rage, excess creative energy' to be annihilated by society (Cixous and Clément 1986: xii). The witch (like the bastard) takes on a life of her own as a damned being. Her independence from patriarchal order gives her a personal radiance and one channel of her creative energy is sexual, her ability to produce children outside the conventional family. Jules Michelet's *La Sorcière*, published in 1862, celebrates witches as rebels against the patriarchal Christian church. He claims that the witch's lifestyle releases a feminine energy which endows her with second sight

and 'la sublime puissance de la conception solitaire', the ability
to give birth alone:

> Seule, elle conçut et enfanta. Qui? Un autre elle-même qui lui
> ressemble à s'y tromper. Fils de haine, conçu de l'amour. Car,
> sans l'amour, on ne crée rien . . . La Sorcière vraiment fit un être.
> Il a tous les semblants de la réalité . . . Voyez au contraire, l'impuis-
> sance de l'Eglise pour engendrer. Comme ses anges sont pales, à
> l'état de grisaille, diaphanes! On voit à travers. Meme . . . les
> démons . . . sont grotesques encore plus que terribles; elles sont
> flottantes et baladines. Tout autre sort Satan du sein brûlant de la
> Sorcière, vivant, armé et tout brandi.

> [Alone, she conceived and gave birth. To whom? Another self who is
> so like her as to deceive the eyes. Son of hate, conceived of love, for
> without love nothing is made . . . The witch really made a living
> being. He has all the appearance of reality . . . See, in contrast, the
> powerlessness of the Church to engender. How pale its angels are, in
> a state of diaphanous greyness. One sees right through them! . . .
> Even its demons are grotesque rather than terrible; they are floating
> buffoons. Altogether different comes Satan, out of the burning
> womb of the witch, living and brandishing his arms.]

(Michelet 1952: 9)

In contrast to the artefacts of good and evil produced by the
Church fathers, the witch's bastard has an energetic originality
and autonomy of being which makes conventional morality look
insubstantial. He is frightening because he reminds patriarchal
authority of its own inability to produce living matter (in the
form of children), and woman's ability to do so outside its
control. The witch's power to conceive and give birth to a child
who reproduces her subversive ideas in unadulterated form is
profoundly menacing. The opinions of male demonologists on
the possibility of procreation between humans and spirits try to
deny the autonomy of the witch by arguing that only a man can
beget children.

In *The Discoverie of Witchcraft* (1584), Reginald Scot asserts
that no child can be the bastard of an incubus 'begotten without
carnall copulation (as Hyperius and others write that Merlin
was)', since the incubus, being a spiritual thing itself, is not
able to impregnate a woman with its own seed (Scot 1964: 88).
The opinion that spirits could not produce semen and thus

fertilise human eggs was shared by Kramer and Sprenger, authors
of *Malleus Maleficarum* (*c.* 1486) and King James in his *Daemonologie* (1597). However, it was agreed that devils, taking on the
shapes of succubi and incubi, could obtain semen from a man
(either by inhabiting a dead human body or by making love to a
living man as a succubus) and impregnate a woman in the form of
an incubus. The resulting child was therefore the son of a man, as
explained in *Malleus Maleficarum*: 'Now it may be asked, of
whom is a child so born the son? It is clear that he is not the
son of the devil but of the man whose semen was received'
(Kramer and Sprenger *c.* 1486: 26). These words betray a strong
sense of insecurity, a need to re-assert the importance of man's
active contribution to conception.

The witch's closeness to her own fertile body denaturalises
conventional morality. According to French feminist Xavière
Gauthier, 'witches are bursting; their entire bodies are desire;
their gestures are caresses; their smell, taste, hearing are all
sensual. Their pleasure is so violent, so transgressive, so open,
so fatal, that men have not yet recovered' (Gauthier 1976: 201).
Popular myth associated witchcraft with an excess of passion
which manifested itself in the form of sexually deviant acts.
Quaife (1987) argues that, in England, there was no general
correlation between charges of sexual deviance, bastard-bearing
and witchcraft accusations, but undoubtedly some spinsters with
illegitimate children formed part of the group of vulnerable
women who were accused and these individual cases fuelled
popular opinion. A bastard child was a concrete example of a
witch's sexual excess. In the Essex witch trials of 1582 and 1589
illegitimacy features in the case histories of three of the women.
The aptly named Joan Cunny is described as 'living very lewdly'
and having 'two lewd daughters no better than naughty packs'
who 'had two bastard children: being both boys' (Rosen 1991:
185). In the 1582 trial of women from St Oyses, Ursley Kempe
and Annis Herd both have illegitimate children who testify
against their mothers (Rosen 1991: 109–10, 152). Bastardy,
female transgression and witchcraft are linked in plays such as
Middleton's *The Witch* (1613) where Hecate (who has a bastard
called Firestone), and the other witches enjoy sex with a variety
of men in incubus form. Their incontinence is mirrored in the

supposedly virtuous community of Ravenna, where Francisca conceives and gives birth to a bastard from an affair with Abarnazes, and suspicions of adultery threaten the marriages of the Duke and Duchess and of Isabella and Antonio.

The witch's reproductive power defies the restraints imposed by the Church. Her bastard child challenges the system of ethics produced and reproduced by the Church fathers at the heart of the patriarchal system. The power of his affront comes from his audacious rebellion in contrast with the Church's conformity; his novelty as opposed to its conventions; his fertility in opposition to its sterile repetition of accepted beliefs. Michelet describes his lively protest against the self-authenticating Trinity of the medieval Church: 'Quand on essaye de faire parler les Trois Personnes entre elles . . . l'ennui monte au sublime. De l'une à l'autre, c'est un *oui* éternel . . . Au contraire, ce gaillard, le fils de la sorcière, sait donner la réplique. Il répond à Jesus. Je suis sur qu'il le desennuie, accablé comme il est de l'insipidité de ses saints.' (When one tries to make the Three Persons talk to each other, one takes boredom to the sublime. From one to the other it's an eternal *yes* . . . By contrast, this gallant, the son of the witch, knows how to give a retort. He replies to Jesus. I'm sure he relieves his boredom, weighed down as he is with the insipidity of his saints) (Michelet 1952: 11).

Michelet compares conformist and non-conformist voices as legitimate and illegitimate sons, echoing Hebrews 12: 5-8. The sons of the Church, confident in their inheritance of eternal grace, wait passively. Their activity is limited to the narrow circle of imitation. In contrast, 'le bâtard maudit, dont la part n'est rien que le fouet, il n'a garde d'attendre. Il va cherchant et jamais ne repose. Il s'agite, de la terre au ciel. Il est fort curieux, fouille, entre, sonde, et met le nez partout. Du *Consummatum est* il se rit, il se moque. Il dit toujours <<Plus loin!>> – et <<En avant!>>.' (The accursed bastard, whose lot is nothing but the whip, doesn't keep waiting. He is always searching and never rests. He is always on the move between heaven and earth. He is very curious, rummaging, penetrating, scrutinising. He puts his nose everywhere. He laughs at 'consummatum est', he makes fun. He always says 'Further on!' and 'Forward!') (Michelet 1952: 12). In Renaissance drama, the bastard of demonic parents makes the same trenchant and probing observations about the conventions of his moral world. His identity as the accursed share frees him from the principles of self-preservation and salvation which operate in that world, allowing him to give voice to non-conformist ideas, both religious and secular.

The Seven Champions of Christendom (1635), supposedly by John Kirke but with possible input from Thomas Heywood (Merchant 1978), uses the relationship between the bastard and his devil-father to undermine paternal authority. Only Tarpax is named as Suckabus's father, implying that man had no part in begetting the witch's son. In addition, the play relies on the popular belief that spirits could not beget children. The witch, Calib, and Tarpax repeatedly stress Tarpax's paternity, but Suckabus is never fully convinced. He says 'mothers have so often belide the childes father, that I am very doubtfull whether ever I had any' (C3v). He refuses to acknowledge Tarpax at first, preferring the physical link he has with his mother (he resembles her much more than Tarpax). The text highlights the instability of paternity, and the dangers of using it as a foundation of social and legal identity.

The uncertainty of Suckabus's relationship with Tarpax is mirrored in his fluctuating allegiance to evil. He is a clown rather than a frightening satanic power, though he is governed by vice. He asks the devil to give him charms to 'juggle as well as any Hocus Pocus i' th' world' (H2) and the audience see him using the spells. He tells his master George that he does not like the sound of 'Elizium' because 'it is a place where good and honest men come in and for mine owne part, I am in the minde never to trouble it' (G4v). Suckabus embodies vices of excess – sloth, gluttony and lechery. He thinks in terms of food or sex and enjoys himself most when he has nothing to do but talk about these things. He presents a negative opposite to the chivalric exploits of the Champions of Christendom and their leader, George. Suckabus thwarts their attack on the giant, Brandron, by tempting six of the Champions with thoughts of lechery (K2v–K3).

The witch's son threatens the Christian quest in a more complex way as George's servant. He shadows the hero like an evil angel and, within the play's psychomachia pattern, symbolises the illegitimate side of George's personality – his connection to the powers of darkness. George is brought up by Calib as a bastard whom the witch supposedly saved from destruction at the hands of his parents. Only by escaping from illegitimate identity is he able to recognise and then reject 'evil'. At the beginning of the play he is torn between his affection for Calib and dislike of bastardy. He uses her magic wand to conjure a vision of his parents and they tell him he is true-born and should 'Vomit the thought of Bastard' (Civ). Newly legitimated, he murders Calib and releases the six Champions, whom he leads into battle against the powers of evil. George is undoubtedly a hero but the clarity of the play's moral structure is marred by his close association with Suckabus. Suckabus is George's internal enemy in the 'warre my selfe hath with my selfe' (Ci). He gives a constant reminder of George's potential for vice and the shadowy presence of illegitimacy behind all legitimate structures. Suckabus shows that far from being something totally alien, evil is uncomfortably proximate to legitimate society.

The Tempest (1611) takes this technique a stage further and presents Caliban as a caricature of the evil in the legitimate world which demonises him. John Freehafer (1969) argues that The Seven Champions may be a parody of The Tempest because of the similarities between Suckabus and Caliban as witches' sons who embody transgressive sensuality and treachery. Certainly both function subversively in their texts as projections of vice. Shakespeare uses the devil's bastard to query the ethics behind western patriarchy, as represented by Prospero and the visitors to the island. Prospero refers to Caliban's birth when first summoning him to the stage: 'Thou poisonous slave, got by the devil himself / Upon thy wicked dam, come forth!' (1.2.319). Caliban's mother is the 'damn'd witch Sycorax' (1.2.263) who was exiled to the island (already pregnant with Caliban), for her wicked sorceries. His origins are emphasised in the descriptions 'devil . . . born devil' (4.1.188), 'freckled whelp, hag-born' (1.2.283), and 'Hag-seed' (1.2.365). Caliban's destructive plans, emotions and wishes confirm his identity as an opponent of legitimate good – Prospero's creative magic. At the end of the play the master-magician makes a direct association between

Caliban's bastardy and his evil nature, describing him as a 'demi-
devil / (For he's a bastard one)' (5.1.272). He seems to be the
offspring of an incubus, but three lines later Prospero contradicts
himself, saying 'this thing of darkness I / Acknowledge mine'
(5.1.275). Caliban's evil powers and Prospero's beneficent magic
are not opposites after all. They turn out to be closely related.
The bastard is demonised because he rebels against the good
magician. To Prospero, this unnatural act proves that Caliban is
'a born devil, on whose nature / Nurture can never stick'
(4.1.188). He has not learned the moral precepts which demand
obedience to a higher authority so he is uncivilised. When
Caliban's behaviour is compared to that of the other characters, we see something different. Instead of confirming Caliban's
lack of nurture, his actions demonstrate his closeness to civilised
society. His rebellion is a microcosm of State politics in Milan,
Naples and the island. It copies the misconduct of many of the
characters, from dukes to drunken butlers, and implicitly condemns the acquisitive and exploitative principles which dominate
all social levels in the play. The demi-devil's bid for power
identifies capitalist enterprise with lust, gluttony, avarice and
pride, sins which taint those who strive to rule the island and
the territories beyond. Prospero is not exempt from criticism.
Caliban is an image of the dual nature of the Duke of Milan. His
complaint 'this island's mine' reminds us simultaneously of
Prospero's position as a victim of his brother's treachery and
his identity as usurper on the island (1.2.331-44). Later, in the ill-
fated rebellion, Caliban plays out Prospero's less attractive role
as an indifferent coloniser, while locating him as the victim of an
attempted coup. Prospero may condemn Caliban as inimical to
nurture, but forgets that the bastard's plot to overthrow a
usurping power copies his own scheme to regain his dukedom.
    In these two episodes, Caliban is a projected representation of
one element of Prospero and Prospero occupies an opposing,
complementary subject position in each case. One Prospero
(whether the victim or the usurper) is always accompanied by
the other and the two seem to be interchangeable, almost
indistinguishable. Caliban is the link between Prospero and
Antonio, showing that they are reflections of each other: the
Duke of Milan. Prospero hints that his usurping brother might

be illegitimate (1.2.117–20) and, in acknowledging Caliban, he significantly takes responsibility for 'an aspect of Antonio' in himself (Orgel 1984: 217). He admits a likeness to his brother and the fact that his power is also illegitimate, even demonic, when seen from the perspective of those subjugated by it. The projection of Prospero's ambiguous nature in the witch's bastard has a broader didactic function as well. The interrelationship between the roles of victim and usurper suggests that everyone, including the ruler, is a victim of the power structure in which they operate. The pursuit of material gain is a trap and no one, not even Prospero, can escape the brutalising effects of this so-called civilised practice.

Caliban's other crime is a domestic one. We are told in the second scene that he attempted to rape Miranda, a piece of preplay history which is integral to the text's treatment of sexual and family politics. Miranda condemns Caliban as one 'capable of all ill' whose nature will not take the print of any civilised goodness (1.2.353–62). Her opinion matches that of her father on Caliban's unnatural treachery (4.1.188–9). As before, though, Caliban is not something alien. The assault certainly shows his savagery, his evil nature as the child of lust, but his sin is not unique. He represents the danger of ungoverned erotic impulses in all the characters. Mannoni suggests that even Prospero has incestuous desires for Miranda (the only woman on the island) and these lead him to project his evil thoughts on to Caliban, whom he hates 'on the grounds of sexual guilt' (Mannoni 1964: 106). If Ferdinand violates Miranda's chastity before they are married, he will descend to the bestial level of a Caliban, a possibility indicated in his service as a log-bearer. The play implicitly draws a parallel between chastity and slavery. Restrictions must be placed on sexual desire (both male and female) if patriarchal society and its system of primogeniture are to be maintained. Prospero's strict control of Miranda's activities is also figured in his enslavement of Caliban. As a bastard and a potential rapist, Caliban symbolises transgressive female sexuality and ungoverned male desire, both of which threaten patriarchal law from within. The careful balance of fertility and chastity in Prospero's masque (first threatened by Venus and her bastard Cupid 4.1.91–101), breaks down because of the impending plot of the 'beast' Caliban (4.1.139–40). The dangerous appetites he represents are demonised; Prospero calls him a 'born devil' and Stephen Orgel (1984) plausibly argues that Prospero may have invented Caliban's parentage as a projection of his (and perhaps Shakespeare's) fears about family structures and reproduction. Certainly the play shows a heightened insecurity about these things.

Through the figure of Miranda, Caliban's two crimes and the relationship between family and State politics are combined. By his own admission he tried to rape her to people the island with Calibans (1.2.349–51). Miranda is constructed, like the island, as a commodity: the object of male acquisitive desire and a source of production. She demonstrates the 'crucial nexus of civil power and sexuality in colonialist discourse' (Brown 1985: 62). Caliban's wish to colonise her body and reproduce is a grotesquely exaggerated image of how the other men regard her. Stephano is told she will 'become thy bed, . . . And bring thee forth brave brood' (3.2.104). Although Caliban is the only one to give voice to these sentiments, his view of woman is embedded in the speech and actions of the other men. Prospero's masque blesses Miranda and Ferdinand so they will be 'honor'd in their issue' and uses the body–territory metaphor to predict a fruitful marriage (4.1.105). Through careful husbandry, Ferdinand will enjoy 'Earth's increase, foison plenty / Barns and garners never empty' (4.1.110). Miranda will be subjected to a never-ending cycle of sowing and harvest (4.1.114–15). By condemning Caliban as a 'born devil' the play demonises this abuse of the female body. Acknowledging Caliban therefore involves recognising evil in the midst of patriarchal culture.

Bastards such as Caliban and Suckabus question the virtue of the legitimate world by externalising its own propensity to evil. In addition, the witch's son was ideal for exploring relationships between different types of religious belief. The spiritual environment of post-Reformation England included more things in heaven and earth than were dreamt of in the Christian philosophies of conformist and non-conformist groups. In many parts of the country, Christian ideas co-existed with beliefs in magic, popular healing and witches and spirits (Reay 1985: 111–12).

Bastards in plays could illustrate the demonisation of pagan elements by the dominant Christian culture. The anonymous *Wily Beguiled* (1602) explores relationships between traditional folklore and the practices of a commercialised society. Capitalist values are presented unsympathetically in the main love plot where Gripe (known as 'Grandsire Usury'), wants to marry his daughter Leila to the son of a wealthy farmer. In contrast, the play celebrates the the rural community's paganised Christianity, presided over by a wise-woman, Mother Midnight.

Robin Goodfellow, the bastard, is part of both worlds. Like the cunning women, he is in touch with the elements (especially the moon) and boasts that he can make love-potions or predict pregnancies. He plots to destroy the financial match arranged by Gripe and, in this respect, resembles the mischevious Robin of folk tradition whose tricks often favoured the fortunes of the young against the authority of their elders. This Robin's motives are significantly different from those of the folk fairy. Instead of helping Leila and her lover, he uses his magic to promote another financial match between the heiress and Churms (a lawyer). He is a monetary schemer who exhibits a very worldly interest in the commercial dealings of the community. The other side of his character makes him more of a roguish swindler or projector than a supernatural being. His demonic nature is equally ambiguous; he is both a devil and a character playing a devil. He tells the audience 'Ile put me on my great carnation nose and wrap me in a rowsing calf-skin suit, and come like some hobgoblin, or some devil ascended from the grisly pit of hell . . . I'll play the devil, I warrant ye' (268). Repeated references to costume and role locate him as part of a comic performance of magic found in folk rituals such as the Christmas sports. Later in the play, though, he defines himself as intrinsically evil. He admits that he is the bastard of a witch or 'refus'd Hagge' and a 'boatewrites son of Hull' (with a possible pun for Hell). His mother was 'the fittest fiend in Hell / To drive men to desperation' (308) and was sent to earth to win more souls for Satan. Robin says that she chose him as her earthly instrument 'not finding any one so fit / To effect her devilish charge' (308). He is demonically possessed, has 'little hope for heaven or heavenly blisse', but hopes that his evil acts will earn him an elevated

position in hell (309). His satanic nature is clear to other characters who refer to him as 'miscreant imp' (269), 'the devil' (286,
302, 306, 307), and 'witch' (245, 302).

The ambiguities in Robin's character problematise the location of evil in *Wily Beguiled*. The play labels the folk fairy (and
the culture he represents) as demonic but suggests that the real
devilry is to be found in the unscrupulous enterprises of the
lawyer Churms, the usurer Gripe and, to a lesser extent, the
farmer Plodall. This undermines the justice and even the
efficacy of a rigid moral structure. By contrasting the explicit
performance of evil and its implicit practice, the play raises
suspicions about a Christian culture which demonises bastards
and anything else which does not fit in with its orthodox
religion.

Brome and Heywood's *The Late Lancashire Witches* (1634)
draws together the subversive power of the bastard and the
witch in what is, I believe, an allegory of conflicts within the
Christian Church. The play is based on the sensational case of
the Lancashire witches who were transported to London for trial
in June 1634; it may also engage with the religious controversies
of its time by using the witches (and the bastard Whetstone) to
comment obliquely on the policies of the newly appointed
Archbishop Laud. Laud had begun to give official favour to
the practices of popular Catholicism which were still prevalent,
particularly in the north. Lancashire was a notorious centre of
recusant activities (as well as having a high incidence of bastard
births). From the 1560s to the 1630s complaints were raised
against parishes for celebrating saints' days and for using holy
water, prayers for the dead and rosary beads in their services
(Reay 1985: 109). Under Laud's regime, such activities were
legitimised while the egalitarian principles of the Puritan sects
were discredited. Brome and Heywood may be using the play to
caricature this change of direction in religious politics. The god-
fearing community are identified with the pro-Catholic establishment who have begun to demonise all the anti-hierarchical
forces associated with zealous Puritan belief.

The practices of the witch coven promote individual autonomy in opposition to traditional heirarchies based on gender,
class and age, in line with extreme Protestant ideas. The

women's sexual transgression is at the centre of these disruptive activities. Granny Peg Johnson admits to an alliance with her familiar devil, saying that he never failed to give her satisfaction 'twice a Weeke' and was a good bedfellow 'Onely his flesh felt cold' (2,749–56). Whetstone is a product of the sexual excess associated with witchcraft (118–22) and promises to beget a bastard on Mal, a junior member of the coven (2,058–9). The witches help him to take revenge on the gallants Bantam, Shakstone and Arthur who have made fun of his illegitimacy. Their plot borrows from a story told in Heywood's *Hierarchie of the Blessed Angels*, where John Teutonicus (a magician), uses spirits to reveal the paternity of some young lords who have mocked him for his base birth (Heywood 1635: 513–14). Like Teutonicus, Whetstone promises to let the gallants see their fathers. The witches' visions show that, far from being aristocratic lords, Bantam's father was his childhood tutor, Shakstone's was his mother's tailor and Arthur's was his father's stable groom (2,120–63). The trick unsettles the basis of all social hierarchy in the play, linking the gallants' mothers to the free-loving witches. It is part of the wider practice of *maleficium* in the Lancashire community.

The witches cast spells to invert the stratified order of the patriarchal household. They bewitch the Seeley family so that 'The Sonne rebukes the Father old; / The Daughter at the mother Scold[s]' and the servants give orders to their master and mistress (559–67). Rebellions against the gerontocratic order had traditionally been associated with the evils of extreme Protestantism. John Christopher complained that children would make 'a mery mockery of their parents' and Miles Huggarde, author of *The Displaying of Protestants* (1555), claimed that servants had 'in maner become masters themselves' (Brigden 1982: 39). In the community of the play, witchcraft is also blamed for marital discord, symbolised in a scene where Lawrence and Parnell's wedding reception breaks down into complete chaos. The couple are eventually mocked in a skimmington ride, showing the inversion of normal gender roles. Only Whetstone is not horrified by the disorder. He is conversant with the witches' activities and when the wedding breakfast is transformed into live snakes, bats, frogs, bees, hornets, he tells the flustered villagers 'I feare nothing thank my Aunt' (1,140). Arthur says 'though he be no witch, he is a wel-willer to the infernal science' (2,674). His bastardy makes him naturally sympathetic to an 'infernal science' which disrupts weddings. He remains loyal to the witches, even when they are arrested and sent off for trial and death.

As a religious allegory, the demonisation of the ungodly coven illustrates the harsh response to Puritanism by the official Church after 1633 and the persecution of those who dared to dissent from its Laudian policies. The years 1633–4 saw proceedings, instigated by Laud, against John Bastwick and William Prynne. Bastwick was brought before the High Commission, fined and imprisoned for publishing an argument in favour of Presbyterianism. In February 1634, the fanatical Puritan Prynne was sentenced to life imprisonment, a huge fine, the loss of his university degrees and the pillory. Possibly Brome and Heywood are caricaturing the fate of such figures in *The Late Lancashire Witches*. Here, as in previous plays, bastardy and witchcraft represent a disruptive energy which is dramatically attractive in contrast to the rigid moral and social structures of patriarchal culture.

'Our pleasant vices / make instruments to plague us'

Satanic parentage was not the only way of characterising a bastard in league with the powers of darkness. Medieval morality tradition provided a dramatic heritage in which illegitimacy featured on the side of sin in conflicts between Vices and Virtues. In dramatic situations developed from the psychomachia pattern, Renaissance playwrights could debate the nature of evil and its relationship to illegitimacy. To examine some of these bastard Vices, we must consider two theories of evil and the ways in which they inform dramatic presentations.

The oriental religion Manichaeism proposed that evil was a force coexistent with good, equal in power and essentially independent of it. The very structure of psychomachia – with opposing figures who personify Vices and Virtues and move independently around the stage – presents evil as extrinsic. The human protagonist is not the origin but the subject of a cosmic and eternal moral conflict. The Vices have a life of their own and continue to exist after his death. Early examples of the psychomachia with illegitimate Vices confirm the common prejudice that bastardy is an essentially evil 'other'. In the anonymous poem *The Assembly of the Gods*, Pluto says that man and virtue can be defeated only by 'a son of myn bastard / Whose name ys Vyce' (601). Vyce, an autonomous being, appears armed 'blakker fer then soot' (618) and mounted on a 'glydynge serpent' (613). He leads a processions of seven Vices followed by a huge army of sins (635–66) and earthly sinners (667–714) including 'Charmers, sorcerers and many scismatykes' (679), 'hoores and Baudys' (700), 'Homycydes, poysoners and common morderers' (704) and 'Pseudo prophetes . . . with fornicatours' (708–9). Morality plays of the early sixteenth century often follow the model set by *The Assembly of the Gods* and personify vices as bastards. In Bale's *Three Lawes* (1547), for example, Infidelitie appears with his base sons Idolatry, Sodomye, Ambycyon, and Covetousness, False Doctrine, and Hypocrysye.

The Vices in these early plays are external motivating energies and the everyman figure is little more than their consenting instrument (Belsey 1985: 15). The very notion of consent complicates the issue, showing that evil is a human propensity. In yielding to Sensuality or Lust, the human protagonist chooses to turn away from God. Vice is therefore found within the individual as well as outside. The development of an internal struggle between bastard Vices and legitimate Virtues is beautifully demonstrated in a very late example of the morality play, Thomas Nabbes's *Microcosmus* (1637). The everyman figure, Physander, falls victim to the temptations of Sensuality, and is unable to control the Four Complexions – Choller, Bloud, Phlegme and Melancholy – who are the illegitimate sons of the Four Elements (Fire, Ayre, Water and Earth). They represent the various 'passions' of his nature, his ungoverned will. The bastard Complexions are in constant disagreement but unite in their hate of Physander's wedding to Belanima, the symbol of spiritual love. Choller protests 'We shall have morall now instead of Martiall discipline' (180), and Bloud (like the older Vice, Lechery), laments that the marriage will frustrate his libertine activities and 'expectation of so many children begot on severall

mothers' (181). The Complexions plot to separate man from his
reason. When Physander yields to Sensuality, they appear in a
dissolute state: drunk, unhappy and argumentative. Order is
restored when Physander repents and his ungoverned desires
are brought under control by the figure of Conscience. Even
then, the bastards (and the potential for sin) remain an intrinsic
part of Physander's make-up. The virtuous body still contains
its opposite vice.

   The location of evil inside the individual is very different from
the dualistic model and more like that proposed by St Augustine,
whose work was at the forefront of the theological controversy
of the sixteenth and seventeenth centuries. In *The City of God*,
written between 412 and 427, St Augustine argues that evil does
not have a separate existence from good, in fact it has no positive
presence since it is an absence of good. He identifies love as the
common source of good and evil and says that vice is a deliberate
turning away from God and spiritual things in favour of an
inordinate love of earthly things. It is not the things themselves
which are vicious but the perverse desire for them, the will.
Thus, lust is vicious not because bodily delights are evil but
because the inordinate desire for them is a conscious perversion
of spiritual love (St Augustine 1620: 424–5). St Augustine had
personal experience of such perverse desire, as he recalls in his
Confessions: 'I defiled . . . the spring of friendship with the lust of
concupiscence and I beclouded its brightness with the hell of
lustfulness' (Russell 1961: 347). He is describing an affair with a
mistress, something which lasted for many years. The fruit of his
sin was a bastard son whom St Augustine brought up, educated
in religious matters and loved (Russell 1961: 347). Jonathan
Dollimore (1991) notes that there is an intimate connection
for Augustine between sin and pleasure; that he recognises
inside himself a love of perversity precisely because it is evil
(133). If this is so, then perhaps his love of the child was partly
a love of transgression itself – of his own sin. The bastard, the
beloved vice, would have been a constant reminder to the Saint
of the presence of evil, or perverse desire, in himself.

   The personal example alerts us to unnerving contradictions in
St Augustine's idea of 'privative' evil: since evil comes from
within good (it is produced by a falling off from good), good

must produce evil in some sense. And if evil comes from good then only a good being can be evil. The paradox threatens to dissolve divisions between good and evil, showing that each one is present in the other. This is what Dollimore calls the 'perverse dynamic' of St Augustine's theory (137). It has important consequences for the presentation of bastards as embodiments of vice because it dislocates pre-existing moral categories and preconceptions about illegitimacy.

The emphasis placed on conscious choice by St Augustine matches the decline, or rather development, of morality drama in Renaissance England. After about 1550 the conflict between good and evil shifts its centre from the macrocosm to the microcosm – the protagonist. This individual appears as a unified and autonomous subject, a humanised character who takes responsibility for his actions (Belsey 1985: 43). The stage of the world takes over from the stage of the soul, so his moral struggle is usually presented through soliloquy rather than dramatised with opposing figures. Not all plays followed this model; the so-called decline of morality drama may have had more to do with the repressive authority of Puritan divines than any inherent failure in its dramatic form (Gardiner 1967). Evidence of its remaining popularity can be seen in the large number of bastard plays which appropriate elements of the psychomachia.

Sometimes bastard characters are identified directly with the Vices of the moralities. Edricus in the anonymous *Edmund Ironside* (1595), compares himself to the Vice in *Cambises*, boasting that he can play 'an *Ambodexter's* part' (330) with no difficulty. He excels himself in this role, offering evil counsel to Edmund and Canutus and delighting in the suffering he causes. He is a Vice in a moral struggle for the kingdom, a role also played by the bastard courtier, Perin, in *A Knack to Know a Knave* (anon. 1592). Like *Edmund Ironside*, this play transfers the psychomachia pattern to a socio-political allegory, commenting on the dangers of preferring those with no legitimate claim to their positions at court (Dessen 1965). Another bastard who deliberately models himself on the Vice is Codigune in Robert Armin's *The Valiant Welshman* (1612). Codigune constructs himself as Envy and vows to become 'Primate' or leader of the sins like the *radix malorum* of the moralities:

> There's the base,
> Whereon my envy shall erect the frame
> Of his confusion. *Gloster*, I know,
> Is Natures master-piece of envious plots,
> The Cabinet of all adulterate ill
> Envy can hatch; with these I will beginne,
> To make blacke envy Primate of each sin.
>
> (C1v)

Envy was a typical bastard vice; Francis Bacon reflected popular opinion when he noted, in his essay 'Of Envy', that 'deformed persons, and eunuchs and old men and bastards' were prone to it (Bacon 1985: 84). The disadvantages suffered by illegitimates under Renaissance patriarchy made them ideal successors to other morality figures, notably Wrath and Pride (qualities they exhibit in the ruthless pursuit of their ambitions). In *The Misfortunes of Arthur* (1588) by Thomas Hughes, the kingdom is plunged into civil war by 'Mordreds cursed pride' (3.1.36). Mordred is described as a personification of Wrath in the battle:

> And he himselfe the spurre of fiends
> And *Gorgons* all, least any part of his
> Scapt free from guilt, enflamde their mindes to wrath.
> And, with a valure more, then Vertue yeelds,
> He chearde them all, and at their backs with long
> Outreached speare, stirde up each lingring hand.
> All furie like frounst up with frantick frets.
>
> (4.2.123)

Instead of a dagger of lath he has a spear, but he resembles the old Vice as he spurs his soldiers on to sin. The conception of bastards, in the heat of lawless passion, made them suitable figures to take over the role of Lust or Lechery as well since they were incarnations of this sin. In short, bastardy was ideal to create a humanised version of the morality Vices in a secular play while maintaining an easily identifiable evil 'type'.

Borrowings from the moralities seem to confirm the popular condemnation of illegitimacy as the accursed share. In many cases, though, plays which take fragments of the morality patterns do so in order to dramatise a perverse dynamic like that found in St Augustine's theory. *The Misfortunes of Arthur* highlights disturbing similarities between Arthur, a Christian champion, and Mordred, the fiendish adulterer. Mordred is the sinful offspring of Arthur's own perverse lust for his sister, as the hero acknowledges, so good has literally produced evil. The demonic opposite turns out to be the same. This is also the case in Lording Barry's city comedy *Ram Alley* (1608). Its bastard, Throat, is little more than a thinly disguised personification of covetousness who confides his plots to the audience with the glee of the Vice. His villainy is a grotesque caricature of the other characters' behaviour. They call Throat vicious to displace their own moral perversions. He is referred to as 'Ambo-dexter' (35) but in the urban world of *Ram Alley* this name (and the moral structure it suggests), are out of place because everyone is tainted by the financial environment in which they operate. There are no moral absolutes in either the London of the play or that of the audience. Allusion to the morality tradition shows what is absent instead of clarifying the difference between good and evil.

The dramatist who develops a perverse use of the morality most fully is Shakespeare. In *Troilus and Cressida* (1602) and *King Lear* (1605), he warps the psychomachia patterns from within and uses bastard characters as agents of distortion. The battleground of *Troilus and Cressida* is not metaphysical but worldly. It takes place in a city and a camp where the absence of gods – even classical ones – is made strikingly clear by Thersites's parodic prayers to Jove, Mercury and the devil Envy. Shakespeare employs the skeleton of morality drama to interrogate cultural values in this secular world. A conflict between abstract ideals (such as honour, faith) and bodily appetites is played out in a secularised psychomachia involving the title characters. In the scene outside Calchas's tent, where Cressida is tempted by Diomed (5.2), we see the opposing sides of her dilemma represented by the positioning of characters on stage. Troilus – a visual reminder of the vows of faith and chastity sworn by the lovers – watches from one viewpoint, silently urging Cressida to keep her vows. From the opposite side of the stage, Thersites gives voice to the temptation to yield to 'the devil Luxury' (5.2.55). As the son of a whore, he is well qualified to play this Vice. Cressida describes the internal struggle which she experiences:

> Troilus, farewell! one eye yet looks on thee,
> But with my heart the other eye doth see.
> Ah, poor our sex! this fault in us I find,
> The error of our eye directs our mind.

(5.2.107)

The eye which looks on Troilus is the 'virtuous' part of her soul which seeks to uphold the laws governing chastity and condemns the promiscuity which infringes those laws. The 'other' eye – whose direction she has followed – is the eye of error, or perverse desire, represented by Thersites. The soliloquy locates the struggle and the sin of transgression with Cressida. It seems to be going on inside her mind, giving her sole responsibility for her actions and thus apparently confirming the misogynist view expressed so many times in the text. Further consideration of the psychomachia pattern proves that what is going on here is more interesting. Because Troilus and Thersites appear anachronistically in the traditional roles of Virtue and Vice, the battle is externalised as it was in the early moralities. It makes Cressida the victim of outside forces. This does more than excuse her fault; it shows that she is trapped by male ideas of woman and has no freedom of choice. Shakespeare manipulates the psychomachia pattern to demonstrate that everywoman, unlike everyman, is denied the exercise of free will. She is governed by the ideology of male ownership (which promotes chastity) and male sexual desire or lust. She is either the chaste soul of beauty or a whore. She does not have the opportunity to fashion herself.

The gender difference is pressed home when Troilus moves into her place as the subject of an intellectual struggle between reason and passion. Kenneth Palmer (1982) comments that 'Troilus's triumph in this scene is to work out in linguistic terms something that corresponds to the moral interlude he has seen in which the devil Luxury defeated Humanum Genus' (62). Cressida apparently turns whore, and Troilus is tempted to respond passionately, to adopt a debased view of all humankind like that which Thersites holds. The bastard represents the temptation to 'square the general sex / By Cressid's rule' (5.2.132) which would make Troilus lose faith in his mother, his own legitimacy and the values of honour and degree which depend on principles of fixed social identity and masculine control. On the opposite side of the stage, Ulysses represents those values. The presence of the two men does not affect the hero as it does Cressida: he is at full liberty to debate with himself – at length (5.2.137–60). He cannot, finally, eradicate the subversive presence of Thersites, even though he exits with Ulysses. The bastard dominates the stage in Act 5, seeing 'nothing but lechery' in the world around him. His malicious observations indicate the power which perverse desire holds over so many of the characters. If they are 'all incontinent varlots' (5.1.98) then he is probably no more vicious than they, and they no more legitimate than he. The play purportedly locates Thersites and the transgression of cultural laws as a demonic 'other' but in fact it reveals the origin of such debasement within the dominant order.

According to Potter (1975) homiletic tragedy develops the psychomachia structure by humanising the everyman figure as a tragic individual. Structurally, the sub-plot of Shakespeare's *King Lear* follows this pattern. Edmund and Edgar are 'like back to back pictures of vice and virtue in an emblem book' (Reibetanz 1977: 45), engaged in an allegorical struggle over Gloucester's soul. Edgar, who retrieves his father from the edge of damnation on a cliff of despair, symbolises virtuous reason and faith. He encourages his father to 'bear / Affliction' (4.6.75) with patient thoughts. Edmund is the incarnation of sin, in that he is the product of Gloucester's lust. Gloucester's haste to believe the worst of Edgar and his wish to commit suicide are the result of Edmund's influence: acts of passion. Edgar finally defeats Edmund in the duel, showing the triumph of virtue over vice. Gloucester's heart bursts 'smilingly' (5.3.199), perhaps indicating salvation, but his fate is determined by a retributive justice linked to the humanist belief in free will and responsibility for one's actions. The price of his lust is his eyes:

> The gods are just, and of our pleasant vices
> Make instruments to plague us:
> The dark and vicious place where thee he got
> Cost him his eyes.
>
> (5.3.171)

Edgar defines Edmund as an external representation of Gloucester's sin, his fall from good. Faith in this judgement on bastardy is diminished because of the conflicting belief systems in the play. In addition, Shakespeare complicates the morality pattern with role-play: the virtuous Edgar plays the devil in the person of Poor Tom, possessed by a 'foul fiend' (3.4.46) who talks of Satan and the 'lake of darkness' (3.6.7). Edmund initially appears to the other characters as a 'Loyal and natural boy' (2.1.84). The performed reversals of good and evil make the location of these opposites infinitely more complex than it first appears.

The importance of acting is taken up in Stephen Greenblatt's fascinating essay 'Shakespeare and the exorcists' (1988), which discusses the play's treatment of one of its sources: Samuel Harsnett's *Declaration of Popish Impostures* (1603). Greenblatt shows how *King Lear* engages with society's confusion over spiritual authority. It illustrates the peculiar nature of religious rituals by simultaneously 'emptying them out', revealing them as theatrical frauds, and re-creating the need for them. Harsnett's *Popish Impostures* discredits the exorcisms performed by a Jesuit priest, Father Edmunds, in line with the Church's wish to eliminate such practices. Greenblatt argues that *King Lear* gives a more sympathetic treatment of exorcism to undermine the orthodox position put forward by Harsnett. By presenting Edgar (disguised as Poor Tom) as an explicitly theatrical example of possession within a fictional context, it encourages the view that rituals, even when demystified, are better than no rituals at all (127). Greenblatt tentatively proposes that the Gloucester plot may express sympathies to Catholic recusants. However, as he suspects, the plot does not easily resolve into 'an allegory in which Catholicism is revealed to be the perse-cuted legitimate elder brother forced to defend himself by means of theatrical illusions against the cold persecution of his skeptical bastard brother Protestantism' (121). A neat reli-gious allegory over-simplifies the distinction between Edmund and Edgar, and doesn't take proper account of the connection between Harsnett's document and Edmund's performance role.

Shakespeare's Edmund and Harsnett's Father Edmunds are kith and kin. Edmund, like the illegitimate aspirant to religious truth, pretends to exorcise his father's house of a foul fiend and unnatural son, only to prove that devil himself. Harsnett claims that the dialogue between Edmunds and the devil was, in fact, a conversation beween 'the devil Edmunds and Edmunds the devil for he played both parts himselfe' (Harsnett 1603: 86). This is also true of the bastard. He sighs with a villainous melancholy like Tom o' Bedlam (1.2.135–6) and then transfers this demonic persona on to a supposedly unnatural Edgar who was, he tells Gloucester, 'Mumbling of wicked charms' (2.1.39). The devilish and fictitious Edgar whom Edmund quotes is no less than the illegitimate elements of Edmund himself. His account of Edgar's villainy (2.1.42–77) is an attempt to execute a self-exorcism, to escape from the evil role which bastardy obliges him to play if he is going to succeed in the legitimate world. The confusion of the brothers' identities blurs distinctions between good and evil. Its perverse dynamic shows the presence of each in the other, the production of wickedness by legitimate society and the potential for virtue in the bastard. Edmund reports that his brother mocked him when he vowed to discover Edgar's villainy, and quotes Edgar's words:

> 'Thou unpossessing bastard, dost thou think,
> If I would stand against thee, would the reposal
> Of any trust, virtue, or worth in thee
> Make thy words faith'd? No . . .
> . . . Il'd turn it all
> To thy suggestion, plot, and damned practice.'
>
> (2.1.67)

By placing this prejudiced view in the mouth of a villainous Edgar, Edmund suggests that it is evil. His story about Edgar trying to displace his own immoral actions on to a bastard 'other' is a direct reversal of his own behaviour, yet it contains an element of truth. Legitimate society (personified by Edgar) is the ultimate source of the evil bastard. Its laws produce the plots and damned practices of the disinherited.

Edmund's fiction drives Edgar into adopting the role of the possessed like Father Edmunds' victims. As Poor Tom, Edgar speaks from the position of the demonised bastard. He is be-devilled, marginalised and disowned by his father (1.2.78). Edmund is the arch-manipulator, making Edgar a fraudulent example of the possessed so that Edmund can be fraudulently

possessed of Edgar's inheritance. The interchangeability of the
role of devil between the brothers highlights the artificial distinction between 'base' and 'legitimate' and leaves us uncertain
about the bastard's evil nature. Is Edmund inherently wicked
because of his base birth or is he only playing the part of the Vice
to get what he wants? The text remains tantalisingly ambiguous.
His role-swapping with Edgar would suggest the latter, and his
demonic performance is, at times, comically artificial. He even
sings '*fa, so la, mi*' (1.2.137) like the Vice in *King Darius* (66).
On the other hand, its consequences for Edgar, Gloucester,
Cordelia and Lear are terrifyingly real in the *Lear* world. We
may doubt whether demystified rituals like Edmund's are better
than no rituals at all. His appropriation of elements of exorcism
means that he cannot be seen simply as the 'skeptical bastard
brother Protestantism'. He is much more equivocal, a personification of the inconsistencies and contradictions within the
English Church, a site of its dangerous debates – in which
people were martyred or exiled.

Illegitimate faiths

The implications of St Augustine's definition of evil were manifested in a very real form in post-Reformation England. Here, it
was no longer a case of identifying an antichristian satanic force
but of locating evil, or perverted good, in the houses of God
themselves. Renaissance society was struggling to distinguish
between legitimate and illegitimate claims to sacred truth put
forward by opposing religious groups within the English Church
and outside it. Dramatists could, and did, enter into the debate
by presenting explicitly religious subjects on stage. Illegitimacy
was employed in the campaign to discredit rival faiths. To depict
the representative of any denomination as a bastard was to
question the legitimacy of that religion, to suggest it was
damned from within. These plays shifted the accursed share
from its marginal position as demonic 'other' to the centre of
power. There was danger in such a reorientation: the bastard's
inclusion within a Christian context destabilised the biblical
authority which excluded him from the congregation of the
Lord. It could undo society's clear distinction of the base from

the legitimate. Nevertheless, illegitimacy was a powerful weapon and the risks involved did not prevent some writers from using it to slander so-called enemies of the faith.

After the death of Mary Tudor, Catholicism became the main target of hostile religious polemic. Identifying the Pope as Antichrist was widely accepted doctrine in the Church of England during Elizabeth's reign. By 1581, John Field concluded that to prove it was 'needless considering how it is a beaten argument in every book' (Hill 1971: 18). Condemnations of Catholicism used bastardy, the accursed share, to blacken their pictures of the Romish faith. The pamphlet entitled *A True and Plaine Genealogy or Pedigree of Antichrist* (1634) traced the Roman Church's bastard descent from the devil:

> He by a stranger without Matrimony
> Did then beget the *Churches Patrimony.*
> Then *Mammon* of *Iniquity* his sonne
> Begot a Child, as his Father had done:
> A worthy sparke, *Abundance* was his name,
> And of *Abundance, Ease,* (a gallant) came.
> Ease begot *Cruelty,* and he *Dominion*
> *Dominion, Pompe;* and *Pompe, Ambition:*
> And of this man old *Simony* did grow,
> A bribing Knave, how cleere soever he show,
> This man of issue was not without hope,
> For why? he liv'd to see his sonne the *Pope;*
> Who in this world doth beare a great renowne,
> And on his head doth weare a triple Crowne.

The tradition of slandering the Pope and his Church with bastardy stretched back to the early days of Protestantism when Clement VII (Pope from 1521 to 1534) was, in fact, illegitimate. The Protestant divine and martyr Richard Barnes attacked Pope Clement in a supplication to Henry VIII, written from exile in Germany. To Barnes, the 'whore's sonne' who could find twelve Cardinals to say he was legitimate (and so able to assume office) was a supreme example of the hypocrisy of the Romish faith (Barnes 1573: 199). Early Protestant drama took a similar line. In Bale's *King Johan* (1538), England pleads to King John to save her from the seduction of the Roman Church, saying that its clergy are not her children but the bastards of Rome (69–73). Sedition, who wreaks havoc in Church and State, is the son of the Pope (179–184), and so is Iniquity, the Vice of the anonymous morality play *King Darius* (67). Catholic churchmen are condemned as fornicators in Bale's *Three Lawes* where Sodomye, Hypocrisye and False Doctrine tell Infidelitie how members of the Church enjoy illicit sexual relationships and either father or give birth to bastard children. In *The Discoverie of Witchcraft* (1584), Reginald Scot suggests that the myth of the incubus-father was fostered 'speciallie' to disguise the lechery 'of idle priest and bawdie monkes; and to cover the shame of thier concubines' (Scot 1964: 88).

The majority of Renaissance plays linking bastardy and the Church do so to criticise Catholicism. There are exceptions, as in Middleton's *The Family of Love* (1602), where the nonconformist sect's preoccupation with carnal rather than spiritual love is shown in a series of accusations involving illicit pregnancies and base-born children. Bastardy exposes religious hypocrisy in the play. On a more positive note, the unborn child of Maria and Gerardine represents a celebration of fertility and a critique of the restrictions placed on desire by religious or paternal authority. The Church comes in for more general criticism in Thomas Nabbes's masque *The Spring's Glory* (1638), where the seasons of the religious calender are personified to show the practice of in-house fornication. Shrovetide, Christmas and Lent boast about the numbers of bastards they have sired and Lent's own bastardy is hinted at.

The Protestant polemic found in many plays may have disguised criticisms of religious groups in England. Donna Hamilton (1992) argues that anti-Catholic rhetoric was appropriated by both conformists and non-conformists to launch attacks on rival sects and on the established Church. Their obsession with Antichrist reflected a concern with the 'purity and integrity of the community of the godly' rather than an attack on an external force (Lake 1980: 162). The non-conformist view was summed up in the first Martin Marprelate tract, generally known as the *Epistle* (1588), which condemned the bishops and priests of the official Church as 'petty Antichrists, petty popes' (39). The Church's High Commission, responsible for making ministers conform, was the very throne of Antichrist,

according to Henry Barrow (Hill 1971: 52). The same kind of
attacks continued into the seventeenth century. The conformist
camp responded by claiming that anyone trying to weaken
English ecclesiastical authority was making the country vulnerable to the threat of Catholic invasion from abroad. James I saw
Puritanism, with its notions of parity, as a threat to his own
sovereignty. This made it no better than antichristian Rome;
James's *Premonition* of 1609 declared '*Jesuits* are nothing but
Puritan-papists' (James I 1918: 126). In a climate of vicious
internecine attacks, dramatic representations of bastard clerics
were probably designed to criticise religious institutions within
England as much as Catholicism abroad.

Illegitimacy of birth had been declared a canonical impediment to ordination so bastards were unable to hold clerical
positions, just as they were denied a place in the congregation
of the Lord according to the Bible. Luther commented that the
bastard was 'completely imbued with the profane traditions of
men and the opinions of the flesh. That is, he will always be
much less fitted for the ministry of the Word. He is also a
disgrace to the church and he takes away from the glory which
we have from Christ' (Luther 1960: 235). In practice, bastards
were appointed to positions in the Church by means of special
dispensations, as in the case of Cardinal Wolsley's son who was
made Dean of Wells. To give reminders of the illegitimacy of
such a figure was to undermine the Church he represented.
Luther argued 'What indeed are the bishops today but bastards
in the whole world' (Luther 1960: 235). *The Blind Beggar of
Bednal Green* (1600) and *1 Henry VI* (1592) both make reference
to the Bishop of Winchester's descent from the bastard line of
the Swynford family to discredit his character. In *1 Henry VI*,
Gloucester calls the Bishop 'thou bastard of my grandfather'
(3.1.42). He is a 'prelate' whose 'audacious wickedness' includes
'lewd, pestiferous, and dissentious pranks' and pernicious usury
(3.1.14–17).

In James's reign, anti-Catholic polemic became even stronger
as a result of the gunpowder plot in 1605. James swiftly introduced an oath of allegiance whereby all Catholics had to swear
that he was the rightful king and that the Pope had no authority
to depose him. The Pope ordered English Catholics not to

pledge allegiance to James and in 1606–7 three anti-Roman plays linking Catholicism with illegitimacy appeared: *The Whore of Babylon* by Dekker, *The Devil's Charter* by Barnabe Barnes, and the anonymous tragedy *Claudius Tiberius Nero*. Dekker's play is based on the description of the whore in Revelation (17: 1–6), which Protestants interpreted to mean the Roman Church. James remarked that Babylon was 'called a whoore for her spiritual adulterie, having seduced the *kings of the earth* to be partakers of her Spirituall fornication' (James I 1918: 146). Dekker's attack follows this view: the Kings of France, Spain and the Holy Roman Empire are sons to the Whore Empress. When they launch a naval attack on England and its ruler Titania (representing Elizabeth I), they are referred to as bastards of the 'scarlet-whore' (5.2.28). After the attack, news comes of a bastard child born in the camp (5.6.34–52), perhaps suggesting the birth of illegitimate Romish practices in England (the gunpowder plot) or even in the English Church. Separatists insisted that they were in the midst of Babylon since its hierarchy and assemblies were antichristian.

The Babylon of Rome features again in Barnes's play *The Devil's Charter* (1606). Barnes was the son of the Bishop of Durham so it is possible that his anti-Catholic bias may include criticism of non-conformist sects in England. His *Divine Centurie of Spirituall Sonnets* (1595), dedicated to his father's successor, already indicates contempt for the Roman Church. Sonnet 33 appeals to God to strengthen the voice of true religion which will 'subvert ambitious Rome'. Sonnet 78 describes the 'shamelesse strumpet of proud Babilon' who destroys true faith with her 'Antichristian route' (Barnes 1875: 177, 200). In *The Devil's Charter*, Barnes loses no opportunity to attack the papacy when retelling Guiccardini's history of the Borgia family. The Prologue introduces Rome as the '*Strumpet of proud* Babylon' whose cup is filled with 'fornication' and whose children form a community of sin (7–8). By alluding to the whore–mother, Barnes implies the figurative bastardy of all the Roman hierarchy. Rome's corruption is the result of God's high wrath for her adultery with the Pope. The devil tells Alexander VI '*Rome* Which once was thy gorgeous concubine / Hath now forsaken thee: now doth she finde, / Thy falshood which did her adulterate' (3,076).

The Pope's children and Alexander himself are the bastards of this adultery. In reality, Roderigo Borgia (Pope Alexander) was not illegitimate, although Caesar, Candie and Lucretia were. The second scene of the play presents them all as bastards. A gentleman complains that Alexander has risen through demonic ambition and now shamelessly 'Displaies his bastard wings' in the nest of power he has usurped (212). Here, he begets a brood of 'ravenous Harpies' and promotes his 'gracelesse, impious' sons to dominate Church and State (214–15). Under their government, Rome has been transformed from 'Vertues Paradice' to a 'wildernesse of vice' (206–7). The gentlemen are horrified that there is no shame, truth, 'Faith nor religion' (165). Their list of complaints, with its repeated rhymes, suggests an interminable procession of vices:

> Nay such prophane and most monstrous *Sodomie*,
> Such obscure Incest and Adultery,
> Such odious Avarice and perfidie,
> Such vinolence and brutish gluttony,
> So barren of sincere integritie.

> (159)

Alexander, Caesar and Lucretia indulge in all these sins. There are references to incestuous relationships between father and daughter and between Lucretia and her brother Caesar. Instead of solemnising vows, the Pope makes 'marriage sacrament a laughter'. Lucretia becomes Alexander's 'onely daughter, wife, and daughter in law' (270), a brothel bride (297–302). She is ruthless as well as lecherous, murdering her second husband, Gismond, to prove herself Caesar's sister and 'deepe in bloudy stratagems as hee' (556). She calls upon the 'griesly Daughters of grimme *Erebus*' (573) to give her strength and then makes her husband sign a suicide note before stabbing him some six times, a chilling combination of brutality and policy which will (she feels) earn the respect of Caesar and Alexander. Her hypocrisy, when the death is discovered, mirrors that of her father and brother on other occasions.

Alexander's love life involves sodomy as well as incest and adultery. He has abused a young prince, Astor Manfredi, with 'vild brutish and unkindely lust' (1,167). In the manner of a skilful morality Vice, he tempts Astor with fruits, confections, wines and riches before murdering him. Both Alexander and Caesar are clever murderers who cover their tracks; Alexander poisons Astor and Philip with asps, reporting that they have died from excessive heat after a game of tennis. Caesar follows in his father's footsteps so there is an obvious irony in Alexander's remark 'Caesar the Divill hath bin thy Schole-maister' (1,951). He murders Lucretia by means of a poisoned face cream and hires a villain to kill his brother. He then dispatches the assassin, confident that he will not be detected, since 'many crimes / Lurke underneath the robes of Holinesse' (1,685).

Hypocritical disguise is taken to an extreme by Alexander who is 'No Pope but *Lucifer* in *Peters* Chaire' (1,027). He demonises Lodovick Sforza for rebelling against the mother Church, only to be mocked as a sham:

Blasphemous exorcist, heere are no divills
Which thou canst conjure, with thy divilish spirit.
We charge thee render up that triple Crowne . . .
Saint *Peters* Chaire wherein (like Antichrist)
Thou doest advance thy selfe thou manne of sinne.

(1,049)

Alexander's pact with the devil is made explicit in several scenes. In the final moments of his life, he discovers the devil '*sitting in his pontificals*' and telling him 'Vaine are thy crosses, vaine all exorcismes' (3,072). This suggests there is something inherently evil about the papal seat, that even after Alexander's death the devil will continue to occupy it. The play revels in heresy to expose heresy, showing that what is supposedly good contains its demonic opposite. Its anti-Catholic sentiments would certainly have been popular in 1606, even if criticisms of English believers lurked beneath.

In the following year, the anonymous play *Claudius Tiberius Nero* presented an equally unattractive picture of Rome, ruled by a bastard emperor. The dramatist has invented Tiberius's bastardy to emphasise his illegitimate nature. In soliloquy, Julia asks 'Shall I call him a Bastard? true it is' (643). The citizens of Rome complain that they see the 'Temple blasted of fidelitie' (537) and turned to the sexual gratification of Tiberius. The corruption has a Christian context, made clear when Germanicus says that Rome has been overtaken by 'a new devis'd Religion, / Of the inconstant Jewes cal'd Christians' (528). Sejanus wishes that Tiberius had never come to power

> Then had not Vestaes Tapers beene defil'd,
> Nor th' Altars turnd to irreligious uses:
> When thou didst make her never dying lampes,
> Serve for the Torches to thy burning lust,
> The whilest her Temple made a brothel-house,
> And all her virgins prostitute to thee.
>
> (2,709)

The play has numerous biblical echoes; in one scene Tiberius comes to murder Agripina with a poisoned apple like the serpent in Eden. He tempts her with earthly power, promising she will be 'Mistresse of the world' (2,884) before giving her the poisoned fruit (2,906–10). Such details link his government with the antichristian forces of the Roman Babylon. The play's Protestant polemic, like that of *The Devil's Charter* and *The Whore of Babylon*, was highly pertinent in the wake of Jesuit plot against James and his government.

The marriage of James's daughter to Frederick V, the Count Palatine, provided the opportunity for the expression of more anti-Catholic sentiments. Frederick's grandfather had established Calvinism in the Palatinate in 1563 and the match cemented a Protestant alliance between the two countries. *The Hector of Germany*, performed in 1613 in celebration of the marriage, refers to 'that Prince which in this Kingdome late, / Marryed the Maydenglory of our state' (3). The play is a commentary on contemporary events. Its author, Smith, rewrites fourteenth-century history in the spirit of the seventeenth century, blatantly altering events to idealise the Protestant union between the English nation and the German Palsgrave, and to slander the French and Spanish. Their attack on the Palsgrave is led by a bastard, Henry of Trastomare, who tries to seize the German Emperory for himself. He is a 'dangerous Foe for Treachery' (44) and is villainised in complete contradiction to the historical sources, where the bastard rescued Spain from the tyranny of his legitimate brother Pedro the Cruel. In *The Hector*

of Germany, Peter of Spayne is virtuous but cowardly; he leaves
the Palsgrave to the mercy of the attacking forces and disappears
from the play early on. There is no other character to balance the
negative view of the French and Spanish. Henry is accompanied
in his assault by two bishops: 'Mentz of a Cleargie-man is stout
and prowde, / Trier his like, in nature and in vice' (21). Even the
common French soldiers are slandered with bastardy (1,598).
The dispute between illegitimate French and Spanish powers
and the virtuous Palsgrave, supported by the English, forms a
thin disguise for anti-Catholic feelings.

Bastard atheists

So far, I have discussed bastards in terms of demonic forces: as
children of devils and witches, embodiments of vice, or antichristian elements within the Church. This leaves out another
distinct threat to the Christian hierarchy: atheism. The relationship between illegitimacy and disbelief contributed to the bastard's role in religious politics. The Bible's exclusion of
illegitimates from the kingdom of heaven is a starting point for
characters who, instead of being allied with satanic powers, are
utterly detached from religious doctrine, unnervingly atheistic in
outlook. These characters make an outright rejection of the
moral order which labelled bastardy as the accursed share. Fears
about new rational thinking were actually exacerbated by the
Protestant culture. Individual reading of the Bible encouraged
independent opinions and some feared that an appeal to human
reason would open the door to atheism (Hill 1993: 349). Characters whose illegitimacy was combined with a horrifying rejection
of God are an expression of common anxieties. The bastard in
Markham and Sampson's play *Herod and Anipater* (1622) is
typical in his denial of heavenly powers in favour of an egocentric
religion. Antipater develops a materialist godhead, saying 'what's
a king? a god: and what are gods, but kings?' (1.3.335). He argues
that earthly power is sooner obeyed than heavenly and concludes

> Kings greater then; nay, better then, then gods:
> Then but a king or god, naught with Antipater;
> And rather king then god; no god; a king, a king.

(1.3.339)

The play tries to recuperate faith in a theocentric world by presenting Antipater's rejection of it as demonic. Dumb shows of devils appear on stage to help in his evil plots. He behaves like a Vice in a psychomachia pattern for Herod's soul, encouraging Herod to murder his family. The King complains that Antipater has polluted his virtue (5.2.250–4) and adopts a tone of false piety to declare 'This bastard sonne hath onely ruined me: Hell never knew his equall; all my sinnes / Are but the seeds he planted' (5.2.176). The psychomachia pattern does not sit easily alongside Antipater's very worldly observations on the operation of power. His voice undercuts Herod's definitions of good and evil. It shows that psychomachia is a tool to deflect attention from the ruler's own unwise or immoral actions which are necessary to maintain that power. Because of Antipater's comments, we are encouraged to think that gods are not king-makers; rather, kings make gods and use religion as an ideological weapon to keep men in awe.

To a Renaissance audience, Antipater's view of the world must have seemed evil but perhaps it had a certain dangerous appeal. It allowed freedom from moral restraints to achieve personal goals and to celebrate individual autonomy, potential and achievement, which was exciting. Characters such as Antipater radiate self-assurance and possess a perverse energy which is undeniably seductive in dramatic terms. Once isolated from the moral order which condemns them, they acquire 'a recognizeable figure, which now radiates intimacy, anguish, the profundity of living beings' (Bataille 1988: 59). The worldly philosophy of these characters is attuned to the emergence of a society whose beliefs in an exclusively theocentric universe had begun to be challenged, nowhere more so than in the work of Machiavelli. Christian condemnations of Machiavelli, like Gabriel Harvey's *Epigramma in Effigem Maciavelli* (1578), related his ideas to atheism. In Harvey's poem, Machiavelli declares 'Fraud is my greatest virtue; the next is force. I know no other gods' (Meyer 1897: 22).

This popular view led to the creation of characters like Machevill in Marlowe's *Jew of Malta* (1589) who counted religion 'but a childish toy' (14). The villainous stage-machiavel was a projected image of the spiritual insecurities which haunted post-Reformation England. He believed in no god but himself and viewed the world from the standpoint of the individual rather than sharing the theocratic collectivist ideals of the medieval period (Praz 1958: 96). His rationalist philosophy considered only practical and physical factors in determining the individual's orientation in society. Although such an approach seems anathema to Renaissance England, a secular view of politics already characterised Tudor society long before Machiavelli's writings appeared. The Reformation encouraged people to interrogate discrepancies between *de jure* and *de facto* government and the Elizabethan response to Machiavelli's political writings was dualist in nature: it accepted the truth of detailed examples of his observations, seeing these in contemporary practice, even though it refused to acknowledge his secular presuppositions (Raab 1964: 70). Thus Machiavelli represented both an astute political thinker and the horrific threat of atheism.

The ideas of Machiavelli, mangled and demonised in official quarters, fitted perfectly into the mouths of bastard characters who could give a vision of the havoc which machiavellianism might wreak within the Christian world. Many of the bastards already discussed in this chapter make casual references to Machiavelli's precepts in the pursuit of their villainous plots. Codigune in *The Valiant Welshman* says that as he plots, 'my brayne / Italianates my barren faculties / To Machivilian black-nesse' (C_{IV}). In *The Hector of Germany* Henry sets out his strategy using images of the lion and the fox to represent strength and manipulative skill, the foundations of machiavellian government. He explains that he will supplement military force with conspiracy since 'twere good to peece the Lyons skinne / Where it too short falls, with the Foxes skinne' (766). Barnabe Barnes (author of *The Devil's Charter*) denounces this policy as a bastard miscegenated form:

> Vile is that wretched analogue, which the corrupt Florentine Secretarie Nicolo Machiavelli servant to Duke Petro di Medici, did in his puddle of princely policies produce betwixt a true Prince and a mixt monster; resembling him . . . unto a lion and a fox.
>
> (Eccles 1933: 238)

Barnes owned copies of *The Prince* and *The Discorsi* (Bawcutt
1982: 411). In *The Devil's Charter*, he appears to be quoting
Machiavelli's ideas 'with malice aforethought' (Meyer 1897:
113). Alexander and Caesar continually echo *The Prince*; they
ask Candie to 'Looke what large distance is twixt Heaven and
Earth, / So many leagues twixt wealth and honesty' (459) and
tell him that 'Princes of this world / Are not prickt in the bookes
of conscience' (B3v). Caesar says that in a hypothetical situation
where two other princes are at war, it is expedient to join forces
with the stronger side and yet seem charitable to the weaker
(446–52). He follows machiavellian ideas himself, certain that a
combination of 'Excellent valour, and deepe policie' (2,170) will
bring success. By putting such precepts into the mouths of his
bastard characters, Barnes moves beyond an attack on a particular Church or sect. The use of machiavellianisms gives a
cautionary picture of a world devoid of religious authority
and moral precepts, a world which may have seemed frighteningly close to a society where belief was fragmented between
conflicting doctrines and institutions.

To summarise: the context of spiritual plurality and turbu-
lence in Renaissance England inevitably complicates the relationship between bastardy and evil. Dramatists drew on popular
prejudice and biblical authority to create demonised characters
but, as I have argued, not all these reinforced the conservative
ideas which formed their starting point. Witches' bastards
embodied a subversive female power which unsettled patriarchal order. The child of sin was not necessarily an evil
'other' since he could appear as a scapegoat for the immoral
practices of the legitimate world. Moral judgements on the
accursed share were made more ambiguous by the breakdown
of absolute spiritual authority and writers used bastardy to
intervene in the religious debates of the period. Characters
who were barred from bliss and traditionally associated with
vice, were ideal stage-machiavels; they could put forward an
alternative non-Providential view of the world. In all cases, the
bastard's identity as damned gave the character an autonomous
energy to comment on the values of the society which
condemned illegitimacy. The full consequences of this isolated
position can be appreciated only when the evil bastard is

considered in a wider social context. The type no longer had
any philosophical connection to a community whose codes of
behaviour were modelled on moral values of right and wrong.
His evil nature had significant social repercussions, which will be
the subject of the next chapter.

3

Unnatural children

Renaissance society was made to feel acutely aware of the horror of a breakdown in social order. Riots and minor rebellions were a recurrent feature of urban life and, so far as can be ascertained from court records, crime rose rapidly at the end of the sixteenth century, peaking in the 1590s in some areas and in the 1620s in others. The governing powers exaggerated the dangers posed by such disruptive activities and warned of the imminent collapse of order (Sharpe 1987: 106–14). *An Homilie Agaynst Disobedience and Wylful Rebellion* (1570) took a typical line, proposing that chaos of apocalyptic dimensions could be prevented only by unquestioning maintenance of the existing social heirarchy. The rightness of this political system was evidenced by the fact that it was part of a divinely controlled pattern and that it was simultaneously 'natural'.

In *The Valiant Welshman* by Robert Armin (1612), Cadallan gives a typical definition of the so-called natural orientation of the individual in society:

> each true man should know,
> To what intent dame Nature brought him forth:
> True subjects are like Commons, who should feede
> Their King, their Country, and their friends at need.

(B2)

Cadallan's words emphasise the importance of deference (to one's social superiors) and paternalism (care for others) in an unequal hierarchy. The true subject should place himself or herself at the service of monarch, country and friends and should nurture them as necessary. Both forms of behaviour are presented as natural. The concept of nature is used to ratify a social structure which relied on the all-pervasive principles of elaborate stratification and inequality (Wrightson 1982: 17). By believing that such a system was natural, people perpetuated its effective operation. The powerless accepted their position without question and thus legitimated the hegemony which subjugated them. In return for their subservience they could expect to be protected by those above them. According to the idea of natural law, rulers were bound to care for their dependents. King James describes the relationships between governor and subjects using a family model:

> By the Law of Nature the King becomes a naturall Father to all his Lieges at his Coronation: And as the Father of his fatherly duty is bound to care for the nourishing, education, and vertuous government of his children; even so is the king bound to care for all his subjects.
>
> (James I 1918: 55)

Under this system the sense of deference paid to one's paternal masters, spiritual and temporal, was an extension of a so-called natural reverence of children for their parents.

Natural behaviour also included harmonious co-habitation with effective equals in a community where the rather vague term 'neighbourliness' covered the maintenance of co-operative relations and the responsibility for not laying unreasonable burdens on the tolerance of others (Wrightson 1982: 51–7). Thomas Starkey's treatise on the English constitution (*c.* 1530) pointed out that man was governed by laws which were

> stablyschyd by nature . . . commyn to al mankynd, as by exampul ther ys a certyn equyte & justyce among al natyons & pepul, wherby they are inclynyd one to dow gud to a nother, one to be benefycyal to a nother lyvyng togyddur in a cumpynabul lyfe.
>
> (Starkey 1989: 9)

Starkey's theory of an unchanging law of nature is essentially conservative. As well as inclining people to civil order, it dictates 'a certayn temperance of the plesurys of the body' where sexual delights are 'for lawful incresse of the pepul', the begetting of legitimate children (Starkey 1989: 9).

The bastard is born outside natural law. He is not like the true subject who knows 'to what intent dame Nature brough him forth'. Codigune, the villain of *The Valiant Welshman*, is a 'Bastard, begot at the back doore of Nature' (I3v). In *Herod and Antipater* (1622), Antipater describes himself and all fellow bastards as 'Nature's Out-Casts' (1.3.358). Barred from God's kingdom, fatherless children are also alienated from the moral and patriarchal principles which bind society together. They are 'unnatural', and, as such, ideal to characterise as a menace to social order. The label 'unnatural child' seems to reinforce the rigid binary opposition natural/unnatural but the descriptions 'Nature's out-Casts' and 'begot at the back doore of Nature' point to a more complex relationship between the two terms. They show that there is no essential difference between an unnatural child and a supposedly natural community; the former is actually a product of the latter. As 'Nature's out-casts', bastards' origins are in nature, they are conceived at its back door. Society produces its own unnatural opposite which it then constructs as an alien element, an 'other', in an attempt to displace the tensions inherent in its structure.

A wider consideration of the legitimation of power in society is therefore necessary to locate the bastard as a symbol of disorder. David Beetham (1991) proposes that the legitimation of State structures in all historical societies depends on three essential criteria. The first of these is the most obvious definition of legitimacy: a conformity to legal rules. Any power acquired in contravention of these rules is illegitimate. The second criterion of legitimacy is a justifiability of the State's rules in terms of a system of shared beliefs – belief in natural law in the case of Renaissance England. When the legal rules find only weak justification in terms of accepted beliefs about the proper source of authority or ends of government, the ruling order experiences what Beetham calls a 'legitimacy deficit' (205). The unnatural opposite in this case is within the community rather than totally alien to it. As we shall see, the bastard character tunes in to a legitimacy deficit and provides a focus for dissenting voices in Renaissance society. Beetham's final criterion for the legitimation of power is the active expression of consent by those ruled, achieved by openly co-operating with the governing body in sanctioned actions. When people act in ways which demonstrate the withdrawal of their consent such as public demonstrations, strikes and acts of civil disobedience, a process of delegitimation occurs. Public forms of noncooperation can make the controlling order appear illegitimate.

Bastard characters, whose birth identifies them as a living contravention of legal rules, make explicit breaches of the law by usurping positions of power in the family and the State. Their actions are not the isolated behaviour of deviants. As a 'son of the people', the bastard is part of a much wider undercurrent of dissatisfaction in the community. His words and actions give voice to the dissent of its members, their non-conformist beliefs and their sense that the ruling laws are by no means natural. His rebellious activities are an exaggerated expression of their own withdrawal of consent from the governing body. In plays which characterise bastards as rebels, the open transgression of rules by the bastard plays out the disruptive tendencies of other groups in society.

A description of social disorder in west Suffolk shows how the unnatural child was part of a wider malaise in Renaissance England. Directions for the admission of offenders to the House of Correction in Sudbury (1624) categorises illegitimacy amongst a host of anti-social types in the population. The House was to take in and set to work any

> that shall be noisome and offensive to any [of] the inhabitants of this town: being common hedge, pale, gate or stile-breakers . . . robbers of orchards and fruit trees, milkers of other men's kine against the will of the owner, and of all such women as have or shall have any bastard . . . and of all persons that be not in the book of the subsidy being judged reputed fathers of base children . . . and of all such men, women and children as shall refuse and will not be put forth to service or to be apprentices
> (West Suffolk Record Office: 121)

The bastard is born into a multitude of dissenters who do not conform to the natural laws of community and hierarchy. Their crimes of noncooperation include destructive protests against enclosure (breaking down hedges, fences and gates) and unneighbourly behaviour – stealing milk or fruit. Individuals who refuse to place themselves under the supervision and protection of a master, as a servant or apprentice, are also in breach of natural law.

Research into popular protest has identified several groups who were prone to act unnaturally towards the community. These ranged across the social scale. Amongst the lower classes, protesters were involved in food riots and fence breaking, forms of insurrection related to the crisis of poverty which had been exacerabated by poor harvests, the exportation of grain, the drop in trade and wages and increasing unemployment. Economic conditions were a primary cause of the increasing problems of bastardy and vagrancy, which represented serious threats to order in the eyes of the authorities. Disruptive groups like unemployed troops or labourers and apprentices were part of a wider 'youth problem' in Renaissance England, when the expansion of population led to a huge increase of young people entering a job market where permanent employment was becoming harder to find (Brigden 1982). Social alienation was not limited to the lower classes. Scholars and clerics with university educations found an insufficiency of jobs for which they had been trained. By 1579, any student who was begging was liable to arrest as a vagrant (Beier 1985: 140). Even the top of the social pyramid was structured around a model of inequality and subsequent alienation: younger sons of the gentry felt that they were unjustly dispossessed of inheritance by laws of primogeniture. They were percieved as a malcontented and subversive group (Thirsk 1969).

The fatherless child had a close social kinship with many of these alienated people. His lack of definite ties to any patriarchal structure likened him to vagrants whose broken bonds with families and employers made them 'masterless men' and therefore dangerous. They frequented alehouses, were supposedly involved in petty crime and were a highly visible group, haunting both town and country. Illegitimates made up a noticeable part of the vagrant population since unmarried mothers often took to the road and unwanted bastard children were given away to beggars. This may have been another discreet form of infanticide, as in the case of Margaret Breakell's child who was taken by its putative father and 'put . . . unto a beggar woman whoe wandreth up and downe the Cuntrie insoemuch that the said chyld is lyke to be starved and famished for want of releefe' (Wrightson 1975: 16). Illicit sexual unions and marriages of

dubious authority were common amongst beggars and this so-
called 'promiscuous generation' produced bastards themselves
(Beier 1985: 65). In addition, bastard children were likely to
become vagrants because of parental neglect. In 1600, Norwich
officials ordered a putative father to 'keep his bastard at the town
of Cringelford and not to suffer him to run roguing about'
(Beier 1985: 56). Although bastards did not make up the majority of the itinerant population, their presence significantly determined the reputation of these groups (Slack 1988: 102). Brome's
play *A Jovial Crew* (1641) examines the related problems of
vagrancy and bastardy, presenting a beggar world whose festive
romance is undercut by the harsh realities of poverty. Oliver
points out that to beget a bastard on a beggar woman relieves
a man of 'the punishment or charge of bastardy' since beggar
whores will not seek out maintenance charges for their children
but rather 'will steal other folks' to travel with and move com-
passion (3.1.260–6). Springlove, the bastard of a beggar and a
gentleman, is hailed as the monarch of a crew of vagrants from
many different social backgrounds and professions. On one level,
the resolution of the play stresses the need to reintegrate these
disaffected and poverty-stricken people.

Bastards have a strong link with members of the upper classes
who were discontented because they were excluded from property and position. Characters in the drama are disgruntled by
their lack of inheritance rights, which put them in a similar
position to younger sons dispossessed by primogeniture. Tracts
by John ap Robert (1624) and John Earle (1628) set forth the
younger brothers' grievances at length and in 1640 their cause
was taken up by the Levellers, perhaps because John Lilburne
and William Walwyn were younger sons of gentry. Younger sons
who received an annuity were usually dependent upon the grace
and favour of their elder brothers for its furbishment, just as
bastards were dependent on the good will of their legitimate
social superiors (Thirsk 1969). Sometimes dramatists make an
explicit link between the two as in *King Lear* (1605), where
Edmund is malcontented because he is 'some twelve or fourteen moonshines / Lag of a brother' as well as being 'base'
(1.2.5–6).

The malcontent's unnaturally seditious activities are explained as the result of exclusion and frustration. Field's *A Woman is a Weathercock* (1609) argues

> we see those happiest in best parts
> And fortunes under-born unto their merits,
> Grow to a sullen envy, hate and scorn
> Of their superiors; and at last, like winds,
> Break forth into rebellious civil wars
> Or private treasons: none so apt for these
> As melancholy wits, fetter'd with need.
>
> (63)

Bastard characters, like younger sons, unemployed graduates, soldiers, courtiers, feel their fortunes are 'under-born unto their merits' and rebel with private treasons or rebellions. They are a focus for the grievances and anti-social tendencies of these malcontented groups. In Massinger's play *The Maid of Honour* (1621), Bertoldo leads a military campaign from his native Sicily to Siena and, as a servant reports to the King,

> All ill affected spirits in *Palermo*
> Or to your government, or person, with
> The turbulent sword-men, such whose poverty forc'd 'em
> To wish a change, are gone along with him.
>
> (2.1.12)

Bertoldo is an energetic character who attracts sympathy for these unemployed men. He explains their position, saying that the King should not 'for want of imployment / Make younger brothers theves' but allow them to go to war to make their fortunes (1.1.218–19). The issue has immediate relevance for a Jacobean audience at the Phoenix Theatre. Bertoldo says 'if examples / May move you more then arguments, looke on *England*' (1.1.220). His war-rousing speech is probably related to current dissatisfaction with England's lack of involvement in the Thirty Years War.

Bastards who rebel against authority in the family or the State are characterised as unnatural villains to demonstrate the horror of transgression. What becomes clear from the plays is that presentations of the rebel can make as strong a critique of the legitimate hierarchy as they do of the unnatural bastard. When the characters explain their actions, they express in a public arena

the radical ideas shared by the alienated dispossessed who
threatened the social order in Renaissance England.

Bastards and the family

Unnaturalness towards members of the family was regarded as
typical bastard behaviour, indicated by the bastardising of legitimate children who behave inappropriately. For example, in *Ram
Alley* (1608) when William Smallshanks woos his father's mistress, Oliver Smallshanks addresses him as 'degenerate bastard',
as Lear does Goneril in *King Lear* (1.4.254). The most extreme
case is in Webster's *The Devil's Law Case* (1617) where the
unnatural behaviour of Romelio and his mother culminates in
the scene in which Leonora declares him illegitimate (4.2). The
label is an appropriate one for Romelio. He is 'a totally self-
possessed egoist' (Berry 1972: 161) and carves out a future for
himself, ignoring ties of love which should bind him to his sister
Jolenta and his mother. He forces Jolenta to accept the wealthy
Ercole as a suitor against her will and, later, asks her to pretend
that she is pregnant by Ercole so that Romelio's own bastard
(begot on a nun) can inherit the estate. To persuade Jolenta,
Romelio says that their mother plans to have an affair with
Contarino, the man Jolenta loves. This 'most unnatural falsehood' (3.3.89) is actually not far from the truth since Leonora's
desire for Contarino makes her behave unnaturally towards both
her daughter and her son. Romelio does not have a monopoly
on rampant individualism or, for that matter, on bastardy. It is
something which implicates Leonora, Crispiano (the supposed
father), Jolenta, Angiolella (the nun) and even the servant
Winifred (1.2.175–6). In the court scene Romelio points out
that everyone is potentially illegitimate (4.2.302–11). The recurrent metaphor of bastardy symbolises the breakdown of natural
relations in a mercantile community where the pursuit of personal interest has become paramount. Romelio is the main
culprit, but the play shows that other characters also act against
kind and nature.

Bastardy and unnaturalness in the family had biblical and
classical precedents. The Bible includes the story of Gideon's

base son Abimelech, who slaughtered sixty-nine of his seventy legitimate brothers on a stone (Judges 9: 1–6). Sir John Fortescue cites this as evidence of the degenerate nature of bastardy in his *Learned Condemnation of the Politique Lawes of England*, translated by Robert Mulcaster in 1573. He says that 'thys mysbegotten chylde wickedlye slewe all those lawfullye begotten children, one onlye excepted . . . whereby it is perceyved, that there was more wickednesse in one bastard childe, then in lxix lawefull sonnes' (96). Plato's *Gorgias* offered an equally stark example of family massacre from classical history. Polus describes the career of Archelaus, the base son of King Perdiccas. After his father's death Archelaus kills his uncle Alcetas, his cousin, and then his legitimate half-brother – a young boy of seven – whom he throws down a well. By destroying all the legitimate heirs to the throne, he becomes King of Macedonia. Jenny Teichman refers to these two figures as 'proto-bastards' (Teichman 1982: 127). Base-born villains in Renaissance drama certainly follow their example.

Evil bastards are indifferent to laws governing kinship relations and invariably try to pull the patriarchal family apart. Even their love is destructive. In an essay on *The Revenger's Tragedy*, Jonas Barish (1976) shows how Spurio combines his plots to destroy his stepbrothers, father and stepmother with a perverted form of intimacy: his incest with the Duchess (150). This relationship is born of hate for her, her sons and the Duke (1.2.193–6). It is designed to fragment the family rather than unite it through natural love. Texts right across the period show that damaging incestuous or adulterous passions are characteristic of bastards. Arthur and Mordred, the hero and the villain of Hughes's *The Misfortunes of Arthur* (1588), are both guilty of incest and adultery. Arbaces, in Beaumont and Fletcher's *A King and No King* (1611) and Alcidonus, in Wilson's play *The Swisser* (1631), both attribute their apparently incestuous desires for their sisters to their supposed illegitimacy. For Arbaces, the 'wilde passion' he feels for Penthea confirms his identity as 'the despised fruite / Of lawlesse lust' (5.4.124–8). Alcidonus draws the same conclusion about his feelings for Selina, telling Antharsis it is 'the effect of that curs'd fate by which I am yours' (4.3.79). The crime of adultery is another (un)natural

consequence of base birth. In *Andromana, the Merchant's Wife*
(1642), the King tells his son that his love of the merchant's
wife would be understandable if the Prince had been a bastard:

> Hadst thou been the offspring of a sinful bed,
> Thou might'st have claim'd adultery as inheritance;
> Lust would have been thy kinsman,
> And what enormity thy looser life
> Could have been guilty of had found excuse
> In an unnatural conception.

(209)

The bastard villain's destructive attitude towards marital bonds is
best summed up by Robin Goodfellow's words: 'the chief course
of all my life / Is to set discord betwixt man and wife' (*Wily
Beguiled*: 309).

Many bastards in the drama fail to show the proper affection,
obedience or filial duty towards their parents. In the opening
scene of *Edmund Ironside* (1595), Uskataulf refers to Edricus as
'degenerate bastard, falsely bred / foul mother-killing *Viper*'
(166). Edricus does not kill his mother but he disowns her,
insults her and her husband and commands their son Stitch to
beat the husband until they leave (491–564). The scene is a
complete invention of the playwright. If it was designed as a
comic routine, its humour (at the expense of the parents) would
have perhaps had a dangerous edge. It also stands as a counter-
foil to the fondness between Emma and her legitimate sons,
Alfred and Edward, shown in Act 4 Scene 2. More often than
not, plays present anti-maternal actions as frightening, though
they can still cause dramatic excitement. In Heywood's *The
Golden Age* (1610), Calisto rushes on stage in terror of being
savaged by her base son Archas. She describes his animal-like
brutality, finally entreating Jove 'Let not the sonne the mother
sacrifice' (44). Sacrificing his mother to further his career is
what the bastard does in *Claudius Tiberius Nero* (1607). Julia
responds to news of his plots by losing all maternal feeling for
her son:

> Not mad *Orestes Clitemnestraes* Sonne
> Was so unnaturall as this beare-whelpe is.
> I did conceive the villaine in my wombe,

Which now I hate because it fostered him.

(1,622)

Matricide is only one element of Tiberius's unnaturalness since he contrives the murders of his son Drusus, his adopted son Germanicus and all Germanicus's family (a wife, two sons and their guardians). He even murders the innocent servants who come to report the victims' deaths, and his dying fantasy is one of genocide. He wishes all the people in the world had only one neck 'that at one deadly blowe, / I might unpeople all the world' (3,332). Such a philosophy is noticeably unsuitable for an emperor and Tiberius's government of Rome is as unnatural as his behaviour towards his family. Germanicus describes Rome in terms which must have sounded frighteningly familiar to an audience experiencing anxiety about an imminent collapse of order:

> The Legions discontent and mutinous:
> The Pretors tyrants in their Provinces:
> The Navie spoil'd, unrig'd, dismembred:
> The Cittie made a brothell house of sinne:
> Italians valour turn'd to luxurie.
> The field of Mars, turn'd to a Tennis-court

(513)

Unnaturalness between bastards and their fathers features more prominently than anti-maternal behaviour in the plays, perhaps because unconventional paternity is the direct cause of the bastard's disadvantage. The oedipal desire to kill the father is all the more extreme in the case of bastards who will never inherit their fathers' positions by legitimate means. Their unnatural rebellions against paternal figures are a major source of dramatic action. Codigune in *The Valiant Welshman*, Mordred in *The Misfortunes of Arthur* and Antipater in *Herod and Antipater* are all guilty of parricide by more or less indirect means and many other bastard villains attempt to kill or injure their fathers. They also fail to show the proper respect; in *The Misfortunes of Arthur*, Mordred's line 'Come sonne, come sire, I first preferre my selfe' (1.4.110) encapsulates the attitude of the ambitious bastard son whose egotism eclipses any sense of filial duty. Robin Goodfellow in the anonymous *Wily Beguiled* (1602) speaks for many bastards, declaring 'if it be to betray mine own father, I'll do it for half a fee' (247). In *King Lear*, we see this realised when Edmund's treachery brings promotion for him and torture and blindness for Gloucester. Contemplating his unnatural act Edmund says

> This seems a fair deserving, and must draw me
> That which my father loses: no less than all.
> The younger rises when the old doth fall.
>
>   (3.3.23)

In Sidney's *Arcadia* (1593), a source for the Gloucester sub-plot, Leonatus repeats the adjective 'unnatural' to describe his bastard Plexirtus, who 'threw me out of my seat and put out my eyes, and then, proud in his tyranny, let me go, neither imprisoning nor killing me, but rather delighting to make me feel my misery' (Sidney 1977: 278). Shakespeare's Edmund is not present when Gloucester is blinded of course, but one senses that he takes a sadistic delight in anticipating what will happen when he reveals the contents of Cordelia's letter (3.5.10) and is subsequently named 'my lord of Gloucester' by Cornwall (3.7.12).

Edmund's line 'The younger rises when the old doth fall' (3.2.25) would have had a particular resonance for the Renaissance audience since, throughout the period, tensions between the younger generation and their elders were recognised as a source of social problems, ranging from the growth of radical Protestantism to disruptions within trade guilds (Brigden 1982). Pierre Spriet (1984) argues that *King Lear* engages with the difficulties which accompany a transfer of power across the generations by showing that 'la vérité du fils', the inevitable process whereby the son supplants the father, must be qualified by the laws of civilised society. The loyal son (like Edgar) will still support the fictional hierarchy which demands the obedience and respect of children to parents whilst surpassing his father in material power. The bastard recognises only the son's power to supplant the parent. Edmund shows his true colours in the lines of his trick letter which may well have struck a chord with younger members of the audience: 'This policy and reverence of age makes the world bitter to the best of our times; keeps our fortunes from us till our oldness cannot relish them. I begin to find an idle and fond bondage in the oppression of aged tyranny, who sways, not as it hath power, but as it is suffer'd' (1.2.46). The letter points out a legitimacy deficit in Renaissance society, a discrepancy between the rules of natural law and beliefs held by the younger generation. By attributing the letter to Edgar, Edmund suggests that its ideas are held, even if unconsciously, in the legitimate world. Edmund's parricidal tendencies reinforce popular prejudices about bastardy while debating a current social problem. His cool pragmatism argues the case of younger members of the Globe audience who were fighting to grow and prosper in Renaissance London.

Bastard villains behave unnaturally towards siblings as well as parents, usually in the pursuit of their ambitions. The most fully developed example of an illegitimate attack on the family is in Markham and Sampson's *Herod and Antipater* (1622), where Antipater wants to rip every branch off the royal family tree. The play presents his demonically inspired grab for the throne in a domestic context. His bastardy is the invention of the dramatists, although a French play on the same topic – *La Mort des enfants d'Herodes* (1639) by Gauthier des Costes de La Calprenède – also bastardises Antipater. His very name builds up expectations of his unnaturalness towards his father, Herod, which is central to the plot. Antipater sees their relationship in terms of Edmund's maxim 'The younger rises when the old doth fall'. He rejects the principle of filial duty:

> Curst be he (in this case) that craves his father's blessing;
> My throane must be my fathers monument;
> My raigne built on his ruine.
>
> (2.1.600)

Antipater's determination that his father should be murdered first, 'that order be observ'd' (1.3.385), is a mocking perversion of respect for genealogical hierarchy. Herod is an obstacle in his way rather than a person to whom he is bound in a relationship of mutual love. The King's death is 'Excellent, excellent: noble, happy newes' (5.2.33) and Antipater asks 'Why, what heart could wish better?' (5.2.34). Herod is shocked by this reaction. He refers to Antipater as 'bastard', automatically linking illegitimacy with unfilial behaviour:

this bastard's faith,
On which so much I doted, to be lost
Thus against kinde and nature; 'tis a sinne,
That teares my heart in pieces.

(5.2.226)

Antipater's legitimate brothers, his rivals in power after Herod, are the subject of further plots made 'against kinde and nature'. Like Abimelech and Archeleus, Antipater refuses to recognise primogeniture, legitimacy and naturally fixed positions in a family hierarchy. He believes instead in the machiavellian ideas that 'Power makes all things lawful, all things sound' (1.2.31), and 'Who can resolve, can doe' (1.3.375). Wit rather than birth is the true foundation of success according to Antipater, who uses his aunt and her barber as tool villains in a plot to turn Herod against his legitimate sons. By forging letters (very much in the manner of Edmund), Antipater persuades Herod that Alexander and Young Aristobolus mean to murder him. Salumith and her barber add evidence against the Princes and Herod has them strangled, telling Antipater 'Ile make thee tread upon them; this day shall / Be thy coronation; but their funerall' (2.1.584). Fratricide and illegitimate success are bound together.

A demonic vision which inspires Antipater cements the link between bastardy and unnatural murder in the audience's mind. A dumb show depicts Jugurth, bastard son of the King of Numidia, who murdered his legitimate brothers because they refused to allow him to sit in state with them beside the throne. Thomas Heywood's translation of Sallust, *The Conspiracie of Cateline and the Warre which Jugurth Maintained* (1609) was probably the source for the dumb show. In it, Jugurth hands Antipater a scroll with the machiavellian maxim '*Non mordent mortui*: dead men do not bite'. Antipater responds with the words 'True, noble bastard' (2.1.607–8) and resolves to murder everyone who stands in his way. He wants Jugurth, and all bastard villains, to join with him and sing a plainsong on the word 'kill'. It rings like a knell in the subsequent lines:

The base sings deepely, kill: the counter-tenor, kill;
The tenor, kill, kill; the treble, kill, kill, kill,

> In diapasion kill is the unison, seven times redoubled;
> And so oft must I kill.
>
> $$(2.1.593)$$

Antipater imagines destruction on a huge scale and with gruesome pleasure. He will heap 'heads on heads, to climbe a kingdomes skye' (1.3.353). He plans to set the royal family on a self-destructive course by provoking them to behave unnaturally: 'Whetting against my father both his wife, / His sister and her husband; some by feare, / Some by beleefe, and some by jealousie' (1.3.408–10). Salumith plots against her own husband and nephews and Herod sentences his wife and sons and Joseph to death, breaking a 'linke in Natures best chaine' (2.1.433). The unnaturalness of these crimes is ultimately attributable to Antipater. True, his plots could not have worked had it not been for the shortcomings of other characters, but Herod, Alexandra and Salumith are petty villains in comparison. Antipater embodies a terrifying indifference to all social bonds. His unnaturalness assumes cosmic dimensions:

> Cloze fountains, rivers dry; pluck up the roots bowes perish;
> Banish the sunne, the moone and starres do vanish:
> And, were it to obscure the world, and spoyle
> Both man and beast, Nature, and every thing;
> Yet I would doo't; and why? I must and will be King.
> Kingly Antipater.
>
> $$(2.1.624)$$

Antipater's imagination privileges individual will above everything. He has no respect for the natural laws which create and hold the world together; he suggests that even these laws are not fixed. To the audience at the Red Bull it must have seemed a nightmarish vision of the destructive potential of self-interest which was concealed within the hierarchy of natural order. At the same time, Antipater's wit, determination and daring make him very exciting to watch. The audience must have been fascinated to see just how far his unnaturalness would allow him to go. Perhaps they recognised something of themselves and their own selfish desires. If so, Antipater's translation of those suppressed unnatural impulses into actions must have had a perverse appeal.

Plays showing unnatural attacks on kin were only one way of using the bastard villain to demonstrate the horror of disorder in the family. The 1652 tragedy *The Bastard* (probably by Cosmo Manuche) gives a disturbing picture of the disruption a base-born servant could create. Bastard children, bound as apprentices or servants, occupied a doubly marginal position since their job reinforced their liminal status. Apprentices were 'put into other families of which they were a part and yet always apart; they were *in* but not *of*' (Smith 1973: 160). Their uneasy position, both inside and outside the authority of paternal control, led to problems of disorder in the community. Apprentices were a notoriously subversive group which included malcontented younger sons forced to learn a trade as they were not going to inherit. They played an active part in civil disturbances, particularly in London. In June 1595 the Lord Mayor argued that 'the great disorder of multitudes of rebellious apprentices . . . shall not be suppressed untill some of them be punished according to the martiall lawe' (Brigden 1982: 48). In *The Bastard*, the treachery of the title character, Gaspar, shows the dangerous potential of groups who found themselves at the mercy of their masters. Gaspar is a cashier to the merchant Alonzo but his position is complicated by the fact that Alonzo promised to make Gaspar his son-in-law in return for his services in the past. The conflict over Gaspar's position as servant or member of the family is quickly established when Alonzo reveals his plans to betroth his daughter to Balthazar. Shocked, Gaspar asks 'Married Cousin?' (B2), using the familiar form of address to remind Alonzo of his promise. The merchant retorts 'How now Bastard? . . . thy tainted blood / Thinks to pollute mine?' (B2). It is bastardy which makes Gaspar an unsuitable family member.

Gaspar's place in the household encompasses both intimacy and subservience. The tension between these forms an undercurrent which runs through the whole plot. When threatened with dismissal unless he accepts his subservient position, he throws himself into the role of powerless dependent, telling Alonzo

You're my Fate, your tongue

Hath power to transform my thoughts, create
Anew my resolutions; I confesse
From you I have my meat; my life depends
On your beneficent Genius: I offend
Ev'n to damnation, should I be ingrate
In my respect to you.

(B2)

This is a fine piece of acting which completely fools Alonzo by flattering his vanity. It mocks the elitist assumption that masters can dictate even the thoughts of their dependants because Alonzo, far from having power to change his servant's mind, is himself the subject of Gaspar's manipulations. Gaspar's performance of deference masks his secret purpose: the 'polluting' of Alonzo's noble blood. The audience, who are in Gaspar's confidence, probably take a subversive pleasure in the secret status reversal.

Gapsar's continued protestations of humility look increasingly ridiculous as his plots grow more treacherous, warning of the danger of covert insurrection in the household. He succeeds in thwarting the match by arranging a liaison between Mariana and Chaves, which he allows Balthazar to discover. Alonzo offers his daughter to Gaspar again, anxious to arrange a quick match to cover her dishonour, but Gaspar's response reminds Alonzo of his earlier contempt

Honest! I dear swear
She will be truly vertuous, but the meanness
Of my poor fortunes makes me worthless, I
Have a spot in my blood, which would dishonour
Your family.

(G2v)

His lines point up Alonzo's hypocrisy, which is made even more obvious when the merchant breaks his promise again and betrothes Mariana to Picarro, another nobleman.

Gaspar's subsequent behaviour is blatantly anti-social, though only to the audience at first. He addresses himself to hell and longs for power to pull 'the Crystall Axell that supports the Spheares, / Down to the earth, that all the world might perish' (G3v). His plotting causes death upon death and makes the final scene 'a bloudy Poppet-play' (L2v) and 'horrid spec-

tacle' (L3). The other characters see him as essentially evil.
Picarro says Gaspar was born in hell and nursed by a Harpy,
but now he has grown to such a 'vast height in sin' that he will
not be allowed to return because he would outshine even the
'prime fiends' (L1–L1v). Mariana borrows lines from *Richard
III* to call him a 'dreadfull minister of Hell' and her exclamation
'Villain, thou knowest no Law of God or Man' (L3v) seems born
out by Gaspar's death. He is proud rather than penitent, declaring amidst the bodies of his victims, 'They're all o're reached by
one poor Bastard's wit' (L3). When his villainy is discovered by
the few remaining characters, he resigns himself to death with
the thought that his evil will outlive him.

The play's final view of Gaspar is not allowed to go unchal-
lenged. Many of his speeches remind us that his treachery is
thrust upon him by the world in which he lives. He sees himself
as part of a community of villains and his horrified reactions to
his misfortunes emphasise Alonzo's cruelty. Details of Gaspar's
past duty to the family establish his character as faithful and
hardworking (B2) so when he complains that he has been
treated unjustly, the audience are inclined to agree. He pleads
eloquently on the part of the dispossessed, pointing out that
since ''tis gold / That rules the law now' (D1v) he has no legal
means to fight his cause. At the end of the play he claims that it is
not his bastardy but Alonzo's moral bastardy that is the real
cause of the tragedy (L4v).

Gaspar exposes the sophisticated society of Seville as nothing
more than an elaborately costumed pack of 'treach'rous animals'
motivated by self-interest (D1v). His plots against the suitors can
succeed only because of their willingness to destroy each other to
achieve their own material ends. He celebrates his organisational
skill with the words:

> I'm rid of all:
> *Balthazar* kils *Picarro*, then himself
> Suffers; *Praepontio*'s kild by *Chaves*, whom
> The Law for that fact strait shall apprehend,
> And soon condemn as guilty; so not one
> Is left to be an obstacle.
>
> (H3v)

This speech undoubtedly shows Gaspar as the selfish and villainous schemer he is, but his wish to be 'rid of all' is shared by his tool villains; it is a guiding principle of the society in which he lives. Roderigo even tells him 'Your policy is orthodox' (F4). According to the values of Seville, Gaspar is as honest as the next man. Picarro tells him 'thou art / (If any good be on the earth) an honest / Plain-dealing man' (I4v) and his other victims agree. Honesty is a relative value; Gaspar's dishonesty is only one type among the many which govern social transactions in the play. When Alonzo borrows a line from 2 Henry VI to tell Gaspar 'hide not thy poison with such sugar'd words' (L4) he reveals a charactersitic of Seville's dominant discourse. Gaspar is not, finally, an anti-social force but an embodiment of the dangerous desires of avarice and self-improvement which motivate all the male characters. He is the play's hero as well as its villain, its greatest achiever. The cultural law which describes them as natural and Gaspar as unnatural is patently unjust. As he says himself, he is 'a proper man' (D1v). This unorthodox treatment of bastardy is perhaps explained by the fact that the probable author, Cosmo Manuche, was the son of a bastard, James Manucci, the illegitimate child of an intelligence officer (Phelps 1979). The play refuses to place blame solely on its title character and its epilogue cautions the audience not to cast '*hasty* Censures' on Gaspar (M1). If they do, they will be as blind to their own faults as are the legitimate characters in Seville.

Seville's condemnation of the bastard represents what Dollimore (1991) calls 'a displacement of disorder from within the dominant onto the subordinate achieved via a mapping of the natural/unnatural binary onto the dominant/subordinate hierarchy' (111). The bastard is called unnatural in an endeavour to externalise ideas and desires whose energy is centrifugal, pushing outwards or upwards in opposition to the binding force of natural law. This kind of scapegoating is exposed brilliantly in Shakespeare's *Much Ado About Nothing* (1599) where the cardboard villain, Don John, is used to highlight the opposing forces of individual self-interest and social co-operation in a domestic context. From his first entrance, the bastard is presented as an anti-social type. He does not engage in the witty conversation of the opening scene and emphasises his lack of engagement in his

very first line: 'I am not of many words, but I thank you'
(1.1.157). Social alienation is an essential element of his character:

> I cannot hide what I am. I must be sad when I have cause, and smile
> at no man's jests; eat when I have stomach, and wait on no man's
> leisure; sleep when I am drowsy, and tend to no man's business;
> laugh when I am merry and claw no man in his humour . . . it better
> fits my blood to be disdain'd of all than to fashion a carriage to rob
> love from any.
>
> (1.3.13)

Don John's blatant misanthropy is diametrically opposed to the
social bustle of Leonato's house with its feasting, dancing,
flirting and hospitality. It is, as Don John acknowledges, the
mark of a 'plain dealing villain' (1.3.32). While the other characters go to the feast with great cheer Don John wishes that the
cook were of his mind and would poison the guests (1.3.72).
Because his motives are so thinly drawn in the play, his desire for
'Any bar, any cross any impediment' (2.2.4) to the proposed
wedding smacks of an antipathy to the institution of marriage.
As a bastard, he is naturally inclined towards the unnatural
destruction of social and spiritual bonds. When his plot is
discovered, the other characters label him simply in terms of
knavery. Don Pedro says 'He is compos'd and fram'd of
treachery' (5.1.249) and, at the examination, the Sexton is
required to 'Write down Prince John a villain' (4.2.41).

Unequivocal condemnations like these show the legitimate
world protesting too much. Dogberry has hit on a truth when he
declares that it is 'flat perjury, to call the prince's brother a
villain' (4.2.42) because Don John's criminality is not self-
contained; it reflects the socially destructive impulses of the
other characters. In one sense his plots are a negative reflection
of Don Pedro's creative ones to promote marriage but the
bastard brother mirrors the legitimate in a more sinister way.
He embodies Don Pedro's own resistance to dominant forms of
interpersonal bonding. Don John's schemes work because of an
implicit, perhaps even unconscious, antagonism to marriage in
Don Pedro and Claudio. This is shown in their protective
attitude towards an all-male society based on military comrade-
ship, perhaps arising from fear of the unknown feminine 'other'.

Levin (1985) argues that there is evidence of a latent homosexuality in the male characters (particularly Don Pedro), making them ripe for temptation to abandon the wedding when Don John brings news that Hero is unchaste. Even if this is not the case, their desire to preserve the all-male community represents a significant threat to the perpetuation of a society based on a conventional family model. As Benedick says, 'the world must be peopled' (2.3.242); a widespread withdrawal of consent from marriage would mean either extinction or a community of bastards.

The potential tragedy of *Much Ado About Nothing* is caused by another weakness in the social structure: a lack of faith in female fidelity amongst the male characters. The bastard is an appropriate scapegoat for their sexual insecurity. Leonato jokingly casts doubt on Hero's legitimacy when he introduces her (1.1.105) and this sets the tone of suspicion which culminates in the church, where not even he has enough faith in her to assert her innocence. The value which Claudio places on his own self-esteem and 'honour' makes him unable to see the plot for the sham it is, revealing an unattractively selfish side to his nature and a crucial lack of faith in the basis of social bonding, on which Don John's practices ride easy.

The self-interest shown by the protagonists – exhibited in exaggerated form in Don John – is dangerous. Choosing independence rather than co-operation in social practices like marriage challenges the dominant order. However peaceful such independence may be, it represents a withdrawal of consent from these social structures and thus de-legitimises them. Since many of the characters refuse to co-operate actively in marriage bargains at some point in the play, Don John's actions may be an explicit expression of a much wider malaise concealed beneath the play's ostensible celebration of wooing and wedding. Beatrice and Benedick are the most vocal dissenters from the social norm and their vows to remain single are a cause for concern. Their pride and self-determination is potentially as menacing as Don John's misanthropic schemes, particularly in the declarations of sexual equality and independence expressed by Beatrice. In fact 'Beatrice's solipsism is ultimately to be seen as containing the seeds of a Don John's revolt' (Taylor 1973:

149). Bastardy therefore provides a grotesque caricature of the self-centred energies which could so easily pull Messina apart. Although the bastard is expelled from the stage in the final scene of betrothal, the social problems he represents are not. Don Pedro will not be coerced into getting himself a wife. His isolation, a blatant withdrawal of co-operative consent, is a dark reminder that potentially destructive forces remain. Messina selects and victimises Don John but the play criticises such futile attempts to project insecurities outwards by constructing and then blaming dispossessed groups as creators of disorder.

Don John's unnaturalness in the family is supplemented by details which present him as a rebel. At the opening of the play he has just been defeated by Don Pedro's forces (1.3.21 and 66–7) and he now occupies the position of conquered prisoner (1.3.32–6). His name may have reminded a Renaissance audience of the enigmatic figure of Don John of Austria, illegitimate son to Emperor Charles V and half-brother to Philip II of Spain. Don John's spectacular military exploits at Granada (1569–70), Lepanto (1571) and the Netherlands (1576–8) represented a valuable repulse of forces alien to Catholic order but his illegitimate energy could not easily be recuperated and controlled by the legitimate world. His military skill, combined with an autonomy of action, alarmed Philip II, particularly when the bastard pursued plans to overtake Tunis in 1573 and repudiated the Treaty of Ghent (1578). Don John of Austria (like Don John of Messina) reminds us that an unnatural child could also be a dangerously unnatural subject.

Unnatural subjects

The connection between unnatural behaviour in family and State is a common one in plays with bastard villains. The two insititutions existed in a mutually validating relationship, which meant that a failure to recognise primary bonds in the microcosm of the family was itself a form of rebellion. Many bastard villains are, like Don John, the sons of rulers, so their domestic mutinies are automatically offences of treason. Stow's abridged English chronicle (1611) gives an account of bastard treachery in

domestic and national contexts. It tells how Prince Edward
sent forces to help 'Peter of Spaine, who was driven out of his
kingdome by Henry his bastard brother . . . & in a bactell at
Nazers, put to flight ye foresaid bastard . . . but not long after,
Henry the bastard, whiles K. Peter sate at a table, suddenly
thrust him through with a speare' (137). Henry's illegitimate
military coup is repeated in the microcosm of the family. Having mauled the body of the kingdom with civil war, he savages
his brother in the home.

The image of the bastard as a herald of national disorder is
even used to describe heroic characters like Bertoldo in Massinger's *The Maid of Honour* or the bastard in Shakespeare's *King
John*. Chatillon names Sir Richard as leader of the malcontents
who accompany King John and Queen Elinor to attack the
French:

> With them a bastard of the king's deceas'd;
> And all th'unsettled humors of the land –
> Rash, inconsiderate, fiery voluntaries,
> With ladies' faces and fierce dragons' spleens –
> Have sold their fortunes at their native homes,
> Bearing their birthrights proudly on their backs,
> To make a hazard of new fortunes here.
>
> (2.1.65)

Bastardy is part of a monstrous feminine power with 'ladies' faces
and fierce dragons' spleens' which menaces the patriarchal State.
Bacon's interpretation of the myth of 'Typhon, or A Rebel'
expands this idea by reading Typhon's birth as an act of female
revenge. Juno forces the gods to grant that she might 'bring
forth something without Jupiter' since he has given birth to
Pallas without her help. She strikes the earth and out of it
springs the bastard Typhon, a monster who wages war on
Jupiter. Bacon analyses the story as an allegory of 'the rebellions
that occur from time to time in monarchies' (1857–61, 6: 703),
defining Jupiter as an autocrat who has failed to take proper
account of the wishes of his kingdom (Juno). The people
become disaffected, unite their force and break out

> into open rebellion; which, because of the infinite calamities it
> inflicts both on kings and peoples is represented under the dreadful

image of Typhon, with a hundred heads, denoting divided powers;
flaming mouths, for devestations by fire; belts of snakes, for the
pestilences which prevail, especially in sieges; iron hands, for
slaughters; eagle's talons for rapine and plunder; feathery body,
for perpetual rumours.

(6: 703)

The monster rebellion is a mother's son, the product of a
feminine grievance against patriarchal dicatorship. Bacon points
out that while rebellions are usually organised by the peers and
nobles, 'the disaffected' include the majority of the population –
the 'vulgar' – whose 'malignant' dispositions give a body and a
life to the plots of their superiors. Public actions constitute a
widespread withdrawal of consent on the part of the country and
a consequent delegitimation of the monarch's power. Contemporary fears of such unnatural behaviour were widespread in
Renaissance England, encouraged by the official response to
recurrent popular insurrection. Food riots, protests against
enclosure and disafforestation, and urban disorders (like the
apprentices' uprising of 1595) were condemned by the Privy
Council, whose powerful rhetoric demanded the punishment
of offenders for the safety of the country (Sharp 1985: 274–97).

The bastard's identity as 'ye sonne of the people' (Fortescue
1573: 93v) makes him an ideal representative of popular grievances. The label indicates his role as a champion of the common
sort, belonging to everyone, and his dangerously ungovernable
nature, fatherless and therefore responsible to no one. The plays
Sir Thomas More (1595) and *The Life and Death of Jack Straw*
(1591) both include references to bastardy in their pictures of
popular protest. The subject would have been highly sensitive
given the frequency of rioting in the 1590s caused by the
poor harvests and increased poverty. The scene ascribed to
Shakespeare in *Sir Thomas More* portrays the events of the May
Day rebellion of 1517 and shows a group of London apprentices
demonstrating against high food prices, the result of foreign
imports. They say their behaviour is caused partly by the eating
of parsnips and their leader, John Lincoln, describes the vege-
tables as bastards: 'these bastards of dung – as you know, they
grow in dung – have infected us, and it is our infection will make
the city shake, which partly comes through the eating of

parsnips' (12). Here bastardy is literally the root cause of urban disorder; it supposedly infects the population with a plague of insurrection by becoming part of their own civic body. In *Jack Straw*, a dramatised account of the peasants' revolt of 1381, the protesters are led by a bastard. Straw marches on London with an army of 'unnatural Rebels' and is stabbed to death by Lord Mayor Walworth who sentences him with the words

> Villaine I say whence comes this rage of thine,
> How darest thou a dungell bastard borne,
> To brave thy Soveraigne and his Nobles thus.

(946)

Jack Straw's bastardy is a complete fabrication of the dramatist. It makes him a suitable figurehead for the group of 'base and common men' (318).

In the earlier part of the play the view of Straw as an 'accursed villain' (971) is counterbalanced by lines which celebrate his defiant acts. Ball sees his attack on the tax collector as 'good service to thy country', an attempt to restore 'civill' order (50–1). Food rioters made the same argument, saying that they were trying to uphold the country's laws (Sharp 1985: 284–5). The inclusion of a more sympathetic attitude to popular protest contrasts sharply with descriptions of Straw's rebellion as unnatural. By accommodating these two viewpoints on the action, the play dramatises a contradiction in the government's response to food riots. Extravagant verbal condemnation of the protests was often accompanied by increased efforts to help the poverty-stricked rioters and provide relief, thus acknowledging the justice of their claims while publicly castigating their actions. The whole process of riot was, in some senses, theatrical (Wrightson 1982: 174). The antagonists' extreme words and actions were undercut by more conciliatory attitudes. Shouts for liberty and fair prices were matched by a wish to sustain the social order rather than overturn it; behind the government's threats was a concern for the rioters' welfare. Buchanan Sharp (1985) argues that 'food rioting had theatrical characteristics, with each side playing a role whose function and limits were well known to the other' (284). If protesters stepped beyond their appointed roles, however, the government was ready to match its threatening rhetoric with action, executing offenders who abandoned the conservative principles of the food riot to attack the ruling order. *Jack Straw* demonstrates the dangers of moving from a theatrically staged confrontation (as in a food riot) to an outright rebellion. In the first part of the play there are lines which encourage sympathy for the rebels as champions of 'the poore people of the Countrie' (23). Reading the rebellion as a staged performance makes Straw's claims for 'wealth and libertie' (704) and his wish to see 'all the Rich men displaste' (113) less threatening. It also makes the exclamations of the courtly characters look over-exaggerated. Sir John Morton's view that the 'Land will come to ruine' (383) is elaborated by the Lord Mayor, who reports that the rebels are 'Making fowle slaughter of your Noblemen, / Burning up Bookes and matters of records', defacing property and beating down 'the better sort' (650–4). Up to this point there has been no evidence of widespread destruction. We are told that Straw invades Sir John Morton's castle and takes his family hostage but this is to gain access to the monarch. The rioters are angry when King Richard breaks his promise to speak to them on the banks of the Thames but the Lord Mayor's report is not substantiated by anything we see on stage.

The scene in which King Richard meets Straw and his followers is the turning point of the play. It shows the Kentish rebels crossing the boundary line from an officially sanctioned protest for their common rights to anarchic revolt. Richard offers a 'generall pardon' (738) and promise of liberty. Two contrasting responses to this conciliatory gesture draw a clear line between legitimate and illegitimate types of protest. The Essex men accept the offer; having 'far more better mindes' (891) they part company and return to their homes. Their faith in the King to right their wrongs defines them as activists willing to work within the confines of the staged riot and to accept the authority of the government as an agent for social change. The Kentish company reject this moderate line. Straw says 'I came for more than to be answered thus' and pours scorn on the Essex men (754–6). From this point on he and his followers are presented as frighteningly destructive. Straw's vow 'I came for spoile and spoile Ile have' (757) is a 'dangerous and unnaturall resolution' (899) which will lead to nothing but havoc (896). The condemnation of the Kentish forces comes to a climax in the label of bastardy. Straw is defined as a 'dungell bastard borne' (947) and those who are pardoned are 'unlike Englishmen, degenerate from your naturall obedience, & nature of your country, that by kinde bringeth forth none, or at least brooketh none such, but spits them out for bastards and recreants' (1,089). *Jack Straw* thus recognises the need for popular protest as a means to enforce basic rights of subsistence, but clearly counsels against more extreme forms of insurrection by condemning rebels as unnatural bastards. The play draws on popular prejudice against illegitimacy to reinforce its essentially conservative viewpoint.

A more radical effect is achieved in Heywood's *1 Edward IV* (1599). The play depicts an infamous historical figure, Thomas Neville, Lord Fauconbridge, whose bastardy and rebellious activities are described in Stow's *Survey of London* (1603) and Sir George Buck's *History of King Richard the Third* (1619). Buck actually makes bastardy synonymous with rebellion: the loyal Fauconbridge is 'nor basely nor *dishonourably descended'* but by becoming a 'seditious rebel', he is transformed into 'the famous and mischevious pirate Thomas Neville, alias Fauconberg, the base son of Sir William de Neville' (Buck 1982: 19). In Heywood's play, Falconbridge is a unsympathetic (though courageous) villain who attacks the city of London, is defeated, and finally executed. Within this framework the play develops a complex relationship between the bastard and the 'vulgar' sort of rebels through which Heywood is able to level criticisms at those in authority.

At the opening of the play news is brought of Falconbridge's uprising from the south. King Edward claims he saw 'Black discontent sit ever on his browe' (8) and a messenger reports 'to him the malcontented commons flock / From every part of *Sussex, Kent* and *Essex*' (7). This sets up expectations of the bastard as a champion of popular protesters from these regions who followed the tradition of the peasants' revolt by staging food riots in 1586–87 and 1594–98. Rioting occured mainly in clothmaking areas and in market towns through which large quantities of grain were shipped (Sharp 1985: 276). The rebel captains in the play seem, at first, to be modelled on figures like

Tyler, Cade and Jack Straw: Smoke is a smith of Cheapstead, Chub is a chandler of Sandwich and Spicing is an apothecary from Kent (10). Smoke compares his followers to 'a troop of hungry travellers / That fix their eyes upon a furnisht feast' (10) and the rebels cry 'Liberty, liberty, liberty, general liberty!' (9). Falconbridge's first long speech contradicts this image. When his men shout for liberty, he asserts, quite unequivocally,

> We do not rise like Tyler, Cade and Straw,
> Bluebeard, and other of that rascal rout,
> Basely like tinkers or such muddy slaves,
> For mending measures or the price of corne,
> Or for some common in the wield of Kent
> Thats by some greedy cormorant enclos'd,
> But in the true and ancient lawfull right
> Of the redoubted house of *Lancaster*.
>
> (9)

The 'ancient liberty' (9) he proclaims as his goal has nothing to do with equality or common rights; he is purportedly fighting for the Lancastrian cause of Henry VI. Falconbridge is royalist rather than republican, an association which proves increasingly subversive as the play continues. His contempt for the Kentish peasants makes a clear distinction between his rebellion and protests against poll taxes, enclosure or corn prices. Heywood indicates that he does not want to attribute blame here. Nor does the play blame those usually associated with riot in the city. The citizens who defend London include a group of very loyal and orderly apprentices who describe themselves as peaceful by custom unlike the pilfering rebels who raise up alehouse brawls and disappear like cowards in time of war (18).

Heywood uses Falconbridge to make a covert though trenchant attack on the nobility and the monarchy. The working people, masters and servants alike, are the heroes of the play and Heywood's villains are those who steal rather than earn. These include the elite as well as the unscrupulous tradesmen Chub, Spicing and Smoke. The rebels' anarchic ideas can be read as examples of the exploitative behaviour of the aristocracy. The captains imagine how they will pillage the shops of velvet, silks and satins to clothe themselves, drink unlimited supplies of wine and take chains of gold and plate (10). Because of Falconbridge's

royalist associations these details indirectly criticise behaviour at
the court, suggesting that its extravagance is also based on theft.
Chub's speech about feasting makes a pertinent comment on the
behaviour of the nobility:

> The costermongers fruite us,
> The poulters send us in fowl,
> And butchers meate without controul:
> And ever when we suppe or dine,
> The vintners freely bring us in wine.
> If anybody aske who shall pay,
> Cut off his head and send him away

(11)

The lines describe the unreasonable power of those with authority
to command what they want on pain of death. They remind us
that King Edward and the court have just retired to spend the
night in feast and jollity. The King is noticeably absent from
the city's defence preparations and tells the Mayor 'you may
condemn us / Of too much slackness in such urgent need' (32).

Falconbridge is a caricature of royal tyranny whose exaggerated speeches encourage a critical response to Edward. Having
rejected kinship with Tyler, Cade, Straw or Wyatt, he declares
'We will be masters of the mint ourselves, / And set our own
stamp on the golden coin' (10). He plans to establish a court at
Westminster and expand it 'to receive our men' (10). The 'we'
he uses is not a communal fraternity but the royal 'we'. The
rebels see him as 'a king, a *Caesar*' who will license their looting
(26). Details of sexual aggression link the outrageous behaviour
of Falconbridge, his men and the court. The rebels imagine that
they will be able to rape maidens and evade the law as easily as
lords (19). Spicing says 'we will be kings tonight / Carouse in
gold and sleep with merchants wives' (30). Edward's seduction
of Jane Shore recalls this imagined abuse of power and the
demand for Shore's wife forms an explicit parallel between the
King and the bastard. Falconbridge announces 'Shore, listen: thy
wife is mine, thats flat. This night, in thine own house, she sleeps
with me' (16). His brutal ultimatum remains a verbal threat but
the King exploits his *droit de seigneur* with complete indifference
to Shore, who had helped to defend the city. The goldsmith had

refused a knighthood and Edward had promised 'Some other
way / We will devise to quittance thy deserts' (33). Shore's
deserts hardly seem just. The King's betrayal of his subject is
echoed by Falconbridge's betrayal of his men. He calls them 'the
dirty scum of rascal peasantry' (20), yet praises them to keep
their support and exploits them heartlessly. The play implies that
the real rebels against the people are not popular protesters, but
the King and nobles whose conflicts and causes (which the
people are obliged to support) are motivated by nothing more
than self-interest. Falconbridge is invading London in the hopes
of recovering his family's property. The lines where he proclaims
his rights make a disturbing comparison between bastard and
monarch:

> He that keeps your Soveraign in the tower
> Hath seized me of my land and robbed me of my right
> I am a gentleman as well as hee
> What he hath got, he holds by tyranny.
>
> (25)

If Falconbridge is as good a gentleman as the King then
Edward's power, as well as being tyrannical, is illegitimate.
The unnatural corruption represented by the bastard is located
inside the social structure. It appears to attack the city as an
invading force but exists within the city walls which mark only a
superficial boundary between order and disorder. An apparently
extraneous soliloquy given by the Mayor, John Crosbie, reinforces this idea. Crosbie confides to the audience that he was
found abandoned as a baby by Cow Cross, from which he got his
name (57). Details of his case history, his base birth, his fostering
at the Hospital, his apprenticeship to a grocer, all suggest he is a
bastard. Crosbie is a virtuous character, the personification of
order, but his speech shows that illegitimacy exists at the centre
of city authority. Attempts to displace disruptive forces on to a
bastard scapegoat will not solve social problems.

Grievance over the loss of land, like that shown by Falconbridge in 1 *Edward IV*, is the motivating force behind all the
other military rebellions mounted by bastard villains. The threat
such figures posed to national order was outlined by King James

who (apparently choosing to forget the suspicions surrounding his own birth) warned his heir

> Have the King my grand-fathers example before your eyes, who by his adulterie, bred the wracke of his lawfull daughter and heire; in begetting that bastard, who unnaturally rebelled, and procured the ruine of his owne Soverane and sister.
>
> (James I 1918: 36)

The bastard referred to is James Stewart, Earl of Moray, who led a rebellion of Protestant forces against his half-sister Mary Queen of Scots in 1560 and again in 1565 when she married Darnley. He had been instrumental in assembling evidence against Mary when she was tried for Darnley's murder in 1568 at the Conference of York. His unnatural behaviour towards his sister may have been part of a wider project to usurp the Scottish throne. He was made Regent of Scotland when Mary was forced to abdicate in 1567 and some sources suggest that he was aiming still higher. As early as 1559, Cecil had instructed his Scottish contact Sadler 'to explore the very truth whether the Lord James do mean any enterprise towards the crown of Scotland for himself or no' and just after Darnley's murder, on 12 March 1567, the Bishop of Mondovi wrote to the Cardinal Secretary 'most people impute the crime to the Earl of Moray, who, being the Queen's brother, has always had the throne in view, although he is a bastard' (Armstrong-Davison 1965: 286–8).

Foreign powers, especially the Spanish, were also discomforted by bastard usurpers. In 1580 Don Antonio (son of the Duke of Beja and his Jewish mistress) persuaded the people that he was rightful heir to the throne of Portugal and was crowned in Lisbon, much to the annoyance of Philip II of Spain who claimed the crown himself. Philip's invading forces defeated Don Antonio, who was eventually forced to retire to England and recieved Elizabeth's protection (Ridley 1987: 235–7). In 1587 another bastard, Arthur Dudley, provoked further Spanish suspicions about English diplomacy. Apprehended and taken to Madrid in 1587, Dudley told Sir Francis Englefield that his mother was Queen Elizabeth and his father, Leicester. He claimed they were planning to elevate him to the throne after Elizabeth's death. Englefield, convinced this was a plot to

promote Protestant rule and disinherit Catholic claimants, wrote
to warn King Philip that 'his claim at present amounts to
nothing, but, with the example of Don Antonio before us, it
cannot be doubted that France and the English heretics, or some
other party, might turn it to their own advantage . . . for
obstructing . . . the inheritance of the crown by its legitimate
master' (Hume 1899: 111–12).

Bastard usurpers in the drama are concerned less with religious politics and more with gaining land and power. The
earliest of these is Mordred in *The Misfortunes of Arthur*
(1588) who is listed in the *dramatis personae* simply as
'Mordred the Usurper'. He is modelled closely on the Senecan
tyrant and is ruthless, evil and destructive. At the opening of the
play he has usurped Arthur's throne and bed in the King's
absence. When Arthur returns from his crusade, Mordred
refuses to give up the crown, showing a complete disregard for
the principle of rightful inheritance. He tells Conan 'Weake is
the Scepters hold, that seekes but right, / The care whereof hath
danger'd many Crownes' (1.4.98) and later insists 'My will must
goe for right' (2.2.41).

The majority of the play is tedious, though it may have held
political interest for its audience in 1588 because of its debates
about government and the relevance of its subject matter to
current events. Mordred's long discussions with Conan analyse
the social consitution of Renaissance England and illustrate the
discrepancy between the ideal principle of reciprocity (or natural love between subjects and rulers) and the reality of
unequal power. Conan, a 'faithfull counsellor', describes a
relationship between monarch and people based on love and
duty but Mordred argues that this would not work because a
ruler's commandments would only be entreaties. He believes 'a
Kingdom's kept by feare' (2.2.32) and that a timorous subject
'dares attempt no chaundge' (2.2.34). These ideas are intended
to shock, to establish Mordred as a tyrant. They also express a
brutal truth behind the system of paternalism and deference
which governed Renaissance society. The elite remained in
power partly because those they ruled dared not change their
position for fear of punishment in this world or the next.
Mordred recognises, with political astuteness, that he can

wield true power over his subjects only by compelling them 'as well to praise as beare' (2.2.80), thus making an outward acceptance of his tyranny and a tacit rejection of any rights of their own. Subordination in the 'natural' hierarchy of Renaissance England worked through just this kind of ideological apparatus.

The play's interrogation of government would have appealed to an audience at the Inns of Court. In a performance before Queen Elizabeth its more subversive elements could easily have been dismissed since the unnatural Mordred gives voice to them. The play possibly had a more specific political meaning, relating to the recent threat of Catholic rebellion from Scotland, Mary's execution in 1587 and the question of succession (Axton 1977). Reese (1945) suggests that the relationship between Mordred and Arthur mirrored that between Mary and Elizabeth, whereas Waller (1925) and Bevington (1968) propose that Mordred represents Bothwell. While the former identification would have justified Elizabeth's decision in executing her cousin for the good of her country, the latter would have avoided making direct allusion to a matter on which Elizabeth was apparently still sensitive. A play linking the younger Bothwell with a villainous Mordred and presenting him in such an unattractive light would doubtless have pleased the Queen.

The Valiant Welshman (1612) is another play which follows a conventional line in depicting the bastard usurper unsympathetically. Its Prologue announces 'a swelling Tragedy / Of discontented men' (A4) and, as the play opens, the Earl of Monmouth is trying to usurp the throne in north Wales. King Octavian fears that his other nobles may have been infected with 'that base Apoplexie of revolt' (B1v). Rebellion is condemned as perverted, greedy appetite and none is more vocal in his criticisms than the King's bastard son, Codigune. Once Monmouth has been defeated by Caradoc, Codigune changes his tune. He is forced to recognise that he cannot inherit when Octavian betrothes his daughter to Caradoc and adopts him as heir. In soliloquy, Codigune vows to wreak revenge:

By her that excommunicates my right
Of my creation, with a bastards name,

And makes me stand nonsuted to a crowne;
Ile fall my selfe, or plucke this Welshman down.

                                                    (Civ)

The shock of Codigune's disinheritance invites sympathy but his
evil nature is quickly established. He refuses to accompany the
wedding party to the church, says that he will stay outside and
curse, devise plots of machiavellian blackness and disguise these
'as brothell sinnes benighted, darkely cleare' (Civ–C2). He kills
his father by poisoning him and without allowing him time to
pray, something which horrifies the 'natural' though adopted
son, Caradoc.

   Unlike Caradoc, the 'trecherous Bastard' (C4v) has no attractive qualities. He is unquestionably evil and rebels against what is
a fully legitimated monarchy. Caradoc accuses him of basely
stealing the crown by 'sinister means, blacke as thy sinnes'
(E2v), words which draw a parallel between his usurpation and
base birth because of the association between bastardy and the
heraldic bar sinister. After he has been defeated in single fight, he
tells the audience 'Ile to the Romanes, and there plot, pell mell.
/ Vessels that once are seasoned, keepe their smell' (E3v).
Rebellion seems to be in his blood and the final scene sums
him up as one whose 'infectious breath' poisons the kingdom
with 'plagues of bloud and death' (I3v).

   Even bastards who are not rebels can represent disorder in the
State. Edricus, the villain of *Edmund Ironside* (1595), is a symbol
of national disunity (Sams 1986: 49). He spends the course of the
play shifting his loyalties between the kings Canutus and
Edmund and engineering conflicts between them. He is
undoubtedly the most interesting and dramatically attractive
character on stage, although his pragmatic philosophy must
have been profoundly disturbing to a Renaissance audience. It
regards the individual's orientation in society as dependent upon
chance and personal will rather than Providence. Edricus
declares 'Pray to the devil. God is not my friend' (1,126). He
is 'the scum of vices, all the ill that may be' (168) and his decision
to retire to Spain identifies his evil nature with Catholicism. For
all its religious allusions, the play is primarily about the dangers
of social mobility. The label 'villain' which sticks to Edricus has

social connotations since he has been raised from a base plough-boy 'to be a duke for all my villainy' (320). He is obssessed with status and takes pride in his ability to 'cloak, cozen, cog and flatter with the king' (291) to win what he wants at no matter what cost to the country. This makes a dark comment on the political interests of statesmen elevated to positions of power, perhaps indicating one reason for the play's revival in the early 1630s. Edricus points out that while he has been promoted 'my betters are exiled the court' (288) and the play unreservedly condemns the social adventurer. In the wake of Buckingham's murder, its message would have been in line with criticisms of the Caroline court.

Illegitimate constitutions

Bastard villains who cause disorder in the family and the State seem committed to an anarchic alternative, a world where the individual position is paramount. Their rebellions strike at the foundations of patriarchal rule and they often put forward an alternative world view which is dangerously persuasive. The unnatural behaviour of characters like Codigune or Edricus can seem reasonable even though they are clearly labelled as evil. In more complex characterisations, the subversive power of the bastard villain is contained in a subtle and interesting way by showing his allegiance to the principles of legitimacy in spite of his rebellious activities. The bastard's transgression of social laws, which appears to be anarchic, is only a means whereby the outcast can re-inscribe himself into the legitimate world order. He rebels not against the legitimate world but against his own illegitimacy and the place to which it consigns him. Many bastard villains reveal a deep-rooted love of the society from which they are excluded. Henry of Trastomare in *The Hector of Germany* is a good example. He attacks the Palsgrave to become Emperor and predicts

> When th' Imperiall Scepter fills my hand,
> And I have *Caesars* wreath upon my brow
> As had my Grandsire, and his royall Father
> I'll make *Iberia* wreake with foes blood.

(78)

Henry vows bloody and unnatural destruction but wants to preserve the traditional genealogical structure. He dreams of owning the imperial trappings which once belonged to his male ancestors even though he can win them only by defying all the laws governing inheritance.

Bastard villains whose final goal is social integration rather than revolution are in tune with the aims of many malcontented groups in Renaissance society. Younger sons wanted to be included in the inheritance of their fathers' property; unemployed scholars, clerics, apprentices envied their colleagues who had permanent jobs and secure tenures. Many of the plays already discussed include details to suggest the bastard's admiration of prizes like title, inheritance, land, dowry. In *The Bastard*, for example, Gaspar's villainy is motivated by his longing to be a full member of Alonzo's family and the society which excludes him. He enjoys calling Alonzo his 'father' (G3), and points out that 'E're long when *I* am married, *I* shall be / Sir *Don* or any thing' (G3). He daydreams that he '*may have noble* blood / *And challenge* Kindred *with the best*' (A4v), showing admiration for social heirarchy. Similarly, in *1 Edward IV*, Falconbridge is proud of his lawfull line even though his birth is unlawful. Since the goal of many bastard rebels is the crown, their championship of an alternative polity is automatically brought into question. Ironically, these villains become upholders of a distorted version of the legitimate world's codes and values in the midst of the chaos they create. The most extreme case is in *The Tempest* where Caliban plans to overthrow Prospero only to recreate his own subservient position in the new regime he will help to set up. Caliban will play the role of 'foot-licker' (4.1.219) to his new masters, Stephano and Trinculo.

The pattern of 'transgressive reinscription' (to borrow Dollimore's term), invariably problematises the opposition legitimate/illegitimate in both the personal constitution of the bastard and the political constitution. Bastard characters who try to recreate themselves within legitimate structures experience serious crises of identity. On a personal level, reinscription means self-annihilation since it necessitates a rejection of the radical 'otherness' of bastardy. The bastard must eliminate part of himself to become an insider and this kind of self-betrayal

usually has tragic personal consequences. It also appears to
maintain orthodox ideologies by showing the domestication of
powerful alien elements. As Dollimore (1986) has argued, the
pattern of transgressive reinscription is not necessarily conservative in nature. It dislocates pre-existing categories and reveals the
proximity of the illegitimate 'other' to the original order, thus
problematising the very idea of legitimacy in a political constitution. The complex relationship between the bastard usurper and
the legitimate world is most fully elaborated in *King Lear* (1605)
and *The Sophister* (1631).

The Sophister is useful to begin with because it is an allegory
about language and centres directly on the bastard's eccentric
relation to the Symbolic order, Lacan's term for the public
language which embodies and creates the abstracted laws of a
culture (in this case, that of Renaissance patriarchy). The play
traces a struggle for the possession of Parrhesia, the kingdom of
the mind, by a variety of personified rhetorical discourses. The
bastard is defined in negative terms as Fallacy. In addition to its
allegory, *The Sophister* appeals to a specific alienated group in
Renaissance England. It was certainly written for an academic
audience and invites a comparison between Fallacy and the class
of dissatisfied intellectuals. In the 1630s and 1640s there was a
large increase in numbers of university graduates who did not
'share all the opportunities, privileges and responsibilities that
were the prerequisites of full unequivocal membership' of Stuart
society (Curtis 1962: 28). They experienced unemployment or
underemployment and were widely regarded as a discontented
and factious group. Their eloquence was dangerous since their
speech was directed against the ruling order rather than contained within it. Analysing the civil war in retrospect, Thomas
Hobbes declared 'the core of rebellion . . . are the universities'
(Curtis 1962: 27). Richard Zouche, the probable author of *The
Sophister*, lived in Oxford and the play begins by presenting
Fallacy as an undergraduate about to 'take's Degree' (A3v).

Superficially, the play constructs Fallacy as an alien 'other'.
Because he is illegitimate, his entry into the Symbolic order is
incomplete. He has no legal father to align him with authority
and is malcontented because he cannot inherit the kingdom of
Discourse, his biological father. The character Definition points

out 'he is base borne and base birth is a vile condition which to them that are unlawfully begotten doth purchase infamy and bereaves them of all hope of succession' (E1v). Fallacy therefore sets out to attack the language which excludes him. He enters 'with a dark Lanthorne' in the manner of the Vice and consecrates his services to the goddess Deceit (A4). He causes chaos by giving Discourse a potion which drives him mad and reduces his speech to a jumble. Fallacy listens gleefully as his father begins to 'talke out of all measure' (B3v), his verse breaking down into prose. The bastard then pretends he has no interest in governing the State and, using the very '*Machivillian* policy' (E2) which he says he hates, works his way to the seat of power. Doing so involves setting his brothers against one another. Fallacy is thirsty for news of their fight and, in truly macabre style, sees their bloody wounds as a triumphant celebration of his own advancement:

> *Fall.*   Bled they very much?
> *Cont.*   Exceedingly.
> [*Fall*]. Well, so their streaming veines
>   Shall serve as Conduits dropping Clarret wine,
>   To sollemnize my Coronation.
>
>   (E3v)

Once in power, Fallacy promotes unnatural relations in the community. He threatens the ancient amities between the kingdoms of Hermenia, Verona and the Isle of Man. Nuptial breaches also ensue. Discourse banishes Lady Method from his bed and Fallacy wrecks the betrothals between his brothers and the daughters of Lady Truth. He enjoys hearing how Lady Truth has been turned out on the streets, has taken to frequenting taverns and has prostituted herself to 'senceless drunkards' and 'most disgract-esteemed hereticks' (H4v). Her daughters Scientia and Opinion have turned to sloth, atheism and prostitution; they are 'only constant in inconstancy' (I1). Fallacy's usurpation destroys natural law which binds the individual to society, society to God and the present to the past. A vivid picture of the apocalyptic breakdown of order, which probably seemed imminent to the audience, is summarised by Judgement:

> Those blessed civill laws are disanul'd,
> Which to so many glorious Emperours,

So many ages, in so many lands,
Have ever beene so justly well approv'd;
There he hath planted rude and practique friends
Which grate the Commons, spoile Nobility.
Betwixt deare brothers and the nearest friends,
Endeavoured to sow vile dissentions.
There the most sacred ordinance of Heaven,
The divine Oracles they falsify.

(H1)

Fallacy's delight at the chaos he has created is only superficial.
He can not destroy enough of the old order to establish a new
code of values because he is in love with the establishment he
attacks. He tries to prevent his brothers' weddings only to
substitute himself as Scientia's bridegroom. He envies Topicus
and Demonstration because they are loved by Discourse, the
nobility and the commoners. Fallacy is distressed to think that he
is held in 'scorn and infamy' and even hated because of his base
birth (B1). He longs to be a full member of the community of
language. Outside it, in soliloquy, he expresses his grievances at
such length and so persuasively that it is difficult not to show
some sympathy for him and disapproval for the ruling order
which discriminates against him.

The new regime Fallacy sets up shows his paradoxical attitude
to the legitimate world. Once he is inside the power structure he
reverts to a form of government like the one he overthrew. He
employs Opposition and Contradiction within a polity whose
basic structure remains the same. It simply involves a cabinet re-
shuffle. He renames himself Great Sophisme and declares:

Let *Definition* and *Division*, both
Be banished the Court, for *Proposition*,
He ne're oppos'd himselfe against me much,
We may procure his love, and use his helpe;
And therefore let him stay. But you
Lord *Opposition*, willingly I make
My sole or chiefest Counsellor of State,
By whom in all affaires I will be rul'd.
You, *Contradiction*, where so e're I goe,
I chuse to beare my sword.

(E3v)

Fallacy rebuilds the old order around him and by doing so delegitimises it. His government is a distorted mirror image of the original and by reflecting it, implies that it was equally corrupt. Earlier speeches prepare for this, hinting that Fallacy is not altogether an outsider in spite of society's wish to construct him as such. He exercised considerable influence in Discourse's kingdom, bestowing his help on all those wishing to 'cloak their foule deformities' (F3v) with lies. He was active amongst the merchants on the Exchange, kept company with 'great Princes' and was familiar with 'most chiefe Statesmen' (B3). A damning picture of the legitimate hegemony emerges so that although Fallacy is the villian of the play, and condemned as such, his usurpation produces a critique of the order against which he rebels.

The serious contradictions in Fallacy's ideology finally cause his downfall. He begins by appointing Opposition as chief counsellor but retains Proposition from his father's government because Proposition 'ne'er oppos'd himselfe against me much' (E3v). As a quasi-legitimate ruler, Fallacy tries to separate himself from the subversive alien energies which brought him to power. He contrives the death of Contradiction and Opposition but cannot escape what is an integral part of his own constitution. Fallacy's followers, who represent the repressed illegitimate side of his nature, run mad and speak in a 'wilde confusion', representing a semiotic language outside the Symbolic (H3). He recognises that his downfall is the result of self-betrayal, asking 'was my selfe the cause, my cursed selfe, / Lulled asleep in fond security?' (H3). He ends the play by leaving his servant Ambiguity and fleeing from the kingdom of Discourse wearing the cloak of Distinction. The cloak distinguishes him as a bastard and re-locates him firmly as an unnatural outsider, but not until he has revealed the fundamental unnaturalness of the order which condemns him.

The process of self-betrayal is explored more fully in Shakespeare's *King Lear*. The goddess Nature to whom Edmund dedicates himself is simultaneously a disruptive force and a champion of his illegitimacy, his difference. Standing up for bastards necessitates a violation of the principles which dictate social stability. In lines exclusive to the quarto version of the play, he prophesies the effects of his plot as

> unnaturalness between the child and the parent, death, dearth, dissolutions of ancient amities, divisions in state, menaces and maledictions against king and nobles, needless diffidences, banishment of friends, dissipation of cohorts, nuptial breaches and I know not what.
>
> (1.2.144)

He imagines anarchy in microcosm and macrocosm, a breaking of social bonds of effective equality (ancient amities) and of inequality (child and parent) so that the correct pattern of deference and paternalism no longer operates. Partly as a result of Edmund's behaviour, these effects do succeed most unhappily. He causes nuptial breaches between Goneril and Albany, Cornwall and Regan and sets the sisters against each other, endangering the kingdom with another division in the face of an invading power. He behaves unnaturally towards his father and brother and is involved in the actual and attempted murders of nobles and monarchs. Edmund's actions seek to destroy a legitimate constitution based on marriage and primogeniture, to promote an illegitimate alternative.

Edmund is not fully committed to this alternative. His energies are directed 'to th' legitimate' not to its overthrow. Capell's emendation 'Edmund the base / Shall top th' legitimate' misreads the character as well as Q1 and F1 by suggesting that he wishes to overturn the existing order instead of forcing his way into it (Pittock 1984: 208). It is Edmund who upholds the principles of degree which Lear and Edgar (as Poor Tom) repudiate in the anarchy of their madness. As Carroll (1987) observes, Edmund becomes a ventriloquist who assumes the speech and values of the legitimate world to get on. He studies deserving by modelling himself on and superseding the legitimate Edgar, the Earl of Gloucester and finally the Duke of Cornwall (whose army he commands in Act 5). His mimicry is a distorted image of legitimate hierarchy, one which matches the government of the *Lear* world all too closely. Edmund is a mirror as well as a ventriloquist, a grotesque reflection of the hegemony which promotes him, demonstrating that its practices are potentially just as unnatural, or illegitimate, as those of the bastard.

Edmund's words to Cornwall 'I will persever in my course of loyalty though the conflict be sore between that and my blood' (3.5.21) hold more truth than Edmund realises. His rise to power causes a fundamental fracture in his character. His entry into the ruling (or Symbolic) order of the play world is profoundly traumatic because he is torn between the contradictory ideologies of the goddess Nature – where all are equal socially – and the stratified legitimate hierarchy. In terms of value systems he is schizophrenic. To achieve success he is obliged to suppress his difference, to deny the illegitimacy which is his nature. His internal struggle is represented dramatically in 2.1 where he lies to Gloucester about Edgar's parricidal tendencies to disguise his plots. The elaborate fiction allows him to displace his own unnaturalness towards brother and father on to Edgar and to reinscribe himself in the legitimate order as a 'Loyal and natural boy' (2.1.84). In the imaginary Edgar, he creates a Frankenstein's monster in an endeavour to deny his own difference and his evil practices, to escape from an identity that he hates. The self-betrayal implicit in the fiction is shown when Edmund quotes both legitimate and illegitimate voices (2.1.45–77) and tells how Edgar cut him with a sword, an injury the audience have just seen Edmund inflict on himself

> I told him, the revengive gods
> 'Gainst parricides did all the thunder bend,
> Spoke with how manifold and strong a bond
> The child was bound to th' father; sir, in fine,
> Seeing how loathly opposite I stood
> To his unnatural purpose, in fell motion
> With his prepared sword he charges home
> My unprovided body.
>
> (2.1.45)

It is not Edgar but Edmund who has cut himself in two by trying to become the legitimate.

The role he plays holds a dangerous fascination for him, one which proves fatal. He may say he stands up for bastards, but he expresses a deep-rooted contempt for illegitimacy when he quotes Edgar's condemnation of him as an 'unpossessing bastard' whose words cannot be trusted (2.1.67–77). Edmund does not celebrate his difference, he tries to efface it. This causes tragedy. Firstly, it forces him to kill Cordelia because she endangers the emergence of his self-created legitimate identity. In *Suffocating Mothers*, Janet Adelman argues that his killing of Cordelia is a recuperation of masculinity which is threatened throughout the play by an overpowering maternal presence (1992: 127–8). For Edmund the problem of Cordelia or the 'suffocating mother' is especially acute because he is a bastard, a mother's child. By reminding him of his maternal origin she destroys the fragile legitimacy which he is trying so hard to construct for himself in spite of the absence of a legal father. He must destroy her and Lear, whose reunion with her represents what could happen so easily to Edmund, a dissolution of the individuated self into the maternal body.

The execution orders complete Edmund's rejection of his maternal identity but this has fatal consequences for him as well as for Cordelia. He wins nothing for 'the base' in his rise to power, in fact he destroys himself. As a ventriloquist, Edmund plays his part not wisely but too well. He becomes saturated with the principles of legitimacy he articulates and is consumed by them. When challenged in the final scene he says he will maintain his truth and honour (5.3.94–5) but he no longer has any truth. In the duel he is already fighting on Edgar's side against his bastardy. He respects Edgar's nobility and is so committed '*to* th' legitimate' (1.2.21) that he cannot choose but accept Edgar's judgement of him as a personified vice (5.3.171–4) and his position as base. His lines 'Th' hast spoken right, 'tis true. / The wheel is come full circle, I am here' (5.3.174), are a far cry from his earlier determination to prove his natural superiority.

Reducing Edmund to an embodiment of evil and baseness seems pitifully inadequate since we know so much about the vices of the other characters. Their ambition, folly and pride cause suffering too, as do the gods, fate or chance. Edmund's progress to the legitimate makes it clear that villainy is not exclusive to outsiders, and ironically it is not Edmund's treachery but Edgar's appeal for his father's blessing which kills Gloucester. Presumably we are not expected to blame Edgar for this, but it problematises his already superficial moral judgement on his bastard brother. Illegitimacy is what Adelman calls a 'protective fantasy', a means to alienate internal corruption,

disease within the legitimate. Lear also uses it, bastardising
Goneril (1.4.232) and Regan (2.2.302–4) because he wants to
disown his part in their disruptive female energy rather than
acknowledge its origin in himself (Adelman 1992: 108–9).
Edmund's reaction to the deaths of his bastardised mistresses
is remarkable: 'I was contracted to them both; all three / Now
marry in an instant' (5.3.229). The union between father's
daughters and mother's son truly dissolves boundaries
between the base and the legitimate; it brings together legitimate hierarchy and illegitimate villainy as one flesh. It is a public
declaration of their sameness and, appropriately, it is neither a
marriage nor an extra-marital union but something poised on
the borderline between the two. In this new-found equality in
death, Edmund can finally acknowledge the mother's part in him
and try to save Cordelia and Lear. As the promised end shows,
even if he tries to do some good 'Despite of mine own nature'
(5.3.245), the problems of the *Lear* world will not be solved.
Although a highly complex villain, he is not the sole cause of
tragedy.

The range of villains discussed in this chapter, to which
Edmund provides a fitting conclusion, shows that the type can
serve a variety of purposes. Popular associations between
bastardy and unnaturalness are the basis of non-socialised characters who are likely to cause conflict in the family and the State.
Dispossessed and malcontented by birth, they have much in
common with other alienated groups whom the authorities
labelled as seditious. Often the bastard gives voice to ideas
which present a challenge to the traditional order. Sometimes
he is only a scapegoat for the faults and tensions within a society
that was founded on the contradictory principles of emergent
capitalist individualism and a system of co-operation. In many
plays, the depiction of the bastard villain as an unnatural child
exposes the binary opposition natural/unnatural as a construct
produced by the dominant order to displace the dangerous
energies which inhere in it and threaten to destroy it. The
paradox of the bastard's position as both 'other' and the same,
inside and outside, is most fully revealed by the fact that in spite
of his unnatural behaviour, the bastard is a natural child.

4

Natural children

In Renaissance England another name for a bastard was a 'natural child'. Agrippa's *Commendation of Matrimony* (1545) explains that 'the frutes of matrimony were of god not of nature. And of this the bastarde children be called naturall: but those that come of matrimony, be onely lawfull' (B7). The adjective 'natural' denotes a bastard's metaphorical exclusion from culture, from divine spirit and human law. Dramatists use its associations of difference to characterise illegitimates in relation to the countryside, animals and plant life or physical appetites. The concept of nature is extremely complex; it signifies something illegal and amoral as well as an unsophisticated innocence. Thus, a diversity of meanings can be generated when bastards are presented as natural children. The image of Mother Nature links them back to their maternal orgins and, sometimes, with a 'feminine' language of the body which subverts patriarchal discourse. They are like the grotesque figure of carnival tradition, intensely conscious of physical needs and desires. As we will see, nature can be used to read bastardy positively, evoking ideas of fertility or regenerative power. More often, the pejorative associations of the label 'natural' are activated to marginalise and subjugate a dangerous 'other' by defining it as foolish or savage. We must begin by discussing some general links between bastardy and nature to demonstrate how contradictions within the latter term are exploited to complicate ideas about the former.

In Act 1 Scene 2 of *King Lear* Edmund has an opportunity to speak for himself rather than being constructed as Gloucester's 'whoreson' (1.2.24). He rejects the 'plague of custom' which labels him as 'base' and appeals instead to nature:

> Thou, Nature, art my goddess, to thy law
> My services are bound. Wherefore should I
> Stand in the plague of custom . . .
>   . . . Why bastard? Wherefore base?
> When my dimensions are as well compact,
> My mind as generous, and my shape as true,
> As honest madam's issue? Why brand they us
> With base? with baseness? bastardy? base, base?
> Who, in the lusty stealth of nature, take
> More composition, and fierce quality,
> Than doth within a dull, stale, tired bed
> Go to th' creating a whole tribe of fops,
> Got 'tween asleep and wake.
>
>   (1.2.1)

Nature is a positive force for Edmund. It allows him to grow and prosper, to mock the word 'legitimate' on which Edgar's super-ority depends, and to reverse the ideology which defines bas-tardy as lack. His choice of goddess is intimately connected to his illegitimacy. It draws on a common belief that bastards, rejected by society, were therefore specially favoured by nature. In Webster's *The Devil's Law Case* (1617), Contilupo points out that although civil law discriminates against base children 'com-passionate nature / Makes them equal; nay, she many times prefers them' (4.2.244). John Donne shares this view, observing that 'sith Lawes robb them of Succesion and civill benefits they should have some thing else equivalent . . . so Bastards *de jure* should have better witts and abilities' (Donne 1980: 32). The type's superior intelligence was accompanied by physical strengths and a natural vigour, according to popular opinion. In Brome's play *The Damoiselle* (1638), Wat tells Dryground 'I love a bastard naturally / Ah they are bouncing spirits' (418).

Bastards' natural gifts are explained with reference to their conception. Jerome Cardan (1580) puts forward the view that children born out of wedlock are more robust because, when they are conceived, 'the seeds [of the parents] are mingled on account of very vigorous love' (465). Thomas Milles (1613) agrees and adds a less clinical explanation, saying that bastards are 'begot . . . with more agreeable conformity of willes, and far sweeter Union of the spirits' than legitimate children. The relationships of unmarried parents have to be conducted

through 'ingenious deceipts' and are filled with more excitement and danger than is found in the 'setled condition of
marriage' so bastard children inherit ingenuity and 'sprightly
judgement . . . commonly accompanied with beseeming corpu-
lence of bodie' (723-4). This idea is widespread. In Renaissance
Italy, Leonardo da Vinci may have been making a wry allusion to
his own bastardy when he observed that the children of passion,
whose parents enjoyed 'great love and desire on both sides',
were of 'great intelligence, full of wit, liveliness' (Bramly 1992:
41). Edmund's first soliloquy in *King Lear* radiates energy and
gives life to the idea that bastards take 'More composition, and
fierce quality' because they are begot in the 'lusty stealth of
nature' (1.2.12).

In direct contrast to positive associations surrounding the
conception of illegitimate children, the name 'natural child'
reflects the unfortunate circumstances in which many unacknowledged bastards were born and brought up. The case of Jane
Jaquet, an umarried mother from Maidstone, illustrates one way
in which the base child was abandoned by society to the elements. Jane was thrown out by two parishes, neither of which
wanted financial responsibility for her bastard, and was forced to
give birth 'in a wad of straw under a tree' where she was 'at last
delivered of a sonn in a litle straw . . . in the common highe waie
in a cold nighte, no better provided then you here' (Martin 1926:
258). Unmarried pregnant women took to the road because they
were expelled by the parish, by their masters, or were encouraged to leave by their parents. Some left home by choice, overcome with shame (Beier 1985: 53). These vagrant women risked
giving birth in similar circumstances to Jane Jaquet. Bastard
babies not murdered at birth were often abandoned by their
parents in fields or ditches. William Gouge (1622) complained
of the large number of 'lewd and unnatural women as leave their
newe-borne children . . . many times in open field' (507). Gri-
mold, a character in Davenant's play *Albovine, King of the
Lombards* (1628), draws on a common knowledge of this practice when he appeals to the King for money:

> I cannot tipple like a duck
> In a green pool, nor feed on berries in

A hedge, like some lost remnant o' my father's
Scattered lust.

(1872–4: 33)

Works of fiction frequently show that it is nature rather than
society which nurtures the bastard. What kind of an environment
'nature' is varies greatly between texts. In the first part of
Richard Johnson's prose narrative *Tom a Lincolne* (1599), the
eponymous hero is abandoned in a romanticised rural landscape
with which he seems to have an affinity. He is 'the sweet darling
of nature' (Johnson 1599: 350) who smiles up at the elements and
attracts 'a number of little birds' which sing for the baby until it
falls asleep 'as sweetly as though it had beene laid in a bed of
softest silke' (239). Tom appears as part of a greater harmony
of nature, which effectively invalidates criticisms of his base
birth. For many bastards, nature is a place of retreat. In *Titus
Andronicus* (1594), Aaron vows to save his baby's life by taking it
to the country where it will 'feed on berries and on roots / And
feed on curds and whey, and suck the goat' (4.2.177). The
idealised pastoral image collapses when Aaron says he will bring
his son up to be a fearsome warrior. We are reminded that nature
represents savagery as well as simplicity. Its wildness is emphasised in Shirley's *The Politician* (1639) where Haraldus reacts to
the news that he is illegitimate by turning away from society to a
community of animals:

Where shall I hide my life? I must no more
Converse with men – . . .
I will entreat my mother we may go
Into some wilderness, where we may find
Some creatures that are spotted like ourselves,
And live and die there; be companion
To the wild panther and the leopard.

(117)

As these examples show, there is a strong kinship between
bastardy and natural forces, but the idea of nature is riddled with
complexities which verge on contradictions (Dollimore 1991:
115). The natural world represents presocial innocence and a
state of destructive bestiality; it encourages the pursuit of desire
without social restraint. Bastards who commit themselves to
nature's laws therefore offer examples of a freedom which is

both attractive and repulsive. They are sensitive to the needs and desires of the body but, because the gratification of these desires ignores social rules, they appear savage. Their attitude to love illustrates the contradiction. Their god of love is Cupid, 'that same wicked bastard of Venus' (*As You Like It* 4.1.211) who delights in lawless sexual activity. Natural children usually see the union between man and woman in physical rather than social terms. In *The Bastard* (1652), Gaspar is not dismayed at the prospect of having a promiscuous wife, declaring instead his approval of the 'Happy Age! when all / Were common, when old *Natures* lawes were read' and when 'every man was free / For every woman' (G3). Curio, a base-born servant in Chapman's *All Fools* (1601), takes this philosophy to an extreme to provoke his jealous master. He claims that there is no such thing as a cuckold: 'what is it but a mere fiction? Show me any such creature in nature. If there be, I would never see it; neither could I ever find any difference betwixt a cuckold and a Christen creature' (3.1.248). An amoral attitude to sex, like Curio's, makes natural children brutish. In Barry's *Ram Alley* (1608), Throat enters Lady Somerfield's house kissing the women and 'making much' of the coachman's wife, behaviour which leads the serving man to describe him as 'nothing for a man, but much for a beast' (355). Paradoxically, what makes a bastard a natural child is exactly what makes him unnatural in the eyes of society.

Associating the bastard's lawless activities with natural impulses inevitably problematises the binary opposition natural/unnatural. It forces a re-examination of this violent hierarchy. The dominant power legitimises its oppressive regime by describing its cultural rules as natural law and displaces its own unnaturalness on to the subordinate term – in this case, the bastard. Many texts use bastards to point out that what is socially unnatural is actually natural in biological terms. Because of this contradiction, nature 'can be used to endorse that which it is ideologically required to suppress' (Dollimore 1991: 115). Descriptions of bastard villains as savage beasts unsettle the dominant discourse which labels them 'unnatural'. Markham and Sampson's play *Herod and Antipater* (1622) offers a good example. Niraleus tells Herod 'Sonnes are no longer ours, then they are Natures' (5.1.146), equating lack of paternity and kinship with nature.

Antipater constructs himself as part of a brutal zoological kingdom. He imagines killing his enemies as 'an hungerstarved tyger'
amongst heifers. He explains his commitment to violent murder
using imagery of animals and sexual desire:

> The tyger, tasting blood; finds it too sweet to leave it:
> The hauke, once made to prey, takes all delight in preying;
> The virgin, once deflour'd, thinks pleasure to grow common;
> And can I then stop in a middle way?
>
> (2.1.620)

By defining female incontinence, of which he is a product,
alongside other predatory appetites, Antipater is able to justify
his current cruelty as the correlative of his identity as a natural
son. A ruthless pursuit of ambition, which takes no account of
the so-called natural bonds between family members, suddenly
appears to be shockingly natural.

The title character in *Claudius Tiberius Nero* (1607) dislocates
the binary opposition by mapping his own unnaturalness back
onto the dominant culture. Legitimate society describes Tiberius
as a 'monster of monsters' (3,002-3), a 'beare whelpe' (1,623)
and a Tygers issue' (2,692), labels which already indicate the
presence of nature within its demonised opposite. The disturbing complement to this idea - the presence of the unnatural
within what society labels as 'natural' - is shown when Tiberius
retires to his orchard to meditate. The scene stands out as the
only obviously 'natural' setting in the play (other than a discussion outside a cave) and it is the only time when Tiberius shows
the least sensitivity to his surroundings. Like the Emperor's
illegitimacy it is the invention of the author. Tiberius considers
the possible threats to his dictatorship through the metaphor of
the plants around him and rationalises his subsequent massacres
as a perverted kind of husbandry:

> These Poppies too much aspire, they are too high,
> I must needes make them headlesse for their pride, . . .
> These marigolds, would follow with the Sunne,
> If I should suffer them to sprout on high,
> But ile confine their stature to my measure:
> So will I doe with all competitors.
>
> (2,031)

Tiberius casts himself as a gardener, pruning and controlling an essentially wild empire. He is a cultivator, improving nature, rather than an inhuman tyrant. A paradox appears: we have a natural child who is behaving unnaturally towards nature by copying the civilised society which constructs and confines everything according to its own 'measure' or values. Tiberius does not deny the label 'unnatural' but identifies himself with the dominant, the so-called natural law which seeks to pervert nature with culture. He delegitimises an ideology which labels him as a savage 'other' by imitating its own practices.

The problematic relationship between nature and culture is examined in detail in Thomas Milles's 'Paradoxe, in the Defence of Bastardie'. Milles argues that it is obvious that 'Nature had some peculier respect of Bastardes' by referring to other 'Bastard thinges'. He first gives the example of mules who can bear greater burdens 'than naturall Horses do or can' and then points to the superiority of grafted or 'Bastard' fruits as more tasty and numerous than those 'as come of Naturall plants' (Milles 1613: 624). The breeding of mules and the grafting of fruit trees can be achieved only by human intervention so these things cannot be said to be 'natural' at all unless, like Polixenes in *The Winter's Tale* (1610), we assume that the art which goes into their creation is itself a form of nature (4.4.89–97). Milles's argument unravels as it develops: he argues for the natural superiority of bastard things and shows that they are culturally constructed. This is not to define them as 'unnatural' in the pejorative sense of the word. Milles ingeniously complicates the opposition between nature and culture to demonstrate that the law which defines illegitimacy is artificial.

The sheep-shearing scene in *The Winter's Tale* follows a similar line. Perdita's rejection of the gillyvors as 'Nature's bastards' (4.4.83) is complicated by the fact that the shepherd assumes she is illegitimate, the result of some 'stair-work, some trunk-work, some behind-door-work' (3.3.72). She is abandoned to the forces of nature on the Bohemian seashore because Leontes believes she is a bastard, even though Paulina tells him that the goddess Nature proves the Princess's legitimacy (2.3.104–5). The opposition natural/unnatural is used subversively, showing that society's efforts to displace illegitimacy (its own cultural construct) on to the world of nature are themselves unnatural. Leontes, an 'unnatural lord' (2.3.113), tells Antigonus to leave the child to the favour of the climate in some 'remote and desert place' (2.3.176–8). He tries to make the murder of a bastard look natural – at least more so than burning the child to death or dashing its brains out. In Bohemia, Perdita is brought up as a natural child even though she is a legitimate princess. Polixenes's defence of 'Nature's bastards' dissolves distinctions between base and legitimate and the audience can read it as a comment on Perdita's own ambiguous position. It obliges them to reconsider the legitimacy of the court's judgements on what is natural, and thus forms an important element of the play's interrogation of the relationship between nature and art.

The natural child is able to confound and confuse the boundary lines between nature and culture in ways which problematise many other binary opposites and, in so doing, reveal the precarious fragility and the oppressive workings of the dominant order. Starting from the living paradox of being both natural and unnatural, the bastard character undoes distinctions between masculine and feminine, sanity and madness, body and spirit, high and low art. The next section will concentrate on the natural child's speaking voice, considering how identification with a feminised nature allows the type to produce a language of difference.

Natural voices

In Renaissace consciousness, nature was perceived as a feminine 'other' according to a set of binary oppositions which identified woman with natural processes outside masculine reason or its controlling discourse. The cultural conflation of woman and nature as 'other' is actually an attempt to displace uncontrollable elements which are common to human experience, repressed bodily desires and natural cycles of reproduction and death. Bastard characters who tune into the natural environment, or their own bodies, develop voices which have much in common with a disruptive 'feminine writing'. Feminine speech or writing is notoriously difficult to define but generally seeks to express those elements which, Lacan argues, are repressed into the unconscious by every child at the point of entry into the Symbolic order when the child acquires speech. French feminist theories identify 'feminine' discourse with the body and nature, with the child's maternal origins and pre-lingual experience where identities, even sexual identities, are not differentiated. It is not a language exclusive to women. In fact, it celebrates a type of sensual pleasure or *'jouissance'* where 'Nature and Culture [are] abolished, all bodies mingled: animals, fruits, and humans in the same intertwining. Flowers penetrate, fruits caress, animals open, humans are like instruments of this universal *jouissance'* (Cixous and Clément 1986: 23). Bastards have an increased sensitivity to 'feminine' language because they are bound to nature and their maternal origins by very strong ties while their relationship with the Symbolic order is more tenuous (see pages 22–3).

It is important to remember that a 'feminine' language does not exist outside the Symbolic order; it disrupts it from within. Refusing to enter the Symbolic at all would relegate the speaker to the realm of incoherence. Instead, bastard characters use conventional speech but introduce elements which decentre the phallus (the master-signifier) from its dominant position. Cixous argues that 'feminine' speech will 'always surpass the discourse that regulates the phallocratic system' and will be spoken by 'peripheral figures that no authority can ever subjugate' (Cixous 1976: 253). Bastards are subjugated by patriarchal law, like women, but their speech can show delight in an excess of meaning, a fluidity, and plurality which undoes the authority of the ruling discourse. Examples from plays across the period will indicate ways in which bastards draw on the natural world to expose an awareness of other languages, consciousnesses, ideologies.

In *The Troublesome Reign of John* (1591), we can see how the bastard juxtaposes the dominant signifiers of patriarchal speech with alien languages. When Philip is asked who his father is, he goes into a trance-like state in which the repressed voices of the natural world begin to speak. He translates what he feels in an extended aside:

The whistling leaves upon the trembling trees,
Whistle in consort I am *Richards* Sonne:

The bubling murmur of the waters fall,
Records *Philippus Regis filius.*
Birds in their flight make musicke with their wings,
Filling the ayre with glorie of my birth:
Birds, bubbles, leaves and mountaines Eccho, all
Ring in mine eares, that I am *Richards* Sonne.

(1. 251)

The speech is full of paradoxes. It is very egocentric, yet it shows
Philip's acute sensitivity to the natural environment, something
which the legitimate characters do not share. The birds, bubbles,
leaves and mountains all define the natural child in relation to his
father. In this respect, they reinforce patriarchal culture and they
use its language, even appropriating pieces of Latin. What they
are celebrating – Philip's illegitimacy – is directly opposed to this
culture. They mimic the voice of mastery only to subvert its
values. Their natural voices show the unnaturalness of a law
which refuses to recognise bastards or record their paternity. A
consciousness of the 'other', which this speech awakes very early
in the play, de-stabilises the monologic authority of subsequent
declarations.

Closeness to natural voices is taken even further by a female
bastard in the anonymous play *Locrine* (1594). Sabren, the child
of King Locrine and the Scythian Queen Estrild, has to watch
both her parents die condemned for their lawless lust, a passion
which has violated Locrine's marriage to Queen Guendoline and
the national identity of Britain itself. Utterly at odds with the
civilised world, Sabren calls on natural forms to help her mourn
for her parents and reaffirm their nobility:

You Dryades and lightfoot Satyri,
You gracious fairies . . .
You savage bears in caves and darkened dens,
Come wail with me the martial Locrine's death;
Come mourn with me for beauteous Estrild's death.

(5.6.137)

Sabren is half-Scythian so her attempt to solicit the land's natural
voices on behalf of bastardy represents a threat to the country's
national integrity. The British Queen, Guendoline, has already
tried to construct the environment as though it is in sympathy
with her, describing how the sun blushes, the heavens weep and

'the very ground doth groan for Guendoline' (5.3.22). She is enraged by Sabren and determines to drown her to 'feed the fishes' (5.6.161–5). In defiance, Sabren merges herself with the natural world. She throws herself into a stream which adopts her name as though she and it have become one (5.6.176–81).

In effect, Sabren has been silenced. She has reconstructed her subversive speech outside the Symbolic order but the voice of the river cannot be understood. Her decision to constitute herself as completely 'other' appears to be self-defeating. This is not altogether true. It would be foolish to read Sabren's suicide in purely positive terms but, as Peter Stallybrass argues, it can be seen as a permanent affirmation of her identity. Instead of becoming the food of nature, Sabren inscribes herself onto the face of the land as the river Severn. She subverts Guendoline's attempts to 'erase the taint of foreignness and exogamy' by engraving the alien 'other' into the body of the nation (Stallybrass 1986: 215). Humber, the conquered Scythian invader, also drowns himself in a river which takes his name (4.4.31–4). Sabren's suicide is more important because she is the bastard of the British King as well as an alien. Her physical self-inscription suggests that division and otherness is endemic to Britain and its language.

The juxtaposition of a bastard's alien forms of speech and ritual with those of the legitimate world highlights the controlling power of phallic law. Nowhere is this more obvious than in Shakespeare's *The Tempest* (1611). The text does not give directions for a non-verbal language so we never hear how Caliban expressed himself before Prospero and Miranda arrived, but many details identify him as a natural child. Prospero calls him 'thou earth' (1.2.316) and 'thou tortoise' (1.2.318), linking him closely with the island. Caliban responds to the sounds, tastes, textures and smells of his environment with what appears to be a natural simplicity. One of his first lines is 'I must eat my dinner' (1.2.330) and his attempted rape of Miranda shows how he follows natural appetites rather than social laws. This act labels him as a villain in the eyes of any civilised audience. Nevertheless, his wish to people the island with Calibans is, in one sense, brutally creative. The horrible crime of rape rallies support for the dominant culture but the incident also focuses attention on

how western language changes Caliban from natural to
unnatural.

What is most striking, as Dollimore (1991) notes, is that
Miranda supposes Caliban did not ever have a language of his
own (110). She tells him 'thou didst not, savage, / Know thine
own meaning', and regards his pre-lingual noises as 'gabble'
which could not possibly endow his actions and purposes with
any kind of sense (1.2.355–8). Caliban's relationship with the
island on which he was born and brought up by his mother
challenges this view. His sensitivity to 'all the qualities o' th'
isle' (1.2.337) is pre-lingual. It alerts us to a polyphony of voices,
'a thousand twangling instruments' (3.2.137), that are not necessarily created by Prospero. Caliban longs to return to a world of
non-oppressive heteroglossia and describes with love the
plurality of sounds that lulled him into a sleep where the clouds
would open and show him riches (3.2.135–43). In this language,
at least, he is not constructed as subordinate or unnatural. Once
Caliban has western speech thrust upon him, he uses it to
celebrate what he has lost and to curse the way it has re-
fashioned him. The very fact that he has learned it belies the
view that he is a creature on whose nature nurture can never
stick (4.1.188). Unsurprisingly, he dislikes the values this language carries because its restrictive codes of chastity and
deference contradict the natural order which grants him equality
and autonomy.

Caliban recognises the power of Prospero's language and
appropriates it to subvert the authority which taught him to
speak. His rebellion against the colonising masculine discourse
is ultimately futile. To empower himself (and communicate with
Stephano and Trinculo) Caliban must adopt his master's voice.
His inability to escape its oppresive nature is shown in a striking
way in Peter Greenaway's film *Prospero's Books*. The film version
of Act 3 Scene 2 opens with the 'echoic music' of the island –
the sound of women's voices – and 'miscellaneous dronings'
(Greenaway 1991: 124). Caliban sits silently on the beach ripping
pages out of Prospero's books. As he describes his plot to
Stephano and Trinculo, Prospero's voice (John Gielgud's) takes
over and the futility of Caliban's endeavour becomes obvious
when he flings more ripped pages into the air and is immediately

'showered with thousands of pages – mocking his efforts' (Greenaway 1991: 126). Caliban cannot overthrow Prospero; the feminine music of the island will always be drowned out by patriarchal speech and writing. However, the natural child exposes the violence within that language; he reminds us that there are others, whose speakers are made into 'others' by voices like Prospero's.

In 'Extreme Fidelity', Hélène Cixous discusses the bastard's aptness for deconstructing phallic law with a language of physical pleasures. She analyses the narrative of Eve and the apple as one which defines femininity in terms of natural pleasure and argues that Perceval, in *The Quest of the Holy Grail*, shares Eve's feminine openness to sensual experiences. She regards his illegitimacy as an important element of his 'wild unconscious': 'Perceval is a woman's son, he does not have a father, he is a boy left to his wild state, he is on the side of pleasure, happiness' (Cixous 1988: 17). Bastards in Renaissance drama frequently take after Perceval. This is evident in Milton's *Mask Performed at Ludlow Castle* (1634) which dramatises the opposition of sensual pleasure and masculine law in an allegorical narrative about female sexuality. Comus, a bastard of Bacchus and Circe, threatens to destroy the Lady's chastity while her brothers represent the ruling discourse which demands it. Comus, whose parentage is Milton's invention, is a mother's son (Milton 1957: 57) and a natural child. His habitation in a wilderness of unenclosed territory is a metaphor for uncontrolled sexuality. The brothers are disturbed when the Lady gets lost in the wood because the free sexual experience it offers looks chaotic and demonic to them. Comus gives an alternative viewpoint. He welcomes joy and feasting, dancing and revelry, telling his followers to 'Braid your locks with rosie twine / Dropping odours, dropping wine' (105). He wants to free youthful desire from the rigorous constraints imposed by 'sowr severity' and 'strict age' (109). Thyrsis warns that what Comus offers is dangerous. His creed of pleasure is like his mother's witchcraft; it will transform mortals into beasts to 'roul with pleasure in a sensual stie' (77). Nevertheless, the arguments Comus presents are persuasive, combining logic and lyricism. He tells the Lady

Wherfore did nature powr her bounties forth
With such a full and unwithdrawing hand,
Covering the earth with odours, fruits and flocks,
Thronging the seas with spawn innumerable,
But all to please and sate the curious taste?

(710)

Images of superabundant fertility, from which Comus himself is conceived, sound attractive. To ignore such bounty would be to offend the 'all-giver' (723), Comus argues. He reverses the conventional construction of identity to suggest that denial of feminine, natural pleasure makes people 'live like natures bastards, not her sons' (727). The Lady abuses nature and 'invert[s] the cov'nants of her trust' (682) by rejecting the sensual delights her own body offers. Comus sees sexual abstinence as unnatural, giving a vivid picture of how it could destroy the earth, 'strangl'd with her wast fertility' (729).

In spite of its moral framework, the masque presents chastity as static. It is true that the Lady actively stands up to Comus and argues her case strongly, but, like her brothers, she can describe chastity only in abstract terms. It is elevated to a 'sublime notion, and high mystery' (785). As such it is unrepresentable, unlike the natural child's values which are fleshed out in three-dimensional form in the scene of '*a stately Palace, set out with all manner of deliciousness: soft Musick, Tables spred with all dainties*' (658). From the audience's point of view, illegitimate pleasure is more accessible. In support of the supreme power of chastity, the elder brother cites the example of Minerva whose shield of Gorgon virginity 'freez'd her foes to congeal'd stone' (449). This image unfortunately locates virginity rather than its enemy as monstrous and the idea it proposes is reversed in the palace, where it is the virgin Lady and not Comus who is frozen 'in stony fetters fixt and motionless' (819). Her creed of absolute chastity traps her in an unnatural stillness.

Only another natural force can release the Lady, and the river nymph Sabrina is an appropriate figure to reintroduce the sensual energy previously embodied by Comus. Like Comus, Sabrina is a natural child. Milton leaves out direct references to her bastardy but the masque alludes to the story of Guendoline and Locrine. The Bridgewater estate encompassed a tributary of the Severn so it is probable that the audience would have been aware of how the river got its name. Sabrina has the power to resolve the binary opposition between 'insnared chastity' (909) and carnal sensuality because she is an embodiment of the former, a 'virgin pure' (826), who is born of the latter. Her body combines chaste purity with a sensitivity to nature and an openness to its powers of change. The description of her metamorphosis from maiden to river emphasises both her virginity and her sensual experience. She retains her 'maid'n gentlenes' (843) even though she has been penetrated by the 'Ambrosial oils' of the river and 'underwent a quick immortal change' which revived and altered her beyond recognition (841). The grotesque and open body of Sabrina is a more appropriate model for the Lady than that of 'chast austerity' (450), with its classical body of 'compleat steel' (421). Sabrina's chastity within sexual experience looks forward to the Lady's marriage rather than fossilising her in virginity. The masque's allegory thus shows the Lady's rite of passage as a form of negotiation, where the bastards introduce an awareness of the female body and its pleasures.

In all the texts discussed in this section, the natural child's voice deconstructs the verbal authority of the legitimate world. It introduces alien elements which reveal that the language on which power depends is a myth, that all monoglossiae are relative rather than absolute. In each case the dominant speech is shown to contain traces of what Bakhtin calls a 'potential for other-languagedness that is more or less sharply perceived' (Bakhtin 1967: 143). Natural children dislocate the boundaries of the text's ruling discourse, ensuring that its instability is most sharply perceived. This practice is menacing to the ruling culture, which responds by trying to disempower the bastard. In *The Newly Born Woman* (1986), Catherine Clément points out that 'dangerous symbolic mobility' encourages society to relegate its subversives to the status of deviants. It redefines them as dangerous, not only to others but to themselves, because they are 'the people who are afflicted with what we call madness, anomaly, perversion' (7). Renaissance plays often follow this containment model, relying on the associations of madness which surround the word 'natural' to label bastards as idiots.

Bastard naturals

The bastard 'natural' is simultaneously foolish and disturbing. His idiocy, like his natural strength (or even his sprightly wit), supposedly stems from his conception. In Clavell's *The Soddered Citizen* (1629), Minona suggests that base children are half-witted because their fathers' minds were distracted by the thought of cuckolding at the moment of conception (1,648–54). Whetstone, the clown in Brome and Heywood's *The Late Lancashire Witches* (1634), admits that his parents 'went to it without feare or wit' (135) and Arthur takes this as an explanation for the bastard's stupidity. Whetstone is a 'meere Ignaro' (163), a butt for the gallants' jokes. Even his uncle, Generous, says he is 'weake and shallow . . . / Dull, as his name' (214–5).

In some respects, bastard naturals occupy the same position as the female hysteric whose body, Clément argues, is a 'theater of forgotten scenes', a site of suffering which plays out a spectacle of the repressed (5). Both bastard natural and hysteric give performances centred on the body and magnify the lower bodily stratum which patriarchal culture has attempted to ignore or suppress. For this, they are branded as deviant, lunatic. In *The Tempest*, Caliban's dangerous symbolic mobility is undercut by his folly. When he worships Stephano and asks to lick his shoe, Trinculo exclaims 'That a monster should be such a natural!' (3.2.32). Caliban suffers in ways which recall the tortured body of the hysteric. He is extremely sensitive to physical sensations and, under Prospero's male gaze, he experiences physical and mental pain. His body is wracked with 'cramps' and 'Side stiches' that restrict his breath (1.2.325). He complains that Prospero's invisible spirits bite, prick and hiss him into madness (2.2.8–14).

Most bastard naturals do not suffer to this extent. Their celebrations of the body are comic, distancing them from the hysteric and making them more like the holy fool. A caricature of their blissful ignorance appears in Brome's play *The English Moor* (1637). Timsy, the base son of Quicksands, is said to be 'the ougliest Arsivarsiest Aufe that ever came / the wrong way into the world' (3.3.88). When Edmond asks 'An Ideot is it?', Buzzard replies 'A very Natrall' (3.3.94–5). Although the real

Timsy does not appear on the stage, Buzzard plays the part of the idiot as a revenge on Quicksands who has unfairly dismissed him. Buzzard's performance supports the impression already given. The 'Child natrall' (4.3.113) talks in nonsense, repeating the phrase 'Hey toodle loodle loodle loodle looe' (4.4.86). Stage directions indicate that he giggles, dances, sings and plays with a hand-operated spinning wheel. In the praeludium to Thomas Goffe's *The Careless Shepherdess* (*c.* 1638), there is an account of how Timothy Rheade performed this clownish role. The Landlord says that he laughed to see Rheade 'hold out's chin, hang down his hands, / And twirle his Bauble' (Brome 1983: 6).

The comic figure of Timsy has an important part in the revenge plots of *The English Moor*. Quicksands is so terrified of being cuckolded that he has imprisoned his wife and disguised her as a Moor. The news that he has a bastard exposes the sexual double standard and, to make matters worse, Buzzard and Arnold make up a story of Timsy's uncontrolled erotic drive causing chaos in the mill where he works:

> Sir by his cunning at the Rock
> And twirling of his spindle on the thripskins
> He has ferkt up the bellyes of Sixteene
> Of his Thrip-Sisters
>
> (4.4.144)

Arnold explains that, by begetting sixteen bastards, the natural child is only following in his father's footsteps (4.4.150). The unscrupulous Quicksands desperately tries to convince the assembled company that Buzzard and not he is the father of the capering 'Ideot' (4.4.127–31).

Exaggerated physical performances of idiocy, like the one in this play, are the exception rather than the rule. Bastard idiots are not marginalised to the same extent as the hysteric (probably because all the examples in the drama are male) and their foolish spectacles are less extreme. Like the hysteric, they become theatres of struggle between culture and nature but they are more fully integrated into social discourse and tend to work verbally rather instead of through a language of the body itself. Foolish bastards offer parodies of the legitimate world's structures and reintroduce elements of the suppressed bodily

stratum within those parodic models. Their humorous performances owe much to a medieval and Renaissance tradition of the
carnivalesque. To approach these characters we must examine
ideas of carnival, folly and the body.

Dramatists found an excellent model for their bastard naturals
in Erasmus's *The Praise of Folly*, translated into English in 1549.
The Praise of Folly uses elements of carnival tradition, celebrating
a common human body and employing parody to degrade the
official culture, sacred and secular. At the beginning of the text,
Folly announces that she is a bastard. She explains that she
wasn't conceived in 'the heavie yoke of wedlocke' but from
the illict union of the gods Youthfulness and Plutus, or abundance (Erasmus 1549: A4). Like most bastard naturals she is
associated with a world of sensual pleasure. Her father had
been drinking generous cupfuls at a banquet when she was
conceived and she is born into a natural utopia, the Islands of
the Fortunate, which are filled with delights to 'satisfie bothe the
sente, and the sight' (A4v). She begins life smiling, nursed by
Drunkenness and Rudeness (A4v). In terms typical of the natural
child, Folly celebrates change and the springtime of renewal,
mocking phallic power and substituting herself as the origin of
life (B1–B1v). She delights in a world where everything is thrown
topsy-turvy (A3v), arguing that, far from being an alien element,
she is the binding force in society (D1v). Her treatise goes on to
demonstrate that nothing happens in the world which isn't full
of folly, performed 'both by fooles, and afore fooles' (E1v).

There is no doubt that *The Praise of Folly* tells us much about
Erasmus's own ideas, but Levi cautions that it is dangerous to
identify Erasmus's voice with that of his speaker (Erasmus 1971:
15–16). What he does not point out is that Erasmus is intimately
linked to Folly and her subversive ideas because of his own
illegitimacy. Erasmus was the base son of a priest and a physician's daughter. A sense of shame about his birth helps to explain
why he tried to obscure its date and said little about his early life
(Schoeck 1990: 29–35). His illegitimacy was well known. Thomas
Milles, for one, refers to him as an example of bastards' natural
superiority, saying that he was virtuous and 'more than meanely
excellent, in the Arts of Grammar and Rhetoricke' (Milles 1613:
724). Erasmus did stand up for bastards in his treatise *On*

Christian Marriage, where he notes that 'from the best of parents the worst of children may be born and on the contrary we sometimes see admirable men born from illicit unions' (Schoeck 1990: 36). *The Praise of Folly* puts forward a similar argument. Folly criticises pride in aristocratic birth and radically reverses notions of illegitimacy, saying that if a wise man dropped from heaven, he might call a man boasting of his ancestry 'a villaine and a bastarde' because he is not allied to virtue 'which is the onely roote of true nobilitiee' (E4). Whether or not this detail reflects a personal grievance, it may be related to Erasmus's sense of his own illegitimacy.

The Praise of Folly uses parody to advance its thesis that folly is central to all social structures. Under the disguise of madness, the speaker mocks the construction of authority in classical declamation by using this form herself. She produces a 'staged' performance of formal rhetoric which undercuts the power of the original. Just before she introduces the idea of base and noble birth, she proposes that life is nothing more than 'a certaine kynde of stage plaie' in which 'men come foorthe disguised one in one arraie, an other in an other, eche plaiyng his parte' (E3v). Folly blurs the boundaries between her own performance and the serious ones she is imitating, suggesting that they are equally foolish. As we shall see, plays with bastard naturals make extensive use of the technique of 'staging'. It is central to the carnivalesque process which Bakhtin identifies in medieval mystery plays, parodies of the classical period, and in Renaissance prose like that of Rabelais. Bakhtin's theory of carnival, with its focus on the body and on parodic travesty, is a useful theoretical framework for reading bastard naturals.

In *Rabelais and his World*, Bakhtin devotes much attention to analysing the grotesque body as a vital element of carnival. He defines it as 'a body in the act of becoming. It is never finished, never completed; it is continually built, created, and builds and creates another body . . . it outgrows its own self, transgressing its own body, in which it concevies a new, second body: the bowels and the phallus' (Bakhtin 1968: 317). The womb is an important part of this ever-changing body and Bakhtin shows the importance of female sexuality in popular comic tradition, where woman 'represents in person the undoing of pretentiousness, of all that is finished, completed and exhausted. She is the inexhaustible vessel of conception' (240). Pregnancy, eating, drinking, copulating and defecating, are emphasised in presentations of the grotesque body which dissolves the confines between itself and the outside world. In this respect it is closely related to the central principles of 'feminine' writing which we have already discussed. The grotesque body of carnival is another disruptive 'language' which comes readily to bastard naturals.

Bakhtin argues that although the body was a central feature of medieval popular culture it was redefined in the sixteenth and seventeenth centuries, where a 'new bodily canon' anxiously tried to impose limits and distinctions to create 'a closed individuality that does not merge with other bodies and with the world' (320). The creation of this canon involved a sharp distinction between official or 'correct' discourse and familiar speech. To establish a ruling monoglossia, that 'which protrudes, bulges, sprouts or branches off (when a body transgresses its limits and a new one begins) is eliminated, hidden or moderated' (320).

Illegitimacy deconstructs the classically 'finished' cultural model by reintroducing the disruptive elements of the grotesque which blur distinctions between self and other. We can outline how this process works in general terms by looking briefly at Boccaccio's prose mythology, *The Genealogy of the Pagan Gods* (1472), which continued to be an important reference manual for sixteenth century writers. Boccaccio, who was himself illegitimate, attempts to build a classically ordered mythic genealogy which he describes using images of the body. He founds the whole genealogy on Demogorgon because, he says, he can find no father to this god. Hyde (1985) points out that, far from being a founding father, Demogorgon was 'in fact a belated bastard, a deified scribal error in a commentary on Statius' (743). Boccaccio's *Genealogy* thus reveals the fictive nature of all authoritarian structures, including that of the new bodily canon which tries to exclude the grotesque. His endeavour to construct an elaborate family tree may have been motivated by his illegitimacy and can be read as characteristic of his time, an 'illegitimate and upstart age' which was 'wishing for legitimacy but unwilling to accept its imaginative restraints' (Hyde 1985: 744). Ultimately, he finds it impossible to order his material into a neat, finished pattern. In the fifteenth book of the *Genealogy* the grotesque figure, with all its protruberances, returns. Boccaccio remarks that his readers 'will above all point to a defect of construction – a broad chest protruding from the pate, legs from the chest, and feet from where the head ought to be' (Boccaccio 1956: 107). The structural disorder caused by illegitimacy in Boccaccio's text is focused more specifically in Renaissance plays, where bastard characters introduce elements of the grotesque body which disorientate the ideas presented in the text and disrupt the dramatic style of the piece.

The grotesque body is a map of 'cosmic, social, topographical and linguistic elements of the world' (Stallybrass and White 1986: 9), nowhere more so than in the case of bastards whose monstrosity manifests physically their illicit conception. Paré's *Monstres et Prodiges* (1573), a medical handbook on deformity, lists the mingling of wrongfully matched seeds as one of the causes of monstrous births (Paré 1982: 4). Bastards, who were produced by a 'wrongful' mixture of seed outside divinely sanctioned marital union, were therefore naturally grotesque. In Ford's *'Tis Pity She's a Whore* (1632), Hippolita tells Soranzo 'Mayst thou live / To father bastards, may her womb bring forth / Monsters' (4.1.96–8). The grotesque nature of illegitimates could take a physical form, as in the satyrs and centaurs whose appearance denotes the adulterous mixture of seed at their conception. In Jonson's *Volpone* (1606), the dwarf, hermaphrodite and eunuch are, Mosca says, Volpone's bastards, begot on gipsies, Jews and Moors (1.5.43–9). Possibly Shakespeare intended Caliban's shape to be grotesque since Trinculo and Stephano call him 'monster' and parts of his body seem to resemble a fish (2.2.33, 5.1.226).

An alternative way of showing bastards' monstrosity was to exaggerate their interest in bodily functions and identify them with a low 'other' centred on eating, drinking, copulation and decay. Michael Neill (1993) argues convincingly that bastards' unconventional (and therefore inherently monstrous) conception makes them the human equivalent of dirt, that grotesque bodily presence from which sophisticated society endeavours to detach itself. The bastard grotesque is preoccupied with food, digestion and waste. Suckabus, in *The Seven Champions of Christendom* (1638), sees life as an alimentary canal. His actions are always motivated by his appetite: 'Oh most astonishable hunger! thou that dost pinch worse than any Fairies, or the gummes of old women' (F3). His love of food is part of the wider theatrical convention of the clown, but his identity as a mother's son gives it a specific origin. He is close to a world of 'feminine' sensual pleasure (signified by his monstrous appearance as a hermaphrodite) and reminisces about his early gustatory experiences with the words 'oh my glorious Mother, what a time of eating had I in thy dayes' (F3). He describes George's victorious military career as a menu of consumable rewards with 'golden gobbets of Beefe and Bacon' and explains how they made a progress through the guts of giants, riding into their bellies and 'out at the But-hole end' (F3–F4). Stage directions have him eating a carrot and a turnip on stage here and later, at Brandron's castle, he enters '*with bread and meate in his hand*' (I3). Suckabus visits the giant Brandron because he hears 'what a brave house hee kept for Victuals' (I3). Inside the castle, the bastard is unable to see the Princesses of Macedon (who have been turned into swans) as anything other then potential goose pies (K1v).

Suckabus's role makes a disturbing commentary on the actions of the heroic plot. Bakhtin points out the ambiguous significance of the gaping mouth as a grotesque symbol of pleasure and of the related notions of swallowing, death and degradation. In *The Seven Champions of Christendom*, the clown's wish to swallow all the food he can highlights the dangers facing the Champions who risk being swallowed up by their enemies and by death. Shakespeare produces a similar effect in *Troilus and Cressida* (1602), via the remarks of Thersites. Thersites describes his surroundings in terms of food. Ajax is 'beef witted' (2.1.12) and Achilles is a 'full dish of fool' (5.1.9), for example. These degrading epithets are reciprocated by Achilles who refers to Thersites as 'my cheese, my digestion' and asks 'why hast thou not serv'd thyself in to my table so many meals?' (2.3.41–2). Images of eating and being eaten echo the desires of the warriors to consume their enemies and the unstinting appetite of the Trojan war for human life. The primary cause of this conflict is sexual appetite, as Thersites constantly reminds us. High ideals of honour, by which the leaders set such store, are like the shining armour used to trick Hector, a glorious cover for a most putrefied core (5.8.1–2). Thersites strips away the rhetorical armour used by the leaders and calls them 'those that war for a placket' (2.3.18). He comments, in the midst of the battle, that 'in a sort lechery eats itself' (5.4.35). Death and sex are bound together as part of the grotesque body's continual process of consumption, decay and renewal.

Thersites has the liberty of the fool to speak his mind; as Achilles points out 'He is a privileg'd man' (2.3.57). Like Folly in Erasmus's text, he uses degrading parody to demonstrate how 'the common curse of mankind, folly and ignorance' (2.3.28) governs all types of human behaviour. His pageant of Ajax (3.3.270–99) satirises military valour and eliminates differences betwen clowns and kings. He delegitimises Ulysses's principle of 'degree' (1.3.85–108), based on so-called natural difference, by describing the military hierarchy as a degree of fools: 'Agamemnon is a fool to offer to command Achilles, Achilles is a fool to be commanded of Agamemnon, Thersites is a fool to serve such a fool, and this Patroclus is a fool positive' (2.3.62). The final judgement on Patroclus invalidates the satirical wisdom of the other comments. It is totally subjective in comparison to the interrelated logic of his previous remarks and mocks the system of relativity which is so important in Ulysses's view of 'degree'. Thersites draws together the elite and the dirt; he takes great delight in turning things upside down, comparing his commanders to animals and suggesting that the animal is superior in each case. Ajax's horse is 'the more capable creature' on two occasions (2.1.17, 3.3.307), and Achilles's mind is smaller than that of a tick in a sheep (3.3.310–12). To describe Menelaus, Thersites gives a long list of wretched creatures and then claims that he would rather be 'the louse of a lazar' than the royal Prince (5.1.48–66). His remarks work in direct opposition to the stratified order of legitimate society. I cannot agree that 'in so far as the play contains an upholder of a true ideal, it is Thersites, whose

rancour must be rooted in some unexpressed moral standard'
(French 1982: 156). Thersites has no ideal; he declares himself
illegitimate in all things. He is 'bastard begot, bastard instructed,
bastard in mind, bastard in valor, in every thing illegitimate'
(5.7.17). This, his final speech, echoes in the audience's mind
as an epitaph to his anarchic philosophy.

Natural performers

Bastard naturals give foolish performances which are marked out
as spectacles, different from the the main text. Their grotesque
roles constitute a 'staging' of carnival within the play world,
performed before both on-stage and off-stage audiences rather
than involving them directly. The aspect of performance has a
significant effect on the subversive power of these characters
which must be taken into account. To do this, it is again useful
to compare their experiences with those of female hysterics.
Clément observes that the spectacle played out by the hysteric
is 'ambiguous, antiestablishment and conservative at the same
time' (Cixous and Clément 1986: 5). It is conservative because its
frenzied expression of the repressed is ultimately contained
within the patriarchal family or institution whose members
make up the audience. Nevertheless, it is subversive because it
introduces disorder, an alien energy which unsettles their established ideas. Clair Willis (1989) examines the idea of performance
and carnival in her article 'Upsetting the public: carnival, hysteria
and women's texts' where she argues that the hysteric's festive
body 'stages' Bakhtin's carnivalesque in ways which disturb
those who watch.

The performaces of bastard naturals have the same ambiguous
quality as the hysteric's 'staged' carnival. The spectacles of folly
which they present are contained by conservative on-stage audiences, yet they retain a dislocative power. Their speech and
actions force the rituals of the legitimate world into a dialogic
relationship with popular parody. Their language activates a
process of objectification where 'every direct word – epic, lyric,
strictly dramatic – is to a greater or lesser degree made into an
object, the word itself becomes a bounded image, one that quite
often appears ridiculous in this framed situation (Bakhtin 1967:

132). Through carnival performances, bastards place social discourse in a 'framed' condition which alienates it and exposes it to critical scrutiny. This deconstructive strategy is especially prominent in Shirley's *The Ball* (1632), Heywood's *Love's Mistress* (1634) and Brome's *The Sparagus Garden* (1635). The bastards all make foolish spectacles of themselves which offer criticisms of behaviour in fashionable Caroline society. As they perform, the conservative audience on stage labels the bastard's parodic representation of its own culture as an illegitimate fraud, a false counterfeit of gentility, and thus re-legitimates its dominant position. As we will see, this technique of containment never quite succeeds in diffusing the bastard's subversive energy.

In Brome's play *The Sparagus Garden* the bastard clown, Tim Hoyden, is an uncouth alien, a 'squab' or 'a lumpe' (138) who comes from Somerset to London to become a gentleman. His education in the social skills turns him into a 'peece of folly' (223). It results in a series of comic performances which expose the sanctimonious attitudes of the civilised world and the dangers of trying to deny the natural impulses celebrated in popular tradition. The play follows a recurrent carnivalesque pattern where the 'high' tries to reject the low 'other' for reasons of prestige only to find that it 'includes that low symbolically, as a primary eroticised constituent of its own fantasy life' (Stallybrass and White 1986: 5). The citizens Money-lacke and Springe trick Tim Hoyden into adopting an ostentatious courtly style. His efforts to quash his natural appetites bring to the surface a current of raw energy which has been suppressed under the façade of civil behaviour.

Brome makes fun of a culture which claims you are what you eat. Tim is told that to become a gentleman, he can only have 'shrimpe dyet and sippings' and other sophisticated but unsatisfying dishes (167). His desire for bacon and bag-pudding exposes a gap between the healthy appetite of a natural child and the menu of the civilised world. Since food is a metaphor for sex in the play, the fashionable diet makes an additional comment on the sexual mores of the city, criticising the way natural desires have been suppressed. Tim's hunger for sex has not been dampened by his civilisation. He determines that, when he is a complete gentleman, his first deed will be to cuckold

Brittleware and beget a bastard on his wife (175). Tim makes
visible the illicit sexual behaviour which runs through the
London of the play. We discover that the two most prestigious
families, the Strikers and the Touchwoods, have associations
with illegitimacy. Striker's housekeeper reminds him that, in
the past, he threw his sister Audrey out of the house because
she got pregnant. Striker is in no position to be sanctimonious
because he is guilty of 'foule incontinence' with the housekeeper
(152–3). Tim's foolery brings out the truth: that Striker 'keeps a
whoor now at three score', a revelation which shames him into
making an honest woman of Friswood (222). Striker's grand-
daughter, Annabell, appears to be pregnant by Touchwood's son
so when Touchwood and Striker use bastardy to insult each
other they come close to the truth:

T.   fill thy house with bastards.
S.   I'le hold them more legitimate than thy brood . . .
     For thou, thy sonne, thy house is all a Bastard.
T.   Beare witnesse, he calls my house a Bastard.

                                                        (183)

Annabell's pregnancy turns out to be a trick to force a marriage
between her and Sam Touchwood but the insults still ring true.
At the beginning of the fourth act, we learn that Tim Hoyden is
the base son of Audrey Striker and Touchwood senior, who
seduced her (176–7). Bastardy, and all it represents in the play,
is part of both houses. Tim's gross appetites are an element of
human nature which will surface however hard society may try to
eliminate them. News of his parentage re-contextualises all
Tim's endeavours to become a gentleman. He is a gentleman
before he begins his civil education. The play shows that fashionable style is, in fact, a grotesque perversion of gentility. Tim
graduates from his finishing school to be presented before his
uncle 'not as a gentleman, but as a gentlewoman', dressed in
women's apparel and carried in a Sedan chair (208–9).

    Tim Hoyden's experience warns of what can happen to an
elite which tries to elevate itself by excluding what is 'low'. His
gentlemanly education censures a decadent society which has
become obsessed with unnatural civil ceremony. This would
have been particularly pertinent in the 1630s which saw the

emergence of a fashionable 'town' society and an enhanced self-awareness about genteel codes of manners. The affectations of the city were also found at the court of Charles I, which attracted criticism from noblemen like William Cavendish, Earl of Newcastle, to whom *The Sparagus Garden* is dedicated. Newcastle complained that the court was full of parasites who 'lived off the king' and 'woulde Jeer the greateste Noble man in Englande iff hee did nott make the laste monthes Reverence A La Mode' (Butler 1984: 195). Newcastle's own comedy *The Variety* (1641) (to which Brome wrote commendatory verses) attacks the new type of courtier, fond of French fashions, so he would have sympathised with Brome's satiric treatment of affectation in *The Sparagus Garden*.

The play's mockery of Tim includes a criticism of court and city fashion. Hoyden determines to acquire a 'sinicall City wit and a supersinicall Court wit' (141), both of which involve skills of flattery and dishonesty. The repartee he learns, composed of compliment followed by 'backsword Complement' (196), is ostentatious to the point of incomprehensibilty. His increased facility with this language is matched by a decreased facility of communication, perhaps reflecting the monarch's failure to communicate effectively with Parliament while cultivating a courtly style. When Hoyden copies down phrase after phrase and gives a performance worthy of Osric, his sophisticated rhetoric is 'framed' and made to look ridiculous. All these details indicate a subversive aspect to Tim's foolery. It makes pointed criticisms of the social elite. Paradoxically, it also reaffirms conservative positions. Because of his bastardy, Tim can never be a true-born gentleman, only a poor counterfeit. His behaviour can be dismissed by audiences on and off stage as an unsuccessful imitation. Tim's performance does not attack the hierarchy of power itself. Instead, it criticises the perversions of true gentility by illegitimate upstarts from court or city, those who would dare to jeer at the Earl of Newcastle or any of the other 'greateste Noble m[e]n in Englande'.

Shirley's play *The Ball* uses its bastard character in an equally ambiguous way as part of its satire on the extravagant foreign fashions adopted by the London nobility. An unsympathetic impression of European influences is given by the foolish

French dancing master, M. Le Frisk, and by Freshwater, a
supposed traveller and projector. The play's anti-European
sentiments are qualified by the view that courtly decadence
may be the fault of the English nobility and its tastes. The
bastard character, Bostock, symbolises corruption from within.
He is a half-cousin to Lord Rainbow and the play highlights his
base birth by including a scene in the second act where he is
tricked into revealing it to Lady Lucina. Bostock is a sham who
uses his illegitimate connections with the aristocracy to domineer
in ale houses

> With tapsters, and threadbare tobacco merchants,
> That worship your gold lace, and ignorance,
> Stand bare, and bend their hams, when you belch out
> *My lord*, and *t'other cousin*, in a bawdy-house.
>
> (62)

He constantly boasts about the 'precious honour' he carries in
his blood, even using it as an excuse to cover his cowardice. He
explains that he could not fight with Colonel Winfield because,
had Winfield wounded him, he would have lost a drop of blood
which 'might ha' been a knight, a lord' or even a prince (71).

These declarations have a certain subversive power. Their
exaggerated claims about the value of noble blood expose the
whole idea to ridicule. Courtly discourse, and the axiologically
accentuated system in it, is 'framed' by Bostock's foolish behaviour which potentially destabilises the self-declared honour and
nobility of the other characters. Because he is base-born, his
comments about his descent appear illegitimate. They put all
references to blood, honour or noble birth into what Bakhtin
calls 'intonational quotation marks' (Bakhtin 1967: 132), allowing no character's speech to escape critical scrutiny. This makes
it difficult to identify exactly where a parodic playing with the
characters' language begins and where Shirley's mockery of
courtly behaviour ends. Indeed, the play was censored because
its satiric treatment of particular individuals was deemed unac-
ceptable at court. Sir Ambrose tells Bostock 'you are [the] gulf
of honor, swallow all' (8). His bastard snobbery threatens to
swallow up the idea of honourable lineage. At the same time,
Bostock's illegitimacy works in precisely the opposite direction.

It distinguishes him from the truly noble characters and dis-
allows his claims to gentility, thus reaffirming the purity and
legitimacy of their elitist positions. There is a delicate balance
between the subversion and consolidation of conservative values,
brought into focus by Bostock's relationship to Lord Rainbow.
    As cousin to Lord Rainbow, Bostock embodies the potential
for corruption in Rainbow himself. When the two noble kinsmen
confront each other at the end of Act 4 Scene 1, they present
mirror images of legitimate and illegitimate nobility. They are
direct opposites, true and false, and yet disturbingly similar.
Rainbow says that Bostock's cowardice is enough 'to make the
blood of all thou know'st suspected' and feels that Lady Lucina
will now think 'I am as base as thou art' (62). The audience are
secure in the knowledge that Rainbow is not the same as
Bostock because he is not a coward or a bastard. However,
Rainbow's comparison – which seems designed to highlight
difference – undermines audience confidence by raising the
spectre of covert bastardy within marriage. The legitimacy of
Rainbow's own claim to noble title cannot be guaranteed absolutely. The situation gets more complex when Shirley shifts
attention to the nature of nobility. Rainbow begins by insulting
Bostock as a 'stain to honour' and attributes this to his birth,
beneath all 'degrees of baseness'. He relates bastardy and despic-
able behaviour to social origin, saying that Bostock was probably
the bastard of a serving man and not a lord (62). This displaces
the idea of illegitimacy from the ruling class and seems to restore
faith in the existing social hierarchy.
    Rainbow then contradicts himself and undercuts his own
position. With the example of Lord Bostock's ostentatious
arrogance before him, he says that birth and title are nothing.
Honour and nobility are won only by merit. He condemns the
parasitical tendencies of those who 'build their glories at their
father's cost' (63), making an explicit attack on Caroline courtiers whose extravagant shows of nobility came to stand for
nobility itself. In direct contrast to his previous attack on
Bostock, he argues that 'our birth / Is not our own act' and
that 'we inherit nothing truly / But what our actions make us
worthy of' (63). By this point, the play seems to be saying that
true nobility has nothing to do with either social class or

legitimacy (like Folly's argument in Erasmus's text). Bostock admits that Rainbow's tirade would make him 'believe I am illegitimate indeed' (63). He is bastardised 'in deed', by his behaviour rather than by his birth. On one level, the exchange reinforces the opposition of Bostock and Rainbow; on another it undermines the idea of noble lineage. Bostock reminds the audience that no aristocrat can be sure of his or her legitimacy and draws attention to the improper behaviour of some aristocrats whose claims to the title 'noble' were spurious.

The play which makes most extensive use of the natural child's performances to provoke questions about the social elite and its tastes is *Love's Mistress; or, The Queen's Masque* by Thomas Heywood. It was performed in front of the court at Somerset House and at the Phoenix in 1634. Heywood's text brings together different aspects of the bastard grotesque's comic and disruptive influence – his closeness to the material bodily principle, his skill in parodic travesty and his ability to disorientate the overall structure of the drama. The natural child's performance is, once again, ambiguous. Heywood uses Corydon to destabilise platonic ideals, courtly masques and elitist notions of art within a form that seems to promote these things. *Love's Mistress* presents the story of Psyche's quest to achieve immortality by becoming the bride of Cupid:

> *Psiche* is *Anima*, *Psiche* is the Soule,
> The Soule, a Virgin, longs to be a bride,
> The soule's Immortall, whom then can shee wooe
> But Heaven? whom wed, but Immortality:
> O blame not Psiche then, if mad with rage,
> Shee long for this so divine marriage.
>
> (106)

As an encomium on platonic love, the play makes a direct appeal to the interests of Queen Henrietta Maria and her circle, perhaps serving as a vehicle to demonstrate in public the Earl of Dorset's devotion to her since it is dedicated to him. Its romantic plot shows how love can be elevated above physical consummation. Psyche is an object of devotion rather than desire. She is 'spotlesse, lovely white' and 'my selfe, my soules *Idea*', echoing the Queen's adopted role as a heroine whose beauty was able to

command love in her courtiers and subjects (Veevers 1989).
Heywood's treatment of the story demonstrates a critical
engagement with these courtly politics. Under the cover of
folly, his bastard character unsettles the conventions of the
platonic idea.

Psyche's ascent to the heavens is fraught with difficulties. It is
a struggle between spiritual and carnal desires. Aided by Cupid,
she must overcome the hostility of Venus, representing Lust.
Interestingly, Heywood cuts out all references to Cupid's bastardy and provocation of sensual passions. The carnal world is
represented instead by the clown Corydon, bastard son of Midas
(115). Cupid is 'true Desire' (107), a spiritual bridegroom whom
Psyche is forbidden even to look at, while Corydon is a fully
fleshed example of the material bodily principle. He enacts the
essential idea of grotesque realism, 'the lowering of all that is
high, spiritual, ideal, abstract . . . a transfer to the material level,
to the sphere of earth and body' (Bakhtin 1968: 19). Cupid and
Psyche's romance is reflected in a lower, comic key in the passion
of Corydon for Amarillis. He celebrates his mistress's physical
qualities in truly carnivalesque fashion. Although Amarillis is old,
wrinkled, and has a long nose, making her 'the veriest dowdy in
all Arcadia', Corydon sings her praises:

> To praise her stil, my Muses will is,
> Although therein I have no cunning,
> Yet is the nose of Amarillis
> Like to a Cock, long, and still running.

> Her eyes, though dimme, do seeme cleere,
> And they of Rheume can well dispose,
> The one doth blinke, the other bleare,
> In Pearle-drops striving with her nose.

> Her brests are like two beds of blisse,
> Or rather like two leane-cowes udders,
> Which shewes that shee no Change-ling is,
> Because, they say, such were her mothers.

> Those few teeth left her in her head,
> Now stand like hedge-flakes in her gumms.
> Full of white Dandriff is her head,
> She puts the Cobler downe for thumbs.

(145)

Corydon constructs his mistress according to Bakhtin's idea of the grotesque. He describes the orifices, apertures and protuberances of the body, emphasising how the confines between it and the outside world are blurred by bodily secretions or broken borders like her 'hedge-flake' teeth. Even distinctions between genders are confused because the image of the nose is related closely to that of the phallus, which it conventionally symbolises in carnival tradition (Bakhtin 1968: 316). Corydon's song is obviously not romantic in the conventional sense; it draws on the ambivalent laughter of the carnival spirit, which is 'gay, triumphant, and at the same time mocking, deriding' (Bakhtin 1968: 11–12). The body appears in a state of decay but with a potential for renewal. This very festive physicality complements the Cupid and Psyche relationship, implicitly commenting on what it lacks as well as what it escapes.

Psyche's story shows the difficulty of constructing and maintaining a perfect, completed body in opposition to the exaggerated but essentially realistic grotesque. For all her identity as 'Spirit' or 'Idea', she is closely related to Corydon's physical world of carnal desire, illegitimacy and reproduction, something which becomes clear when she disobeys Cupid and looks at him in bed. As punishment, she is thrown down to earth, deformed and 'Barren of comfort, great with child of feare' (123). In this dishonoured state – pregnant and apparently husbandless – she returns to her father who immediately bastardises her with the words 'Thou art not mine, but the base birth of shame' (130). Venus also refuses to welcome her or her unborn baby, saying she will not 'prove a grandame to a strumpets brat' (131). Heywood obviously intended Psyche's pregnancy to be noticeable as a symbol of her shame since the text makes several references to her 'great belly' (141). The potentially illegitimate baby represents Psyche's initial failure to escape from the material world occupied by Corydon. Significantly, no further reference is made to the pregnancy when Psyche is finally immortalised by Jove and married to Cupid. The threat of illegitimacy, like her deformity, disappears. Her purity is celebrated, and her jealous sisters (who possibly represent Lady Carlisle, the Queen's rival as a platonic heroine), are obliged to repent for having tempted her to disobey Cupid.

They submit themselves as handmaids and servants to her virtue.

The play's ending shows the superiority of spiritual love above the material bodily principle but Corydon's energetic celebration of the physical and the base destabilises this hierarchy. Cupid and Psyche's imminent marriage is parodied by that which Corydon looks forward to with Amarillis in the temple of Venus or Lust. When he tries to steal Psyche's box of celestial beauty to improve his looks for the wedding, Cupid substitutes another box 'of ugly painting'. Corydon remains ignorant of how 'monstrous' he appears and anticipates a joyous meeting with his bride, a feast of drinking and a busy night ahead of him (153–5). Although he is comically mistaken, his complete confidence in his own celestial beauty questions the value judgements which lie behind the triumphant ending of the Cupid and Psyche story.

Corydon puts the style and symbolism of platonic drama under scrutiny, and thus makes an important contribution to the debate between Art and Ignorance which frames the romantic allegory. The play personifies the binary opposition in the figures of Apuleius (representing Art) and Midas (representing Ignorance), who observe and comment on the action. Corydon, like his father Midas, is 'all earthlie, / Nothing Caelestiall in thee' (133) and prefers popular festive forms. When Apuleius admits that Art must some time give way to Ignorance, Corydon comes on to lead a rustic dance of swains as an interlude to the Cupid and Psyche story. Corydon cannot be contained within the category of 'Ignorance'. More often, his performances confuse the divisions between high and low art. His speeches travesty and mimic the classical style in ways which show the essential sameness of Midas and Apuleius as part-man and part-beast.

Corydon sets out opposed to poetry and begins by degrading it, transferring it from a high spiritual ideal to the material sphere. To show that poets do nothing more than 'fill your head with a thousand fooleries' (114), he subjects Homer's epic to parodic treatment, producing a story where Troy becomes 'a Village of some twenty houses' invaded by Menelaus 'a Farmer, who had a light wench to his Wife call'd *Hellen*, that kepte his sheepe' (113). In Corydon's account of *The Iliad*, Priam is a good hearted but foolish father of 'a great many bowsing lads' who live at the other side of 'a small Brooke, that one might stride over'. Ulysses is a 'Towne-clarke', Hector 'a Baker' and Ajax 'a Butcher' (113). There is a striking resemblance between Corydon's reductive vewpoint and that of Thersites in *Troilus and Cressida*. Both share the natural child's perception of the events in terms of sensual response and seek to deconstruct the Homeric myth. Corydon's attack on classical forms extends to the Latin used by poets. He comments 'What's *Titule tu patule* but Titles and Pages; What's *Propria que Maribus* but a proper man loves Mary-bons, or *Feminno generi tribunter* but the Feminine Gender is troublesome; what's *Ovid*, but *quasi*, avoide' (114). Macaronic parody forces the sacred language of classical literary tradition into a dialogue with the vernacular which transforms it into what Bakhtin calls 'a ridiculous image, the comic carnival mask of a narrow and joyless pedant' (Bakhtin 1988: 151). It shows that a reverential approach inevitably fossilises language, isolating it from the vital, interactive currency of popular speech.

Corydon subjects the language of love to similar treatment. He vows he will describe Cupid's 'stile in Folio' and, to do this, employs a mock-elevated rhetoric and an excess of alliteration. Cupid is, he says,

> King of cares, cogitations, and cox-combes; Vice-roy of vowes and vanities; Prince of passions, prate-apaces and pickled lovers; Duke of disasters, dissemblers, and drown'd eyes; Marquesse of molancholly, and mad-folkes, grand Signor of griefes, and grones; Lord of lamen-tations, Heroe of hie-hoes, Admirall of aymees, and Mounsieur of Mutton lac'd.
>
> (113)

Corydon's abusive language is typical of the familiar speech of the market place, an essential element of popular folk humour. It is semantically isolated from its context and forms a set piece, a performance which simultaneously insults the deity and revitalises him. By mocking Cupid's aristocratic status, Corydon suggests that love is a common human experience, not something enjoyed only by a chosen elite. Cupid's revenge, which involves shooting Corydon and turning him into a lover, ironically brings about that degrading and popularising process.

The next ocasion on which Corydon appears is the key scene of the Art–Ignorance debate, a musical competition between Pan and Apollo. One of the swains comments that the hierarchy of low and high art will be challenged if '*Pans* pipe dare contend with *Apolloes* Harpe'. An outright confrontation is avoided because the gods are represented by their inferiors, Apollo by a page and Pan by Corydon's own 'winde pipe', thus recreating the traditional status reversal found in carnival rituals like the boy bishops. Corydon's song compares Apollo and Pan by juxtaposing classical allusions and references to elements of the popular festival. Verses 2, 4 and 6 of the song give a sense of how he draws on images of cooking and kitchen utensils to celebrate a deity whose name is ideally suited to a series of puns:

> *They call thee Sonne of Bright* Latona,
> *But girt thee in thy torrid zona,*
> *Sweate baste, and broyle, as best thou can*
> *Thou art not like our Dripping* Pan.
>
> *Then thou that art the heavens bright eye,*
> *Or burne, or scorch, or boyle, or fry,*
> *Bee thou a god, or bee thou man,*
> *Thou art not like our Frying* Pan.
>
> *Thy selfe in thy bright Charriot settle,*
> *With Skillet arm'd, Brasse-pot, or Kettle,*
> *With Iugg, blacke-pot, with Glasse, or Can,*
> *No talking to our Warming* Pan

(125)

Corydon's transfer of culinary imagery to a scene of confrontation is charactersitic of popular festive culture in the fifteenth and sixteenth centuries and may also draw on Jonson's recent parody of To-Pan the tinker in *Tale of a Tub* (1633). The substitution of kettle for crown reverses the normal hierarchy of classical over festive forms to show the superiority of Pan over Apollo, satyrs over spirits, body over mind. A comment by Apollo makes it clear that the kitchen implements form the instrumental backing for Corydon's song, which, as Raymond Shadey remarks, 'clearly exceeds his own prediction of a catastrophe' in its ridiculous comic ending to the competition

(Shadey 1975: xciii). Full carnivalesque reversal is achieved when Midas declares Corydon and Pan the winners. Apollo leaves with the arrogant declaration 'My musicke lives unquestion'd, what's amisse / Is not in us, but in their ignorance' (127). Such comments have led critics to believe that Heywood is presenting Corydon unsympathetically, as a symbol of an unfit writer or audience. The comments of the other characters dismiss his performances as foolish and it cannot be denied that much of his speech appears to be anti-artistic. Grivelet (1954) suggests that he is based on Davenant (whose work Heywood despised), a theory that seems attractive in view of Davenant's claim to be an illegitimate son of Shakespeare. Clark (1931) and Bentley (1956: 580–2) both identify Corydon with *Histriomastix*, William Prynne's lengthy treatise attacking actors and the art of the theatre. Even if Corydon does represent an anti-artistic voice, I do not think Heywood intended to support the ideas of high art presented by Apollo. Details remind the audience of the violence inherent in the maintenance of an exclusive artistic hierarchy. Before the singing contest, for example, Midas significantly reminds Apollo that 'poore *Marsias* / For striving with thee had his skin pull'd off' (124). Corydon's popular festive forms are crude but more communal. They celebrate a bodily energy, common to all, which is indestructible and undeniable. His utopian carnival of the common body offers an immortality which is all-inclusive and finally more powerful than that which the spiritual world gives only to specially chosen individuals through a process of denial and self-sacrifice. As Bakhtin remarks, carnival 'affirms the people's immortal, indestructible character. In the world of carnival, the awareness of the people's immortality is accompanied with the realisation that established authority and truth are relative' (Bakhtin 1968: 256).

Thus, although Heywood appears to be writing *Love's Mistress* for a particular courtly audience who were interested in platonic love and accustomed to participating in masques, he uses his bastard character to offer a different perspective on these things. The audience are obliged to watch *The Queen's Masque* (to use its subtitle), against the background of a contradictory reality presented by Corydon, a world which the conventions of the masque cannot accommodate. Corydon's antimasque performances invade the world of the masque, misappropriate its symbolism through parodic mimicry and dislocate its stylised promotion of grace, harmony and hierarchy. In effect, Corydon's role bastardises *Love's Mistress*, making it neither a masque nor a drama but a hybrid since its antimasque elements are not suppressed by a dominant main masque. A similar effect is achieved in Milton's *Mask Performed at Ludlow Castle*, where the disruptive antimasque scenes, in which Comus appears, are expanded to draw attention to the artifice and fragility of the masque form itself.

On a smaller scale, bastards in *The Tempest* and in Brome's plays *The Court Beggar* (1640) and *The English Moor* disorientate the masque genre. Caliban's rebellion is an antimasque which destroys the Prospero's 'majestic vision' (4.1.118) of chaste fertility with reminders of lustful desire. At the end of Brome's *The Court Beggar*, a masque is used to make 'an explicit exposure' of the behaviour of social upstarts and projectors who have infested the court and city (Butler 1984: 227). The corrupt nature of the characters satirised is shown in the casting. Venus and Cupid are played by Philomel, a whore, and her bastard son Billy. Earlier in the play illegitimacy had been associated with the projectors, whom Brome singles out for criticism since they propose a tax on the begetting of children (194–5). In *The English Moor*, Buzzard's performance of the bastard idiot is central to the disruption of masquing in the play and the subsequent revelation of social hypocrisy. Quicksands's masque of Moors (designed to exhibit his triumph over those who threatened him with cuckoldry in a wedding-night masque), is ruined by the antimasque of his 'naturall Ideot'. Buzzard's performance bursts chaotically into the main masque and provides a comic 'catastrophe' to the proceedings, demonstrating that ungovernable natural forces cannot be completely excluded or concealed.

In all the plays discussed so far, the natural child's carnivalesque energy is something disruptive to the dominant culture, even though it may be refreshingly different. I want to conclude by looking at a play which contradicts this pattern. In Brome's *A Jovial Crew* (1641) bastardy is a harmonising force which binds nature to culture. For the first (and only) time, the natural child is presented in an unequivocally positive way. Springlove, whose very name indicates his function, is a symbol of recuperation. He is invested with the power to revitalise and unite a community that is decadent and divided. Legitimate society in the play is stale; courtiers, lawyers and soldiers have been driven to find places in a community of beggars. Oldrents, the father-figure of the legitimate world, laments the decline of his family into beggary. His daughters Rachel and Meriel are discontented and tell the steward Springlove "'Tis a base melancholy house. Our father's sadness banishes us out on't' (2.1.248). Springlove cannot endure the suffocation; each spring he is irresistibly drawn towards the natural world. He is called by the songs of the cuckoo and the nightingale and appeals to Oldrents to release him from office:

> S.   Oh, sir, you hear I am call'd.
> O.   Fie, Springlove, fie.
>   I hop'd thou hadst abjur'd that uncouth practice.
> S.   You thought I had forsaken nature then.
> O.   Is that disease of nature still in thee
>   So virulent?
>
> (1.1.153)

Although Oldrents degrades Springlove's desires as 'uncouth', the play does not share his viewpoint. The bastard symbolises the regenerative, positive power of nature. His identity as a mother's son makes him a natural embodiment of such forces. He admits that only by death 'can this predominant sway / Of nature be extinguish'd in me' (1.1.242) and questions why this should be so. The play explains his behaviour with the revelation that he is the bastard of Oldrents and a beggar. He is bound by nature to nature.

The beggar community, associated with the rural and the physical, is full of bastards. The Patrico is a hedge priest whose wedding contracts follow rather than precede sexual activity and are not recognised as legally valid. During the course of the play, one of the 'doxies' gives birth to a bastard child. Springlove, who was born 'a naked beggar' (2.1.282), is part of this alternative lifestyle. He follows the free-love ethic of the natural child in his relationship with Amie, an heiress who has eloped to escape an arranged marriage. We learn that he 'tumbled her and kiss'd her on the straw', then angered her companion Martin even further

by offering to cuckold him on his wedding night in the barn
(4.2.33–9).

Springlove's retreat to the apparently base lifestyle of the
beggars is a journey to liberty and not to banishment. It appears
so attractive that Oldrents's daughters, Rachel and Meriel, and
their suitors want to follow him there. Springlove leads them
into their 'birthnight into a new world' (3.1.34) of nature. They
are uncomfortable, but the vitality and freedom they enjoy there
are valuable. They become acutely aware of their physical surroundings and of the needs and desires of their own bodies.
Unlike them, Springlove is at one with the elements and even
sleeps through storms (3.1.16–21). His educative role has an
important social dimension. While Oldrents and his children
see the beggars as a jovial crew, Springlove knows from personal
experience that such merriment is made in spite of 'cold and
hunger' (2.1.292), fear of whipping, and unmitigated squalor. He
introduces the lovers to the discomforts and dangers of life on
the road, forcing them to recognise how out of touch they are
with the realities of poverty and to abandon their romantic
perceptions of vagrancy. Outside its story, the text probably
makes a critical comment on the elitist romanticism of earlier
plays like Dekker and Ford's *The Spanish Gipsy* (1623). This play
includes a foolish aristocrat called Sancho who is referred to as a
bastard (2.1.162–7), but his illegitimacy is only sketched lightly
and his folly makes him very different from Springlove. Springlove comments ironically on the lovers' idealised views of freedom, telling them they are likely to be beaten and so 'must . . .
leap hedge and ditch now; through the briers and mires till we
'scape out of this liberty to our next rendezvous' (3.1.419–21).

Springlove has a strong sense of social responsibility even
though he is a natural child. This compares favourably with
the selfish behaviour of Oldrents and his children and forms a
model for them to learn from. Rachel and Meriel see the beggars' commonwealth as a release from their duties in the household to 'absolute freedom . . . the whole country or kingdom
over' (2.1.18–21). When Oldrents abandons himself to a festival
month with the beggars, his merriment 'is overdone' (2.2.115), it
is irresponsible. In complete contrast, Springlove respects his
social ties. He carefully prepares the accounts before he asks

leave to travel (1.1.122–38) and is praised for his efficiency and his charity to the poor. Oldrents is impressed to find one so 'young in years . . . so ripe in goodness' (1.1.140). Springlove's sense of duty to Oldrents is explained by their blood-link. They are bound together by an affection so strong that Hearty believes 'Springlove / Were sure his bastard' (2.2.50). Bastardy represents natural love and duty – a radical reversal of the usual associations of unnaturalness between child and parent. Springlove is torn by guilt at the thought of abandoning the Oldrents estate (1.1.235– 59). The mental battle between his 'duty to a master' (1.1.257) and his 'inborn strong desire of liberty' (1.1.249) is a focus for the play's considerations of freedom and responsibility. His maternal links to illegitimacy, beggary and freedom are balanced by his paternal links to duty and to society. He resolves the dilemma by agreeing to lead the lovers in their beggar progress as a means of curing his master's grief (2.1.270).

The resolution of the play centres on the reconciliation of the different elements of Springlove's character. As Jackson Cope remarks, 'Springlove is the knot which ties nature to society, fertility to liberality' (Cope 1973: 165). The masque of Utopia at the beggars' feast (4.2) presents an ideal balance between social hierarchy and individual autonomy. Springlove's unique identity in the play enables him to combine the two. Having educated the young lovers about the interdependence of social obligation and freedom, Springlove returns them, revitalised, to the legit-imate world's hierarchy. He does this using 'The Merry Beg-gars', a play within the play, something highly artistic which shows his commitment to culture even as it celebrates a com-munity associated with nature. (His interest in theatre and metatheatre is discussed further in my final chapter.) Society is fully renewed by the acknowledgement of Springlove. Oldrents accepts responsibility for his affair with the Patrico's sister and admits Springlove into the family, re-integrating the forces of nature and culture. Springlove also mends ancient rifts between families, giving the characters chance to undo the wrongs of a pre-play history in which Oldrents's grandfather had craftily cheated the Patrico's grandfather, Wrought-On, and reduced him to beggary (5.1.411–14). As the son of Oldrents and the Patrico's sister, Springlove is great-grandson to the original

Oldrents and Wrought-On. He unites the two houses, and the communities, by his bastard birth.

In the context of imminent civil war, Springlove's pleas for tolerance, integration and social responsibility are particularly poignant. Martin Butler (1984) argues that in the play Brome puts forward a 'modern ethic of political obligation' which acknowledges the interdependence of all elements of society (279). The bastard is an important bridging character in this pattern. He has a dual personality, as beggar and steward, and represents the rural and official aspects of the tightly knit provincial community which should not be ignored by any government at Westminster. In his role as bastard vagrant, he speaks for those alienated from the legitimate hierarchy. His inclusion in the family at the end gives an exemplary picture of a ruling order which will listen to the infinite variety of people who make up its population. The natural child in this play shares many characteristics with his natural brothers and sister from earlier texts. He embodies a powerful life force due to his conception in the lusty stealth of nature and is keenly aware of his physical surroundings. As a mother's son he is governed by irrepressible natural desires and, like Cixous's example of the bastard Perceval, he is part of a world of feminine pleasure which constantly subverts and escapes the confines of patriarchal law. What he says and does in the play introduces alien perspectives which unsettle the authority of the ruling order, forcing it to interrogate its own legitimacy. In spite of the challenge he brings, he is not characterised as savage, unlike bastard villains. Neither is he labelled as a fool, the technique used to diffuse the subversive power of so many bastard naturals whose alternative discourse destabilises the monologic authority of their plays. In *A Jovial Crew* the natural child is a hero.

5

Heroic bastards

The strong stage tradition of the bastard villain, bound to wreak destruction on society, did not stop some dramatists from presenting examples of the type which directly contradicted this norm. Illegitimate characters who are virtuous rather than vicious are immediately controversial, even if they do not conform to conventional ideas of heroism. In fact, the bastard's status as outsider makes him particularly suitable to explore the paradoxical relationship between qualities of glorious individualism and service to society which make up the archetypal hero. Heroic or virtuous bastards challenge the officially sanctioned view of illegitimacy as evil and inferior. To temper the threat they pose to the ruling ideology, these positive models are often qualified in some way. Orthodox ideas could be reinforced by making the hero's bastardy a tragic flaw which, in spite of his virtue, destroys him. Such plays confirm society's definition of illegitimacy as a negative 'other' and undermine their own radical starting point. An alternative option, for dramatists who really wanted to stand up for bastards, was to authorise a positive image of illegitimacy with reference to a widely respected figure, text or ideology.

The highest authority to which one could appeal for support was the Bible. As we have already seen, Scripture provided justification for the persecution and demonisation of bastards but the Bible was full of contradictions and its great advantage was that 'it could be quoted to make unorthodox or unpopular points' (Hill 1993: 6). The history of Abimelech, the unnatural usurper in Judges (9: 1-57), was followed by the story of a virtuous bastard, Jephthah (11: 1-30). His legitimate brothers, who threw him out as incapable of inheritance in their father's house, asked him to return as their leader and saviour of Israel. Thomas Becon's *Book of Matrimony* (1564) cites this piece of Scripture to counter the text from Deuteronomy (28: 2) which justified the exclusion of bastards from property and position: 'Jephthah, a Gideadite was a bastard and the sonne of an harlot, and notwithstanding God gave him both his spirit, and made him also ruler and hed over his people Israel' (Becon 1564: DCxlix). Becon regards this as authority good enough to license the election of bastards to public office if they are 'meete and worthye', thus overturning the civil laws based on Deuteronomy. He argues that bastards should also be admitted to the ministry since 'Christ did vouchesafe that bastards shuld be rehersed in his genealogy and stock of kinred' (Becon 1564: DCxlix). Christ's ancestors, listed in the first chapter of Matthew's Gospel, included the offspring of incest (the children of Tamar) and adultery (the children of Bathsheba). Thomas Milles (1613) and Sir George Buck (1619) both allude to Christ's genealogy in their defences of bastardy. As we will see shortly, the Bible proved to be an unexpectedly rich source for dramatists wishing to characterise virtuous bastards.

Reference to classical and historical figures was another way of authorising a positive attitude to illegitimacy. In *The Complete Gentleman*, first published in 1622, Henry Peacham remarks that the worthiness of bastards can be seen from many examples, and asks 'Who are more famous then *Remus* and *Romulus*, who laid the first stone of *Rome*? more couragious and truely valiant, then *Hercules*, *Alexander*, our King *Arthur of Britaine*, and *William* the first? more critically learned than *Christopher Longolius*, *Jacobus Faber*?' (Peacham 1634: 9). Heroes from classical legend and English history prove the excellence of bastards as military leaders and governers. Famous scholars from more recent times, such as Jacobus Faber (who translated and edited Aristotle), discredit the image of the bastard as a 'natural', and therefore uncultured, child. Robert Burton gives a similar list in his *Anatomy of Melancholy* (1621) as a cure to those malcontented by their base birth. He comments 'almost in every kingdom the most ancient families have been at first princes' bastards; their worthiest captains, best wits, greatest scholars, bravest spirits in all our annals, have been base' (Burton 1964: 140). Thomas

Milles cites even more examples in his 'Paradoxe in the Defence of Bastardie' (1613). The need to elaborate the point so fully is striking evidence of the strength of prejudice which writers were fighting against. Long lists do become rather tedious, particularly in a play. Plays with bastard heroes include allusions to famous figures like the ones Peacham quotes, but they tend to be much briefer. For example, in *The Sophister* (1631) by Richard Zouche, Opposition considers that bastardy is a serious impediment for Fallacy, and then argues 'what of his base birth? *Hercules* was base borne, so was *Romulus*, so many Worthies' (D2–D2v)

Dramatists adopt another method, more amenable to performance, to legitimate their unconventional presentation of bastards. They appropriate the very centre of the dominant ideology – its respect for paternity – and use it in the presentation of the hero. The heroic status of most virtuous bastards comes from their connection to a great paternal figure, a god or a king, with whom the bastard strives to identify himself. A play which celebrates a filial–paternal link actually reproduces the patriarchal values which favour legitimacy. The bastard becomes an example of male sexual prowess and male bonding rather than a mother's son. The paradox of paternity within illegitimacy consolidates dominant masculine values instead of promoting subversive feminist ones. There is only one female bastard, in Brome's *The Damoiselle* (1638), who could be called a heroine and her part is not large although she is crucial to the play's subversive critique. The majority of plays depict heroes who are the sons of legendary fathers. This seems disappointingly conventional but it need not necessarily be so. Negative ideas about bastardy are radically reversed by images of demi-gods who are divinely protected rather than being barred from heaven until the tenth generation, and who inherit extraordinary powers because of their birth instead of being socially disadvantaged by it. Some heroes dislocate the conventional ideology of male heroism into which they have been cast. Characters with supernatural paternity can even unsettle the religious beliefs used to legitimate worldly power.

Son of a god, born of a woman

Christ and Hercules are the two most important figures whose supernatural paternity elevates them to heroic status. They serve as prototypes for many bastard heroes in the drama. Christ is the supreme example of virtuous bastardy, a figure taken from the highest authority, the Bible, and connected to the Heavenly Father whose paternity was the model for patriarchal rule. In Matthew's Gospel (1: 1–17), the list of illegitimate ancestors provided an illustrious precedent for Jesus's own illegitimacy which is described clearly in the rest of the chapter (1: 18–25) (Romer 1988: 177). To refer to Matthew's Gospel and Christ's genealogy in a defence of bastardy was implicitly to include him among your list of examples. In *The History of Richard The Third* (1619), Buck clinches his argument on the worthiness of bastards with the words 'And this one example is above all, to wit, that Jesus Christ the greatest and most noble king, was content to descend from Phares, a bastard' (Buck 1982: 112). The word 'bastard' hangs ambiguously at the end of the sentence; it applies to both Christ and Phares.

Matthew's account of the Nativity emphasises its illegitimate aspect. The narrative tells that Joseph discovered Mary was with child and 'being a just man, and not willing to make her a publick example, was minded to put her away privily' (Matthew 1: 18–19). Wright (1992) points out that, by including details of a virginal conception, Matthew and Luke were taking a huge risk. 'They must have known that they were opening the door to the possibility of deep misunderstanding' (83). To misunderstand the story would be to discredit the Virgin Birth as simply another religious hoax, designed to disguise sexual misbehaviour.

Such misunderstanding went back as far as the second century. Celsus, a Greek Platonist, claimed that Jesus had 'invented his birth from a virgin' and was the son of a soldier and a poor Jewish country woman who was turned out by her husband for her adultery and 'disgracefully gave birth to Jesus, an illegitimate child'. The original work was destroyed by Church censorship, but much of Celsus's text survived into the Renaissance in Origen's refutation *Against Celsus* (Roberts 1869: 426–31). Marlowe probably drew on this subversive tradition in allegedly proclaiming that 'Christ was a bastard and his mother dishonest', according to the Baines note of 1593. Richard Cholmley was accused of making a similar suggestion, namely that 'Jhesus Christe was a bastarde St Mary a whore & the Aungell Gabriell a Bawde to the holy ghoste' (Kocher 1962: 28). Goldberg (1984) suggests that the Baines libel against Marlowe speaks from the position of a 'socially sanctioned *double agency*' by recording the voice that the Elizabethan secret service licensed Marlowe to use as a spy (77). If so, then the slander of Christ's illegitimacy appears to be a subversion produced by society only to be contained by a greater authority.

Containment was, perhaps, not such an easy matter since conventional Christian beliefs in religious writings were also haunted by the image of illegitimacy. A fifteenth-century carol 'The Holy Well' describes the children of the rich mocking Christ because he was 'but a maiden's child' (Rickert 1910: 84–6). Oppositions between Christ and an illegitimate Antichrist inadvertently drew attention to similarities between the two. In the 1525 pamphlet *Here begynneth the byrthe and lyfe of Antechryst*, Antichrist is conceived from an incestuous union between Schalus and his daughter Ulcas which parodies the relationship between the Virgin Mary and the Heavenly Father. The text anxiously points out that 'antechryste is as moche for to say in ye Grekes language by interpretacyon as contrary unto Chryst' but, however clearly the right message is telegraphed, the demonic counterpart functions as a subversive mirror to Christ. Protestantism, which promoted individual interpretation of the Bible and the demystification of religious doctrine, made the possibility of a 'deep misunderstanding' of Matthew's Gospel much more widespread. Explaining the nature of the Saviour as simultaneously divine and human led writers like Thomas Becon into dangerous waters. In *The Acts of Christ and Antichrist* (1563) he remarked that Christ 'is the true and naturall Sonne of the livyng and immortall God: and as concerning his humanitie, he is the true and naturall Soone of Marie the Virgine' (A2). As the natural son of Mary, Jesus was, of course, illegitimate.

Christ's bastardy is like his dual nature as the immortal son of God and the human son of Mary; it is deeply ambiguous. On one hand, it reinforces patriarchy since it celebrates the link between a self-sacrificing son and an elevated, mysterious but infallible father. Jesus seems to fit into the conservative pattern of bastardy rather than the radical one. On the other hand, his illegitimacy seriously undermines patriarchal structures because a God who manifests himself as a bastard sides with the outcast and the marginal, outside those power structures. In her book *The Illegitimacy of Jesus* (1987), Jane Schaberg argues that such a God 'cannot be a projection or endorsement of patriarchal ideology' (77). Belief in the Virgin Birth has been a tool of institutional sexism, a means of oppressing women. Reading Christ as a bastard is a way of deconstructing this oppressive regime. Bishop John Spong (1992) draws on the work of feminist biblical scholars to suggest that Jesus may have been conceived by an act of sexual violence (rape) and not by a virgin conception. Not surprisingly, these ideas have caused controversy. N. T. Wright (1992) accuses Spong of unsound biblical scholarship. I am not qualified to make judgements on these views but whatever legitimacy (or otherwise) such radical ideas have, the reactions they provoke testify to the subversive power of Christ's bastardy. In a culture like that of Renaissance England, far more biblical and misogynist than our own, even the lightest allusion to an illegitimate Jesus would have been dangerous.

To see Christ as a mother's son opens up biblical authority to feminist appropriation. It allows for an experience of the sacred in a situation of illegitimacy (Schaberg 1987: 19). Two examples of religious writing by women of the early modern period show how the Virgin Birth can be reclaimed to form part of a wider subversive strategy. Aemelia Lanyer introduces her poem *Salve Deus Rex Judaeorum* (1611) by hinting at Christ's illegitimacy: 'it pleased our Lord and Saviour Jesus Christ, without the assistance of man, beeing free from originall and all other sinnes . . . to be begotten of a woman, borne of a woman, nourished of a woman' (Lanyer 1978: 78). Undoubtedly Lanyer's main motive is to rewrite Christian history from a feminist perspective. Within this, the covert celebration of virtuous bastardy may have had something to do with her personal circumstances. Lanyer was the illegitimate daughter of a court musician. According to the physician Simon Forman, she was also the mother of base

children so it is not unlikely that her early feminism is linked with
a wish, whether conscious or not, to celebrate illegitimacy
(Lanyer 1978: 11–16). A more explicit rejection of patriarchal
ideas is found in *Eliza's Babes or The Virgins-Offering*, a series
of divine poems and meditations published anonymously in
1652. The author compares her poems to fatherless babes,
begotten by God. As well as praising him, the bastard 'babes'
give voice to Eliza's more unconventional – illegitimate – views
on female autonomy. Even when she is obliged to accept a
husband, she continues to privilege her extra-marital affair and
its literary offspring above marriage and natural motherhood.
The metaphor of virgin birth allows her to express radical ideas
under the cover of divine inspiration.

The idea of virgin birth widened the gap between patriarchal
control and female sexuality by suggesting that women could
produce children independently of men. Like promiscuity,
women's active pursuit of virginity could be a 'mode of sexual
revolt' against male-dominated matrimonial monogamy in
Renaissance England. The virgin and the whore occupy similar
positions, as doubles rather than antitheses (Halpern 1986: 92).
The production of children by either type subverts social norms.
Attitudes towards Joan in Shakespeare's *1 Henry VI* (1592)
demonstrate this. Her ambiguous identity as 'Pucelle or
puzzel' (1.4.107), virgin and whore, is shown when she disowns
her father and bastardises herself (5.4.7–41), then claims that she
is virginal, 'Chaste, and immaculate' (5.4.51) and finally begs not
to be burned to death because she is with child (5.4.62). The Earl
of Warwick is keen to have 'no bastards live' (5.4.70) and the
lords joke that she 'hath been liberal and free. / And yet
forsooth she is a virgin pure!' (5.4.82). Their mockery is an
attempt to laugh off the real threats which Joan presents as a
figure of virgin independence and uncontrolled sexual activity.
When they cannot diffuse her power by ridiculing her as a 'holy
maid with child' (5.4.65), they burn her as the demonic opposite,
a witch.

Like Joan, Annabella in Ford's *'Tis Pity She's A Whore* (1632)
appropriates the image of the Virgin Birth to defend herself from
the charge of whoredom. Her pregnant body, with its 'bastard-
bearing womb' (4.3.14), contains the secrets of paternity (and

incest) so her husband, Soranzo, has no access to this knowledge (Wiseman 1990). Anxious to protect her brother, Annabella translates the mystery of her body's secret into a divine mystery: she describes her affair with Giovanni in terms which parody the Nativity, setting him up as a god, herself as a Virgin Mary, and Soranzo as the doubting Joseph. Giovanni is the 'more than man that got this sprightly boy' (4.3.31) and the relationship between them is miraculous:

> This noble creature was in every part
> So angel-like, so glorious, that a woman
> Who had not been but human, as was I,
> Would have kneeled to him, and have begged for love.
> You! Why, you are not worthy once to name
> His name without true worship, or, indeed,
> Unless you kneeled, to hear another name him.
>
> (4.3.36)

She impudently suggests that Soranzo should be proud to 'father what so brave a father got' (4.3.45). The scene echoes the turbulent relationship between Mary and Joseph which derives from Matthew 1: 18–25 and was much elaborated in medieval versions of the Gospel and mystery plays. Like the other pseudo-religious ceremonies between Giovanni and Annabella, it indicates the world they now inhabit, alienated from conventional morality and sexual ideology. Annabella's parody of the biblical story is provocative. It probably attracts sympathy for her cause rather than Soranzo's and, at the same time, it delegitimises the Church which judges her as a whore. She uses Scripture to show that the patriarchal institutions which dominate the Parma of the play are oppressive but fragile.

In Elizabethan England the dangerous combination of bastardy, active virginity and virgin birth was concentrated in the figure of the monarch. Elizabeth I occupied an anomalous position as Virgin Queen, mother to her people and royal bastard (since the act declaring her illegitimate had never been repealed). Her role as virgin mother to the population bastard-ised them in line with their monarch. In addition there were rumours that she had had sexual relations with her courtiers and given birth to their bastards. One report said that she had at least

thirteen natural children (Hibbert 1990: 80–1). Within a cultural
context like this, the characterisation of bastard heroes as Christ-
like figures can be disturbing. They defy the typical view of
bastardy and, more importantly, they draw attention to the
unspoken presence of illegitimacy at the foundations of Church
and State authority.

Renaissance writers imitate the Nativity story in birth narra-
tives to invest their bastard heroes with Christ-like qualities.
Their parodies pay homage to Christ as the highest authority
while subversively dissolving differences between the Christian
narrative and secular or pagan stories of virgin birth. A parody of
the Nativity can make the real thing can look like just another
parody (Wright 1992: 84). We can see this deconstructive process
at work in accounts of Merlin's birth. In an early example, the
anonymous *Lytel Treatyse of ye Byrth and P[ro]phecye of Marlyn*
(1510), a voice from heaven announces to the labourers building
Vortyger's castle 'A chylde in Englonde there was bore / And
begotten without mannes mone' (B2v). The narrator strengthens
the comparison between this child and the Son of God by
alluding to the prophecies of David and Moses:

> that a fend shoulde fonde
> To lye on a earthe by a mayde mylde
> And brynge on her such a chylde
> That sholde, they sed, tho
> All the worlde wyiche wo
>
> (B4)

Biblical echoes prepare for the transformation of Marlyn from
devil's child to hero. They establish him as a Christian champion
and simultaneously undercut Christianity's claim to be an exclusive truth. Accounts of Merlin's birth in Geoffrey of
Monmouth's *History of the Kings of Britain* (c. 1138) – the
source for many Renaissance treatments of Arthurian legend –
and Heywood's *Life of Merlin* (1641) emphasise the virginity of
Merlin's mother and his supernatural paternity. In both texts
Merlin is teased for his bastardy like the Christ-child in the carol
'The Holy Well'.

William Rowley's play *The Birth of Merlin* (1608) follows the
tradition and presents Merlin as a pagan devil's bastard and a

Christlike saviour. His dualistic nature breaks down binary opposites by showing their interrelationship. Prince Uter recognises that 'Vices are Vertues, if so thought and seen, / And Trees with foulest roots, branch soonest green' (95). Merlin is a living example of this principle; he represents the emergence of good from evil and shows that the location of vice and virtue is arbitrary. The absolute authority of Christian faith is shaken, along with common prejudices about bastardy. As part of its subversive strategy, the play uses Merlin to promote radical ideas about female sexual behaviour. Sexual transgression is, quite literally, demonised but the text pays lip service to patriarchal ideology only to undermine it. Joan's liaison with the devil, the greatest evil, is actually the cause of the greatest good. The play's other image of transcendent good is in two gentlewomen who defy their father and fiancés to follow careers of active virginity. They form an appropriate parallel to the 'whore', Joan. Constanzia says 'I have no father, friend, no husband now, all are but borrowed robes, in which we masque to waste and spend the time' (103). Her statement of independence is a conventional dedication of Christian faith and a dangerous defiance of patriarchy. Christianised bastardy is at the centre of a structural principle of reversal in *The Birth of Merlin*. Within its mythical framework of military battles, the play idealises subversive female activity.

The base offspring of classical gods provided other prototypes for bastard heroes. In *Herod and Antipater* (1622), by Markham and Sampson, Antipater appeals to bastard gods or demi-gods for assistance with his plots:

> Men base by birth, in worth are seldome base;
> And Natures out-casts, still are Fortunes darlings:
> Bacchus, Apollo, Mercury; bastards, yet bravest gods:
> Then, why not I a god, a demi-god, or worthy?
> You gods, you demi-gods, you worthies then assist me;
> That, as our birth was like, our worth may beare like price.
>   (1.3.357)

Celebrating the illegitimate fruits of Jupiter's various amours was such a widespread tradition that the character Momus in Carew's masque *Coelum Brittanicum* (1633) criticises 'the

Ribald poets' who, he says, 'to perpetuate the memory and
example of [the gods'] tryumphs over chastity, to all future
imitation, have . . . devolved to Posterity the Pedigrees of their
whores bawds, and bastards' (Carew 1969: 218). Translations of
Seneca's tragedies by Jasper Heywood and John Studley, and
Thomas Heywood's retelling of the myths in his plays of the
Ages (1610–12), kept the celebratory tradition alive. Heywood's
plays emphasise the magical conceptions and births of Archas,
Perseus, Bacchus, Castor and Pollux and Hercules. Each character shows how the superhuman qualities of the father could be
inherited by the bastard son. The most important of these pagan
heroes was undoubtedly Hercules. Milles (1613), Buck (1619)
and Peacham (1634) all cite him as an example of the noble
bastard. Renaissance emblem books proclaim him a champion
of illegitimates. Emblem 124 in Marquale's 1551 collection
asserts that 'being a bastard should not be a cause of censure
for anyone since Hercules, the greatest man ever born among us,
was also a bastard'. Andreas Alciatus's emblem 139 (1621)
appeals to bastards with the motto 'You, the bastards, should
forever celebrate the honours of Hercules for he was the prince
of your class' (Alciatus 1985: 139).

Renaissance texts sought to amalgamate the two leading
figures of classical and Christian tradition by interpreting
Hercules as a forerunner of Christ. The mythologist Alexander
Ross moralises the Hercules myth in *Mystagogus Poeticus*, assert-
ing that 'Our blessed Saviour is the true Hercules, who was the
true and only Son of God and of the virgin Mary,' (Rivers 1979:
31). Ronsard, who had numerous imitators and translators
among sixteenth-century English poets, compares the labours
of the two heroes and their divine illegitimacy in his poem
Hercule Chrestien (1555). English plays develop a Christian
interpretation of the Hercules myth. *The Birth of Hercules*
(anon. 1604) includes details borrowed from Luke's account of
the angel and the shepherds (2,336–9) and Matthew's description of Joseph receiving reassurance from God about Mary's
chastity (2,508–19). Translations of Seneca's *Hercules Furens*
and *Hercules Oetaeus*, in the collection *Seneca: His Tenne
Tragedies* (1581), make allusions to the Harrowing of Hell and
the Crucifixion in their dramatisations of the story.

Royal and noble paternity

Links with a great paternal figure are just as important for noble and royal bastards as they are for demi-gods. In plays, the illustrious parent is often raised to the status of a god, appearing only in abstract, idealised form; off-stage rather than on, dead rather than alive. The bastards of kings and aristocrats were held in high regard. Sir George Buck argues that the most honourable houses have been founded by the illegitimate sons:

> The King of Spaine descended from Henry de Trastamara, base sonne of Alphonsus the Justicer, King of Castile. And some write that the royal Stewarts of Scotland descend from a base son of Fleance. And who hath not and doth not honour the princely race of William the Conqueror, who was the bastard son of Robert, the Duke of Normandy? And there was never a more noble or a more valiant nor a more heroical man than Robert, Earle of Glocester, base sonne of King Henry I.
>
> (Buck 1982: 112)

Such bastards could occupy high status positions in Renaissance society. Thomas Milles (1613) observes that in 'moderne and present times . . . wee shall finde, the greatest houses of Princes in France, Italy, Germany, Spaine and elsewhere to be renowned by Bastardes' (724). The Borgia, Medici and Sforza families, Don John of Austria and Margaret of Parma (both bastards of Emperor Charles V) provided useful source material for plays. To English dramatists a more immediate example of a bastard in a prominent position (apart from Elizabeth I) was Lord James Stewart, who had become Regent for the infant King James VI.

Illegitimacy had an intrinsic appeal to those of lower social status wishing to rise as bastards of their social superiors. For example, in Nashe's *Have With You to Saffron Walden* (1596), Gabriel 'doth nothing but turmoile his thoghts how to raise his estate, and invent new petegrees, and what great Noble-mans bastard hee was likely to bee, not whose sonne he is reputed to bee' (1966, 3: 56). He would be prouder to be the bastard of a lord than the legitimate son of a ropemaker. The motives for raising one's estate in this way were not necessarily material; after all, proclaiming oneself a bastard cut off rights of inheritance. What a famous father could bring was honour. When Davenant claimed to be a bastard son of Shakespeare, it was presumably in the hope of being recognised as the heir of his literary talents, not of New Place. Royal bastards claim illegitimacy in the pursuit of glory rather than wealth. Hall's Chronicle includes the colourful story of Dunios, Bastard of Orleans, who had proudly asserted his illegitimacy at court:

> When the question [of his parentage] was repeted to hym again, he boldly answered, my harte geveth me, & my noble corage telleth me, that I am the sonne of the noble Duke of Orleaunce, more glad to be his Bastarde, with a meane livyng, than the lawfull sonne of that coward cuckolde Cauny . . .
>
> (Bullough 1962: 55)

The bastards in *The Troublesome Reign of John* (1591) and Shakespeare's *King John* (1596) behave similarly so it seems reasonable to suppose that Hall's history provided source material for the drama here. In *The Troublesome Reign*, Philip's discovery of his paternity is highly romanticised. To satisfy Robert Fauconbridge, King John arranges a ritualised test in which Philip has to answer three times to the question 'who was thy Father?' On the third occasion, he cannot preserve false legitimacy or land, and says 'tis honors fire / That makes me sweare *King Richard* was my Sire' (1.277). In Shakespeare's *King John*, the newly titled Sir Richard realises that bastardy has made him 'A foot of honor better than I was, / But many a many foot of land the worse' (1.1.182).

It has been suggested that Philip and, to a lesser extent, Sir Richard are based on a contemporary historical figure, Sir John Perrot, who claimed to be a bastard of Henry VIII. In view of Arthur Acheson's opinion that Perrot 'might have lived in history as a paladin of romance' had he been born two hundred years earlier, the suggestion that he may have contributed to the conception of these two dramatic characters does not seem unlikely. Perrot had been acknowledged as a bastard brother by Edward VI, and accepted into the royal household and court by both Mary Tudor and Elizabeth I. Since the date of neither play can be firmly established, it is possible that they may have been written to rally support for Perrot at the time of his arrest in 1591 (Acheson 1920: 135–43). Sir John Perrot might also have been a source for the character of Stukeley in the anonymous play *Captain Thomas Stukeley* (1596). A rich oral tradition surrounded the figure of Stukeley, who also claimed to be a bastard of Henry VIII.

A brief examination of *Captain Thomas Stukeley* allows us to see how wry allusions to royal bastardy can be woven into a text. The play also alerts us to the fact that illegitimacy, even for a heroic character, can lead to tragedy. Stukeley's birth is referred to only once in the play, by his friend Vernon who attributes the character's vital qualities to his illegitimate paternity:

> Doubtles if ever man was misbegot,
> It is this Stukly: of a boundless mind,
> Undaunted spirit, and uncontrouled spleene,
> Lavish as is the liquide Oceane,
> That drops his crownes even as the clouds drop Raine.

(1,099)

The first three lines would seem appropriate to describe any natural child but the last two imply a reference to Henry VIII, easily identified by an audience aware of Stukeley's royal pretensions. His supposed descent from Henry VIII helps to explain his extreme confidence, his impetuous and yet generous behaviour in the play and the references to royalty which are made in association with the character. He refuses to be commanded by 'any man thats meaner then a king' (1,276) and is completely irresponsible about money (something for which Perrot and Henry VIII were also noted). He spends his wife's dowry to pay off a clothier, a vintner, a supplier of weapons, a buckler, a tennis keeper and a fencing master. The nature of his creditors gives a sense of the extravagant lifestyle he leads, which is perhaps deliberately reminiscent of that of Henry VIII. Stukeley 'tunes his speaches to a kingly keye' (2,298) ready to conquer the world. Spectators are encouraged to regard the bastard as regal and heroic, of 'a gallant mind' (173), a 'fine mettle' and an 'Active spirit' (175).

In spite of this marvellous reputation, Stukeley is doomed. Fighting on the side of Muly Mahamet in the battle of Alcazar, he dies unheroically at the hands of a group of Italian soldiers. Stukeley's downfall is linked to illegitimacy because Muly

Mahamet is also a bastard. His uncle defines him as an unnatural
usurper:

> Dare but my brothers Bastard and a slave,
> that should have kneeld at Abdelmelech's feet,
> send these proud threats from his audacious lips.
>
> (2,638)

Another line calls him 'Base bastard Moore' (2,335) and since the
African scenes show evidence of revision, it is possible that other
references have been lost in the amendments. Even with what
remains, it seems that illegitimacy brings tragedy as well as glory.
Stukeley falls from his elevated position by allying himself with a
typically villainous bastard. Muly Mahamet represents the negative qualities of Stukeley's own illegitimacy which drag the hero
down to ignominy. The pattern sketched out here is elaborated
much more fully in plays where the hero's bastardy is the root
cause of his tragedy, an inescapable flaw which destroys him
from within.

Tragic heroes

To achieve heroic status, royal, noble or mythical bastards strive
to construct a self which accords with the masculine world's
ideas of virtue and nobility. Tragedy occurs when the hero
finally fails to overcome an 'essential' element of his bastardy,
the alien other which is part of his being. The futility of his
attempt to integrate as a pseudo-legitimate likens him to the
unnatural villains discussed in Chapter 3, but unlike these characters, who transgress in order to recreate themselves within the
legitimate order, bastard heroes aim to conform only to transgress as if by instinct. Even the biblical hero Jepthah is doomed
to commit an unnatural act. He promises a sacrifice to the Lord
which forces him to condemn his only daughter to death (Judges
11: 1–30). Similarly, instinctive unnaturalness dooms the bastard
characters in *The Unfortunate Mother* (1639) by Thomas
Nabbes. Spurio and Notho both exhibit some aspect of the
evil bastard which mars their otherwise spotless characters and
brings about their downfall. Spurio is 'a rare example / Of a
great good man' (92) who is impassioned with an incestuous

love for his mother and 'burnes with a corrupted flame' (133).
Notho, a military hero, begins to behave like the typical ambitious usurper when prompted by Corvino, who is the real villain
of the play. The two brothers finally murder each other to the
horror of their mother, Infelice, who asks

> What sad influence
> Order'd this Tragick action? or what motives
> Could teach them to direct it to this end
> This most unnatural end.

(152)

It is the ambitious Corvino who is immediately responsible for
the tragedy but the play suggests that an innate fault in both
brothers, attributable to their birth, makes them behave
unnaturally.

Such characterisations allow dramatists to investigate the process of self-fashioning which 'occurs at the point of encounter
between an authority and an alien' and where 'any achieved
identity always contains within itself the signs of its own subversion or loss' (Greenblatt 1980: 9). The point of encounter
between authority and alien is especially problematic for
mothers' sons whose birth alienates them from the ideals of an
authority which privileges the masculine. To become a hero, a
purely male creation of *virtus*, is very precarious, even for legitimate characters, because it demands an exclusion of the contaminating presence of maternal origin. Janet Adelman explores
this idea brilliantly in her book *Suffocating Mothers* (1992), which
shows how male characters struggle to escape from their identities as mothers' sons to fashion themselves as products of a
purely paternal lineage. The quest for masculine selfhood is all
the more difficult for bastards because their maternal legacy,
which corrupts them at the point of origin, is so much more
powerful. Their unique starting point lends an ambiguity to their
careers: their quests are heroic triumphs over the disadvantages
of illegitimacy and cowardly retreats from their difference.
Invariably bastard heroes are unable to escape their maternal
origins. Their tragic ends are caused by a return of the repressed
'otherness' of bastardy which shatters their endeavours to prove
themselves their fathers' sons and recreate themselves as heroes.

Hercules is an important model for tragic characters who are torn apart by conflicting energies. As Waith observes in *The Herculean Hero* (1962), Renaissance interpretations of the Hercules myth had difficulty in reconciling its contradictory elements. Hercules's glorious triumphs over enemies such as Cerberus and the Nemean lion confirmed his individualistic integrity. His lustful adultery, destructive madness and unnatural murders offended conventional morality. It seemed that there was not one Hercules but two (Shulman 1983). Bastardy provides a key to the paradox of Hercules. He is at once a demi-god and a mother's son, a transcendent hero and a potential villain, a model of superhuman strength and sensual depravity. Seneca's tragedies *Hercules Furens*, and *Hercules Oetaeus* translated by Jasper Heywood and John Studley, focus much more closely on the question of Hercules's parentage than Euripedes or Sophocles had done. The schizophrenic nature of the hero as both demi-god and bastard upstart proves to be his tragic undoing; in *Hercules Oetaeus*, Juno recognises that the best way to destroy Hercules will be to 'let hym / agaynst hym selfe rebell' (Seneca 1969: 212).

Internal battle is the mainspring of Thomas Heywood's interpretation of the myth in *The Silver Age* (1611) and *The Brazen Age* (1611). Waith (1962) sees these plays as 'spectacles rather than coherent dramatisations of heroic character' (210) but if we examine the relationship between bastardy and heroic self-definition, their retelling of the Hercules story assumes unity. Both plays present Hercules's career as a conflict between positive and negative elements of his illegitimacy, symbolised by the divine paternity of Jove and the destructive nature of Juno. Masculine and feminine forces compete to win control of the hero's personality and the plays demonstrate what a superhuman task it is to fashion a 'perfect' masculine self. The paternity of Jove offers Hercules the potential for heroic transendence and immortality (as part of a male-constructed mythic history). Juno represents the contaminating maternal presence which continually threatens to come between Hercules and his divine father, to disrupt the purity of the paternal–filial bond with reminders of bastardy. The opposing influences are introduced at Hercules's birth where the male chorus (Homer) praises him as a 'Iove-bred

Issue famous for chivalry, while Juno refers to him as a 'mechall brat' and 'bastard' (123). She gives constant reminders of his base birth throughout both plays and symbolises his earthly identity as a mother's son. In this respect the plays are conventionally misogynist; they equate femaleness and bastardy as alien elements likely to corrupt the hero. Nevertheless, Heywood's telling of the story demonstrates how easily patriarchal myths can crumble.

Juno tries to destroy Hercules by confronting him with opponents or dangers which represent elements of the dangerous bastard 'other' in himself. He must labour continually to assert his quasi-legitimate identity as Jove's son. He triumphs over monstrous enemies who represent the savagery of the (un)natural child. His defeat of tyrannous rulers endorses his loyalty to legitimate power rather than that of the (typically bastard) usurper. He symbolically detaches himself from the grotesque body celebrated by the natural child by cleaning out the stables of Augeas. Indeed, throughout his labours, Hercules subjects his body (and those of his enemies) to physical pain and hardship, as though trying to destroy his maternal inheritance – his material connection to his mother – to achieve paternal acknowledgement.

The most important enemies Hercules encounters are the Centaurs. They are the bastards of Juno, embodiments of unlawful desire, and in them Hercules finds his alter ego. They meet at the wedding of Hypodamia where the Centaurs behave as (un)natural children, governed only by appetite, and try to rape the bride. Hercules opposes them, standing up for chastity and marriage instead of for bastards:

> Audacious Centaur, do but touch her skirt,
> Prophane that garment *Hymen* hath put on;
> Or with thy hideous shape once neere her cheeke,
> Il'e lay so huge a ponder on thy skull,
> As if the basses of the heaven should shrinke,
> And whelme ore thee the marble firmament.
>
> (142)

The subsequent fight between Hercules and the Centaurs is a struggle for superiority between the bastard of a male god and

those of a female deity. It represents externally the conflict going
on inside the hero. Jove-born Hercules stands for heroism and
legitimate order while the maternally-inspired Centaurs are
associated with the outlawed impulses he must overcome. He
is victorious on this occasion but the illegitimate maternal influence continues to exert a subversive power in the play. It is
through a plot involving Nessus, the only surviving Centaur,
that Juno brings about the downfall of the hero.

In *The Brazen Age*, Hercules shoots Nessus with a poisioned
arrow when the Centaur tries to rape Hercules's bride,
Deianeira. Nessus is fatally wounded but Hercules cannot anni-
hilate his alter ego so easily. The dying Nessus gives his shirt to
Deianeira and thereby introduces the fatal 'flaw' which will undo
Hercules: his infidelity and lust. Handing over the shirt gives a
clear signal of the emergence of these illegitimate qualities in
Hercules. Nessus tells Deianeira

> I know thy Lord lascivious, bent to lust,
> Witnesse the fifty daughters of King *Thespeius*,
> Whom in one night he did adulterate:
> And of those fifty begot fifty sonnes.
>
> (181)

In typically misogynist style, the play presents Hercules's fall as a
return to the female, to his point of illegitimate origin. He is
overcome with an adulterous passion for Omphale (like that
from which he was conceived), and dresses as a woman. His
grotesque appearance signifies his identity as a mother's son; he
is no longer separated from his maternal origins as a positive,
masculine subject. Instead he is a bastard, who can be defined
only in negative terms. The Princes refuse to recognise him since
'hee's turn'd woman' (240) and the hero significantly asks 'How
have I lost my selfe?' (244). Femininity, and the bastardy to
which it is linked, decompose heroic identity.

Hercules accepts the fatal shirt as a symbol of the sanctity of
marriage, hoping to appease Juno as well as Deianeira. His
words 'In this wee'le sacrifice / And make our peace with her
and Jupiter' (248) are highly ironic as Hercules himself is the
final sacrifice. The shirt is immersed in the bastard blood of the
'lust-burnt Centaure' (180) and inflames in Hercules all the

negative aspects of bastardy which he has endeavoured to suppress in the execution of heroic deeds. He suddenly assumes the
most destructive qualities of the unnatural villain: he wants to
pull down the altars, kill the priests and destroy Jove's temples.
He curses his wife, longs to 'spurne mountaines downe, and
teare up rockes' (250) and to make his way to hell by
stamping a path into the earth. At the height of his bastard
fury, he kills Omphale mistaking her for his wife and blaming
her as one who has 'fier'd my bones . . . shortned my
renowne' (253). Again the play lays the blame on the
women – Omphale, Deianeira and Juno – but acknowledges
the power of feminine influence (and illegitimacy) to overthrow patriarchal constructs of honour. Only by destroying
his body can Hercules attain a form of legitimacy. His earthly
self perishes in the sacrificial fire and Jove finally acknowledges his son. Telamon's comment 'His soule is made a star,
and mounted heaven, / I see great Jove hath not forgot his
sonne' (254) links deification with paternal recognition and
bypasses the problem of illegitimacy.

The Hercules myth exerts a powerful influence on plays
whose bastards are tragic heroes. *The Misfortunes of Arthur*
(1588) by Thomas Hughes is closely modelled on Senecan
drama. It contrasts the achievements of the bastard King
with his 'wicked' birth and lust in begetting Mordred. Like
Hercules, Arthur weaves his own destruction by succumbing to
an excess of passion, a sinful contrast to his heroic martial
activities. He is a skilful soldier who returns to England a
victorious Christian conquerer (3.2.53). His wish to rule by
inspiring his subjects' love and loyalty (3.1.101) and his unwill-
ingness to impeach his country's peace with civil war (3.3.51)
contrast favourably to Mordred's ideas of successful rule.
Arthur appears more as 'a paragon of princely virtues than a
sinful member of a tainted stock' (Armstrong 1956: 247). Nevertheless, he is unable to escape the doom of his illegitimate birth
and that of his son:

> Well: t'is my plague for life so lewdly ledde,
> The price of guilt is still a heavier guilt.
> For were it light, that ev'n by birth my selfe

Was bad, I made my sister bad: nay were
That also light, I have begot as bad.
Yea worse, an heire assignde to all our sinnes.

(3.4.20)

Arthur's life is inextricably bound to Mordred, the 'heire' of sins.
The two bastards end their careers by unnaturally stabbing each
other on the battlefield. As they die, Arthur sees in his son's face
a mirror image of the negative elements of his own illegitimacy 'a
witnesse of my crimes: / A fearefull vision of my former guilte'
(5.1.100–1). The hero gazes at the alien other, born from and
contained in himself. He believes that the Fates have linked their
faults alike (5.1.122) to make their unnatural ends a mirror to the
world 'both of incestious life, and wicked birth' (5.1.121).

Another tragic hero from Arthurian romance is the bastard
Tom a Lincoln whose chivalric history was popularised in
Richard Johnson's prose romance *Tom a Lincoln*, published in
two parts in 1599 and 1607. Tom, the son of King Arthur and
Lady Angelica, is a hero but in the second part of Johnson's text
Arthur's deathbed revelation that Tom is 'begot in wantonnesse,
and borne a bastard' (314) causes a series of tragic events. The
Queen turns against Tom with a wrath comparable to that of
Juno, slandering him as 'the base borne seed of lust' and then
cruelly murdering his mother. News of Tom's bastardy has an
even more disastrous effect on his wife, Anglitora, who laments
that she has given up father, friends and country 'for the disloyall
love of a bastard' (318) and becomes an adulteress. She murders
Tom and throws him on a dunghill, his fate and burial recalling
that of so many illegitimate victims of infanticide.

The prose romance forms the main source for a play, probably
dating from about 1611. John Pitcher's introduction to the
Malone Society Reprint of the script (from a manuscript in the
hand of Morgan Evans), argues that it was probably performed
at Gray's Inn and may have been written by Thomas Heywood.
Unfortunately (though fortunately for Tom), the play dramatises only the first part of the story; it emphasises Tom's bastard
birth but ends before this is made public. The writer certainly
knew both parts of Johnson's text and includes hints of a darker
sequel but no dramatic version of Part Two is extant. Nevertheless, in the play we do have, Tom's behaviour causes tragedy

for others and is interesting since it raises questions about the nature and value of the heroic. The drama is a parody of chivalric romance; it glorifies Tom and simultaneously deconstructs ideas of heroism by showing him involved in actions which are certainly not heroic, actions more typical of the bastard villain. Tom grows up as the supposed son of a shepherd who comments that 'he was ever kind, ever courteous, ever affable, ever mild, ever gentle' (397–8). This fulsome praise seems ironically misplaced when Tom unnaturally deserts his foster-father and the poor shepherd collapses from grief and dies at Tom's feet. Interestingly Tom asks the heavens how he has 'transgresst yor lawes' (566) to deserve such a fate and suspects that he might be illegitimate (573). Having shown the cost of Tom's heroic ambitions, the text switches mood again to glamorise his resemblance to his royal father. The 'Charecters / of bright Nobility' (644) stamped in Tom's face make it certain he is descended from princely parentage. He becomes a national hero, leading the English forces who are sent to put down 'base rebellious fRANCE' (856). His role in subduing rebellion rather than leading it moves him further away from the role of base-born villain. However, King Arthur's congratulation 'Rise famowse yowth that makste myne honowre rise' (1,030) contains a note of irony in that Tom is actually the result of Arthur's dishonourable adultery.

After his victory in France, the hero sets out on a quest to find his father and here the play's critical undercurrent deepens. Like Hercules, Tom strives to establish a filial–paternal link and escape his difference as a mother's son. He is distracted from his chivalric exploits in Fairy land, where he has an affair with Caelia, the Amazonian Fairy Queen, and fathers a bastard child on her. Once again, the hero seems to be overcome by lascivious desires which are part of his nature. He deserts the mistress and bastard (who are potent reminders of his own doubtful origins), with the excuse that he must pursue his honourable quest. The play shows him as increasingly dishonourable. He bravely slays a dragon in Prester John's kingdom but causes the deaths of Prester John and his wife as well by eloping with their daughter, Princess Anglitora. The suicides of Prester John and Queen Bellamy are the dramatist's invention (though heavily

endebted to Shakespeare's *King Lear* and *Hamlet*) and seem
designed to undermine a positive reading of Tom's character.
The hero selfishly forgets or ignores his earlier promise to
return to Caelia at the completion of his adventures. Her
reaction highlights the subversive juxtaposition of heroic and
ignoble images of Tom. When she realises that she and her
child have been abandoned, she throws herself into the ocean,
carrying a letter in the hopes that he'll find her dead body. The
contents of the letter contrast dramatically with the reality of
Tom's cruelty. It refers to him as the 'mirrour of all courtesy', as
a 'bright starre of chivalry' and, most inappropriately of all, she
praises him as a 'constant, faithfull, loyall man' (2,764–7). Caelia
knows her words are lies; she constructs Tom as a parody of true
chivalry because she dare not call him false or untrue (2,781). She
bids farewell to him as 'great Brittaines greatest praise' (2,825)
and floats out to his ship, a symbolic female sacrifice to his heroic
image. Her dead body and the paean of praise bound to it give a
stark picture of the price of heroism. Her letter compels the
audience to recontextualise all the panegyric used in the play
and makes them regard its romantic celebration of Tom with
considerable suspicion. Tom thinks of himself as the stuff of 'a
Chronicle of lastinge prayse' (264) and Arthur tells him that his
deeds 'will engrave thy name in Annales pende / untill aeternity
shall have an ende' (1,064). Caelia's words turn these patriarchal
histories into fictions designed to boost the male ego. Behind the
play's romantic view of chivalry lies an unsettling interrogation of
masculine honour.

The bastard hero is used to problematise honour again in a
later play, Massinger's *The Maid of Honour* (1621). The play is
tragicomedy rather than pure tragedy but Bertoldo's bastardy is
a tragic force. Bertoldo is introduced as a Knight of Malta and an
admired soldier who tells his brother 'Your birth, and justly,
claimes my fathers Kingdome; / But his Heroique minde des-
cends to mee' (1.1.237–8). Honour is of paramount importance
to him and, like Hercules, he needs to need to be active as
though labouring against an inherent vice. He argues that
'Vertue, if not in action, is a vice, / And when wee move not
forward, we goe backeward' (1.1.186). These words have particular relevance to Bertoldo, who is doomed to a path of vice

even as he seems to be moving forward. He leads a military campaign to Siena, but commits his forces to a dishonourable cause. He discovers he is fighting against the knights of his own religious order and the leader, Gonzago, is horrified to see that Bertoldo has put on 'Foule vices vizard' (2.5.90). The 'funerall of his vertue, / Faith and religion' (2.5.63) is elaborated more fully in the love plot. Bertoldo is a skilled and attractive courtier, so much so that Camiola praises him as 'North-star / And guider of all hearts' (1.2.83). Her faith in his constancy is misplaced. At each turn of events, his love becomes more selfish and more mercenary. The sincerity of his commitment to spiritual values is brought into question at the very beginning of play when he proposes marriage to Camiola. He seems quite ready to break his oath of celibacy as a Knight of Malta. Later, he makes Camiola his earthly goddess, promising to marry her in return for a ransom to release him from prison in Siena. Once free, he is attracted to Princess Aurelia and thoughts of a crown. He is acutely aware of his fall into sin but seems unable to help himself:

No, no it cannot be, yet but Camiola
There is no stop betweene me and a crowne.
Then my ingratitude! a sinne in which
All sinnes are comprehended! Aide me vertue,
Or I am lost.

$$(4.4.153)$$

What appears to be an inherent vice in Bertoldo triumphs over his virtue and he rejects the maid of honour in favour of the wealthy princess. Marriage is, of course, the only way he can win a crown legitimately so his temptation is understandable. This does not make it any less wicked according to the moral standards of the play. Bertoldo is demonised; when he appears richly clothed before Aurelia, Astutio remarks 'the divell I thinke supplies him' (4.4.56). Like a morality Vice, he inflames lust in Aurelia who is transformed into 'a wanton Helen' (4.4.145) and behaves as though 'some fury hath posses'd her' (4.4.119).

At the end of the play, Bertoldo recognises and repents his deviance from the 'noble tract / Mark'd mee by vertue!' (5.2.178). He is re-admitted as a Knight of Malta but does not

win back the love of Camiola who decides to become a nun.
Base birth seems irreconcilable with a path of pure honour but
Bertoldo is not the only sinner. As Camiola realises, the whole
court is corrupt in these 'more then impious times' (3.3.138) so
Bertoldo's downfall is not surprising (3.3.152–3). Her rejection
of all suitors and of a worldly life groups the dishonourable
Bertoldo with a society of dishonourable men. The play suggests that it is not bastardy but the material life which cannot be
reconciled with absolute honour. Its high ideals are unrealistic.

Lambs for slaughter: tragic victims

Other plays show the tragic effects of illegitimacy on virtuous
characters who are not heroes in the traditional sense. They
appear instead as innocent sacrifices to the ruling culture and
its persecutory practices. Dramatists heighten their criticisms of
an ideology which privileges legitimacy by comparing the virtuous victims to Christ. Imagery of sacrifice is highly developed
in Dekker's *The Noble Spanish Soldier* (1622) and *The Welsh
Ambassador* (1623), two plays dealing with pre-contracted marriage situations. The presentation of the bastards in both texts
attracts sympathy for the female characters and helps to censure
the Kings who use their power irresponsibly. In *The Noble
Spanish Soldier*, Prince Sebastian is described as 'the mark'd-
out Lambe for slaughter' (4.1.62) because the King has bribed
Balthazar to murder him. The Prince in *The Welsh Ambassador*
tells his father 'doe what you will with mee, / Ile stand you like a
little harmlesse lambe' (5.1.135). Such imagery identifies the
causes of the Princes' wronged mothers as good and patriarchal
authority (embodied by the Kings' wills) as wicked. *The Noble
Spanish Soldier* shows the King as full of 'ugliness, lust, treachery'
though gilded with the power of State (5.2.30–1). Oenelia and
Sebastian appear saintly and just. Sebastian retires to a monastery
and, because the King thought him murdered, his reappearance
as his father's confessor is like a resurrection. The King feels that
Sebastian is 'some spirit' (5.4.97) come from heaven to make his
soul 'somewhat lighter' as he repents (5.4.104). Sebastian's words
'Haile my good Sonne / I come to be thy ghostly Father'
(5.4.95) reverse status positions, using a carnivalesque mode

typical of the natural child to serious purpose. The oedipal struggle is transformed from the pattern of unnatural parricide (followed by the bastard villain) into a triumph of good over evil.

Criticisms of the legitimate order are also made by plays in which characters' discovery of their parentage kills them with shame. These bastards are essentially passive, pitiful figures rather than heroic protagonists struggling against an illegitimate identity. In Peele's *Edward I* (1591), the bastard is female. Joan of Acon is an immensely pious character who preaches the values of virtue and justice, and the sanctity of marriage. She is betrothed to the Earl of Gloucester and the dramatist develops a loving relationship between them independent of his sources (Peele 1952–70, 7: 17). The news that she is the fruit of the Queen's illegitimate relationship with the King's brother is too shameful for Joan to bear and she sinks down at Edward's feet and dies. This is again the dramatist's invention, intended to heighten the shock effect of her sacrifice. The King emphasises Joan's innocence which stands in stark contrast to the guilt of her mother.

In Shirley's *The Politician* (1639), Haraldus dies from an inexplicable illness soon after learning that he is the bastard of Queen Marpisa and her lover Gotharus, a scheming politician. He tells his mother 'I cannot live . . . I have a wound within / You do not see, more killing than all fevers' (148–9). Illegitimacy places a curse on him, or so he believes, asking Gotharus 'why should both your lusts / Curse my unsinning heart? Oh, I must be, / For your vice, scorn'd, though innocent!' (117). His protest at the injustice of the bastard's position echoes the arguments put forward by William Clerke (1594), Thomas Milles (1613) and other writers. Milles points out that 'the poore Bastard . . . findeth not himselfe to be in any fault, neither hath broken holy Lawes concerning his birth'. The bastard character in *The Thracian Wonder* (anon. 1595) makes the same claim (F1v) and his own exemplary behaviour (finally rewarded with legitimation) argues strongly against the laws which persecute virtuous innocents for their parents' sins.

Haraldus's virtue is much emphasised in *The Politician*, in contrast to the scheming nature of his mother and his supposed father. He does not share their unnatural qualities, refusing to become the ambitious villain they want him to be. He shows the proper duty of a subject to his king, saying 'I was born with the condition / To obey, not govern' (101) and dying with the words 'My duty to / The King' (151). He also endeavours to show the duty expected of a son towards his parents. To question his mother's honour and his own paternity would be a terrible 'crime', he believes. Haraldus is honest, of a gentle disposition and pious, qualities which make the courtiers feel he cannot be Gotharus's son (94) even though he was probably 'got with more heat and blood' than Marpisa's husband could manage (93–4). Marpisa finally tells Haraldus that he is legitimate, but he feels the curse of bastardy too deeply by this time and dies a pitiful sacrifice to the plots of his mother and her lover. Even though illegitimacy brings death for Haraldus, it does serve a positive function. He refuses to see it as a reason for villainy and ambition and so becomes a figure of outstanding virtue. Illegitimacy offers him isolation from the legitimate court which is riddled with corruption It makes him part of an alien world of honesty. This play therefore combines its use of bastardy as a tragic force with details which present it as a positive metaphor.

Bastardy as a positive metaphor

When the society presented in a play is corrupt, the bastard's status as outsider can offer an attractive position for a virtuous character. The governing hierarchy which constructs a morally upright individual as illegitimate asserts the rightness of its own corrupt rule. In such cases the bastard raises fundamental questions about the constitution of legitimacy. Virtuous bastards offer the dramatist a means to criticise the circular relationship between legitimacy and power, where the rules of exclusion which empower the dominant are also the rules which legitimate them. A regime which excludes virtue can simultaneously legalise itself by requiring others to respect that exclusiveness which is the basis of its power (Beetham 1991: 56–7). The virtuous bastard who embodies values normally characterised as legitimate draws attention to their absence in such a regime. As Beetham points out, 'it is only when legitimacy is absent that we can fully appreciate its significance when it is present, and where it is often taken for granted' (Beetham 1991: 6).

These ideas are explored in Dekker, Day and Haughton's play *Lust's Dominion; or the Lascivious Queen* (1600), where the legitimate Prince, Philip, is slandered with bastardy and forced to flee from the Spanish court. The ruling order bastardises a virtuous figure, thus proving its own lack of moral legitimacy. The court is contaminated by lust and by the ambitious plots of Eleazar, Moorish lover of the lascivious Queen. When King Philip dies, moral and political corruption takes on a sham legitimacy: Fernando inherits his mother's lust as well as his father's crown. Eleazar is promoted to be Royal Protector and abuses his position to further his plan to usurp the Spanish throne. The new regime tries to displace its own illegitimate activities on to Philip who inherits his father's noble qualities. Eleazar warns that Philip has 'sworn confusion to this Realm' (3.2.202) and the friars Crab and Cole, who are bribed to proclaim Philip's bastardy, cast him in the role of pantomime villain:

> *Crab.* How villainous and strong!
> *Cole.* How monstrous and huge!
> *Crab.* The faction of Prince *Philip* is
> *Cole.* *Philip* that is a bastard.
> *Crab.* *Philip* that is a dastard.
> *Cole.* *Philip* that kill'd your King.
> *Crab.* Onely to make himself King.
>
> (3.3.52)

The monks' performance exaggerates the characteristics normally associated with the bastard and applies them, most inappropriately, to Philip. Their comic double act makes fun of the prejudice against illegitimacy and those who follow it. It is a fiction invented by Church and State to sustain an unscrupulous regime. The evils attributed to Philip are acted out by Eleazar. When the two characters meet on the battlefield, the text highlights their symbolic opposition to show how conventional moral values have been turned upside down:

> *Elea.* Bastard of Spain?
> *Phil.*   Thou true-stamp'd son of hell,
> Thy pedigree is written in thy face.   (4.1.40)

Philip is not really illegitimate but the only position left to him is that of slandered 'other'. Legitimacy, which is 'true stamp'd' and has a pedigree, has become the badge of hell and bastardy is now the refuge of virtue. Philip accepts the role of bastard to detach himself from his mother and her lover, telling the King of Portugal 'I may be well transform'd from what I am, / When a black divel is husband to my dam' (4.1.23). Bastardy allows him to act unnaturally, converting all the 'innative duty' he owes his mother into hate (4.1.16–21). Philip fights to relegitimate the ruling hierarchy in Spain as well as to recover his own legitimacy. The latter part of the play associates him with Christ and demonises Eleazar. Philip comes to send 'the damn'd *Moor* and the divels' down to hell (4.4.8–10), until he is betrayed by Cardinal Mendoza, a Judas figure (4.6.21). The action imitates the pattern of events in the Gospels: Mendoza approaches Philip 'in love and peace', reminiscent of Judas's kiss, before arresting him for high treason as a 'traitor and bastard' (4.4.89). A trial scene follows, where Philip is sentenced to bastardy and the Cardinal to death. The last part of the play includes a symbolic Harrowing of Hell in which Philip, supposed dead, delivers the virtuous and repentant characters 'from below' (5.3.109), where they are imprisoned in a hell-like dungeon (5.2.43). He frees the country from lust's dominion and is hailed as its saviour.

The Devil's Charter (1606), by Barnabe Barnes, takes the process of reversal found in *Lust's Dominion* one stage further because the ruling hierarchy is literally illegitimate. All three of Pope Alexander's children are bastards and Alexander is bastard-ised in the text (212). The youngest son, Candie, is different from the rest of the family. While Alexander is in league with the devil, Candie appeals to Heaven for mercy for his sister (1,430-3) and protection for himself (1,463-5). His prayer '*A che me fido, guarda me Dio*' (1,634) links him to Christ as he dies, innocently, in one of Caesar's plots. Candie determines to fight only in 'warres which vertue levies against vice' (468), a policy certainly not shared by the machiavels Alexander and Caesar. The audience are encouraged to agree with Caesar's assessment of his brother as 'an honest man, and fitt for heaven' (1,922) and, as such, a corruption from the typical Borgia characteristics. Caesar highlights Candie's deviance by referring to him as 'A bastard of our house, degenerate, / In whom no sparke or spiracle of honor, / Appear'd to raise the race of *Borgia*' (1,956). What Caesar actually means is that Candie shows no inclination to become involved in the family's evil practices. Ironically, by calling Candie a bastard to a bastard dynasty, Caesar insults him with legitimacy. This indicates just how far the Borgia rule has reversed conventional oppositions and reveals the dangers behind the self-legitimating operations of power.

The Troublesome Reign of John, King of England (1591) uses the bastard's ideological distantiation to criticise and then re-legitimate corrupt State institutions. Bastardy gives Philip an important detachment from political decision-making which King John does not have. John is troubled by the thought of excommunication and prostrates himself before the papal legate, pleading for re-acceptance (10.181–7); Philip shows utter contempt for the established Church throughout both parts of the play. He enjoys raiding the abbeys so much that, in these scenes, it is easy to believe that he shares the amoral viewpoint of the (un)natural child. When the wars are over, he longs to continue the rape and pillage of battle inside the cloisters, where he can 'dive into the Monkes and Abbots bags' and 'make some sport among the smooth skin Nunnes' (4.42). He calls the prayers of Friar Thomas a 'rabble' (6.29) and parodies the ritualised Latin of the Church, using rhyming couplets to criticise the clergy:

Is this the labour of their lives to feede and live at ease,
To revell so lasciviously as often as they please.
Ile mend the fault or fault my ayme, if I do misse amending,
Tis better burn the cloisters down than leave them for offending.
                                                              (6.96)

Philip's brutal candour is not simply the destructive impulse of the bastard villain or an outright attack on religion *per se*. He exposes a country riddled with spiritual hypocrisy or 'fained holines' (10.85), and his purpose is to 'mend the fault', to relegitimate the Church by purging it of lechery, drunkenness and avarice. He is commited to Protestantism rather than to no religion at all, constructing himself as a champion of heavenly virtue against a demonic clergy.

Many of Philip's remarks have a particular anti-Catholic focus.

The Pope, 'the cursed Priest of *Italy*' (10.147), is the object of his special disgust. When King John is murdered by the Abbot, Philip moralises 'This is the fruite of Poperie' (15.113). The play's final scene shows the victory of his Protestant faith. It is Philip, surrounded by the bodies of the corrupt clergy, who tells the dying King 'Forgive the world and all your earthly foes, / And call on Christ, who is your latest friend' (15.92). The simplicity of this spiritual advice contrasts favourably with the rhetoric used by the Church figures earlier in the play. John predicts a victory over the Roman whore of Babylon (15.104–7), and Philip assures the audience that if England unites 'Nor Pope, nor *Fraunce*, nor *Spaine* can doo them wrong' (16.54). His role as a 'folk hero of uncompromising resistance to Catholic treason' (Bevington 1968: 200) is in direct contrast to the conventional use of bastardy in plays promoting Protestant polemic. As I discussed in Chapter 2, illegitimacy is usually a tool to slander the enemy (Catholic) faith but *Troublesome Reign* reverses the pattern and characterises the bastard as a Protestant evangelist.

Its religious politics may engage with the contemporary controversy over Puritan non-conformity in Renaissance England. If, as Donna Hamilton (1992) suggests, the play does displace its discussion of these issues on to a dramatic dispute over legal legitimacy in the first scene, then the bastard can perhaps be identified with a non-conformist Puritan voice, subjugated and used to legitimate the established Church. A possible source for Philip's character is found in John De Verten, a bastard who rose to prominence as an assistant to Henry VIII in the dissolution of the monasteries. This would provide some explanation for the abbey scenes which other critics have found unsuited to the rest of the play. Jacqueline Trace (1980) argues that the memory of John de Verten was kept alive in oral tradition into the 1590s (67–8). The hero of the play may also owe something to James Stewart, the illegitimate Earl of Moray, who led the forces of the Scottish Congregation in defence of their Protestant faith in 1560 and again in 1565. His commitment to Elizabeth was shown in the 1569 Northern Rebellion where he fought against the rebel Earls and Scottish Catholics who supported their interests. In a proclamation issued on 8 December 1569, he condemns those who presume 'to erecte the Papisticall religion in the boundis where they have repaired' (Boyd 1903: 20). After he was assassinated in Linlithgow in 1570, a series of broadside ballads was printed celebrating his virtue and thus making him into the kind of folk hero depicted in *Troublesome Reign*.

To define Philip as a Protestant champion is to ignore another important aspect of his illegitimacy. It is a way of referring back to an idealised past. Richard Coeur de Lion, the last undisputed ruler of the kingdom, personifies an age where right and wrong are clearly distinguishable. Nostalgia for this time runs high in a society where John's right to the crown is challenged by Arthur and ethics are eclipsed by political expediency. Philip's bastardy connects him more firmly to the ideal past than to contemporary politics. He plays the role of chivalric hero, pursuing his father's murderer with a single-minded determination for revenge which stands out from the indecision or inaction of other characters. His victory over Austria consolidates his image as a reincarnation of the heroic Coeur de Lion:

> Thus hath K. *Richards* Sonne performde his vowes.
> And offred *Austrias* bloud for sacrifice
> Unto his fathers everliving soule.
> Brave *Cordelion*, now my heart doth say,
> I have deservde, though not to be thy heire
> Yet as I am, thy base begotten sonne.
>
> (3.146)

It is the 'base begotten sonne' who must uphold the chivalric ideals of the past within the confusion of the present. Philip is brutal and insensitive at times (particularly towards his mother), but he is responsible for keeping alive the principles of loyalty and self-integrity which ought to characterise the legitimate society of the play.

The play's celebration of a bastard hero certainly challenges the stigma of illegitimacy but it fails to undermine patriarchal culture as a whole. Instead, Philip seems to promote the ideas on which this culture is based. He criticises the corrupt hierarchy headed by King John, but the alternative ideology he offers is equally conservative, perhaps even more so since it is based on a chivalric past dominated by a warrior King. For something more radical, we must look to Shakespeare's *King John*. Here, bastardy still offers ideological distance from a corrupt legitimate world but its apparently perverse role as a tool for upholding conventional values is developed in a more interesting way. It is double-edged: destabilising a male-centred culture while purportedly celebrating it. Such subtlety is possible because of the complexity of the bastard character. To dismiss Sir Richard's bastardy as 'rather superfluous' (Draper 1938: 126) is simply wrong since his special relationship to the society of the play depends upon it.

The dominant order in *King John* is lacking in true legitimacy. John is a *de facto* king who has 'done a rape / Upon the maiden virtue of the crown' (2.1.97) to beget an illegitimate reign, and Arthur is powerless to assert his rightful claim. Constance points out that the Kings are 'a counterfeit / Resembling majesty' (3.1.99) in a world where 'law itself is perfect wrong' (3.1.189). Society is riddled with hypocrisy; force and expediency are disguised as honour and religious conscience. Fortune 'adulterates hourly' with the faithless King John and King Philip is a bawd to their adultery (3.1.56–61). The 'vile concluded peace' (2.1.586) which disempowers Arthur is the bastard child of this relationship. In the early part of the play, Sir Richard joins his voice with those of the female characters to subvert masculine authority. He punctuates the arguments over John's and Arthur's claims to the throne with the interjections 'Bastards and else' (2.1.276), and 'Some bastards too' (2.1.279), which draw attention to Coeur de Lion's divided heritage and the lack of clear right. The former reminds the audience of Elinor's remark that John relies on 'strong possession' much more than right (1.1.40), and the latter recalls the accusations of bastardy just made by Elinor and Constance, which would invalidate Arthur's legitimacy. It is appropriate that the interventions are placed in the mouth of the bastard of Coeur de Lion, the monarch whose inheritance is in dispute. Perhaps the idea of Sir Richard as a third potential candidate occurs to the audience although it does not seem to be his intention to suggest this to the other characters.

Sir Richard's subversive advertisement of bastardy makes him 'an "illegitimate" commentator on an illegitimate reign' but he

is not, as Ernest Jones would have him, a total innocent, a 'child
lost in the wood of the world's shocking callousness' (Jones
1977: 147, 238). His bastardy (and its typically negative associations) immediately complicates audience response. His self-
awareness betrays a worldly wisdom which undercuts the
impression of naivety suggested by much of his bluff speech.
At first, Sir Richard seems to be adopting the usual bastard role
of attacking the establishment by delivering 'Sweet, sweet, sweet
poison for the age's tooth' (1.1.213). A series of incidental details
associates him with the villainous qualities of the stereotypical
bastard. Chatillon's identifies him with the 'unsettled humors of
the land' and the threat of national disorder (2.1.65–71). He
promises to play the devil (2.1.134) and cuckold Austria
(2.1.292), copying the behaviour of the morality vice, Lechery.
In Act 5, Salisbury refers to him as 'that misbegotten devil
Falconbridge' (5.4.4), repeating the widely held view that
bastards are damned in their conception. Some of Sir Richard's
'policy' smacks of the bastard machiavel's cold pragmatism.
Michael Manheim (1989) argues that he advances by acting in
an increasingly machiavellian manner 'in which all statements are
dedicated to attaining and retaining power' (131). Reading the
bastard as an embodiment of new machiavellianism explains his
skilful use of rhetoric to sustain the authority of monarchy but it
fails to take into account his resignation of power at the end of
the play.

In the earlier acts, though, Sir Richard's personal ambition is
an unsettling element of his character. His speeches in Act 1 are
dominated by the pronoun 'I' to create an impression of self-
interest. After being knighted, he describes himself as a 'mounting spirit' (1.1.206) and imagines how flattery will 'strew the
footsteps of [his] rising' (1.1.216). He exhibits the potential to
develop as a bastard usurper, so the audience may be suspicious
when he rises to a prominent position, being given 'the present
ordering of this time' at the opening of the fifth act (5.1.77).
Earlier, he declares 'Gain be my lord, for I will worship thee'
(2.1.598) and looks forward to raiding the monasteries, claiming
'Bell, book, and candle shall not drive me back / When gold and
silver becks me to come on' (3.3.12). Here, he shows the
materialistic outlook of the unnatural villain. Sir Richard is

certainly aware of what is happening to him. He is tempted to
become a man of the world rather than a bastard to the time, as
he admits in his soliloquy on 'that smooth-faced gentleman,
tickling commodity' (2.1.573). He knows that this devilish
'daily break-vow' (2.1.569) has made Philip and John compromise their positions, and acknowledges that he is equally
vulnerable to its influence:

> And why rail I on this commodity?
> But for because he hath not woo'd me yet.
> Not that I have the power to clutch my hand
> When his fair angels would salute my palm.
>
> (2.1.587)

Sir Richard stands on the margins of the corrupt world of
commodity rather than outside it. His interest in the issue
focuses important ideas about his heroic status since the word
'commodity' (meaning self-interest) is implicitly set against the
idea of commonwealth or service to society. The bastard considers what kind of hero he will become and recognises that he
could follow the path of self-advancement and outdo the other
rulers at their own illegitimate game.

Casting Sir Richard as the mirror and personification of an
illegitimate world fails to take account of how his role changes
later in the play. Events show that he does not become a disciple
of commodity. Instead, he sacrifices his personal interest for the
legitimate commonwealth, behaviour which stands out in the
biased world of self-interest. The turning point for the meaning
of his bastardy comes with the death of Arthur. Pandulph's
words 'All form is formless, order orderless' (3.1.253) prove
chillingly accurate since Arthur's death symbolises the complete
breakdown of legitimate order in *King John*. Sir Richard views
the body in abstract terms:

> How easy dost thou take all England up
> From forth this morsel of dead royalty!
> The life, the right, and truth of all this realm
> Is fled to heaven; and England now is left
> To tug and scamble, and to part by th' teeth
> The unowned interest of proud swelling state.
> Now for the bare-pick'd bone of majesty
> Doth dogged war bristle his angry crest,

And snarleth in the gentle eyes of peace;
Now powers from home and discontents at home
Meet in one line; and vast confusion waits,
As doth a raven on a sick-fall'n beast,
The imminent decay of wrested pomp

                                                    (4.3.142)

This is the point in the personal microcosm of England offered
by Sir Richard where 'Legitimation, name and all is gone'
(1.1.248). It is a final dislocation of the King's two bodies, an
event which, in legal theory, should never happen (Axton 1977:
109). Arthur is the only character with 'right', so the principles
behind legitimate rule have 'fled to heaven', leaving monarchy as
an empty shell or carcass. The bastard dogs of war, struggling to
'part by th' teeth' the realm of England, are those with power
but not right (John and Lewis). Because the legitimate power
structure has fallen into their hands, its principles of degree,
truth and right must pass into the alien realm of the bastard,
in the reversal pattern already observed in other plays.

Sir Richard's character and actions effect a process which
Danby (1948) calls 'legitimizing the illegitimate' (75). Isolated
from the corrupt and empty shell of monarchy, the bastard
becomes the upholder of traditional patriarchal values. For this
reason, he cannot be an embodiment 'of every kind of illegitimacy' who constantly subverts the process of patriarchal history
(Rackin 1990: 186). Following his destructive criticisms, he tries
to uphold and reinfuse the principles of legitimacy into a hierarchy now threatened with 'imminent decay'. His apparently
amoral attitude is replaced by a strong spiritual awareness
when he is talking to Hubert (4.3.116–34) and when he appeals
to heaven (5.6.37–8, 5.7.60, for example). In politics, his contempt for bargained peace at Angiers is supplanted by a wish to
promote civilised negotiation with the French and the rebels.
Joseph Candido (1989) observes that his 'ideological bastardy
becomes the touchstone of his political superiority' (125)
because it allows him to locate and promote a meaningful
good in an adulterate world of impurity. He leads the English
force himself, taking up arms to 'glister like the god of war'
(5.1.54). He makes mistakes as a military leader but is
romanticised as a hero who 'In spite of spite alone upholds the

day' (5.4.5). Sir Richard speaks as the guardian of a disembodied, idealised kingship in the midst of a world of fragmented authority. When he acts as John's ambassador, his references to a 'gallant monarch' and to images of lion and eagle (5.2.128–58) describe a principle rather than John, the King of 'wrested pomp'. Sir Richard is well qualified to speak for the legitimate monarchy of the past. He is the 'very spirit of Plantagenet' (1.1.67), an ambassador for a 'perfect Richard' (1.1.90).

Sir Richard's identity as the bastard of an idealised Richard I allows him to legitimise the illegitimate but it also makes his position uniquely difficult. In a key scene in the midst of the battle, Hubert confronts him with the problem of his identity:

> *Hub.* Who art thou?
> *Bast.* Who thou wilt; and if thou please,
>   Thou mayst befriend me so much as to think
>   I come one way of the Plantagenets.
>
>   (5.6.9)

The exchange highlights Sir Richard's relationship to his bastardy at the very moment when the audience and the bastard himself are beginning to view him purely as a personification of kingly qualities (something often emphasised in production by costuming him in the lion skin to liken him to his father). Beaurline (1990) finds it difficult to imagine that the bastard is 'tempted to take over the reins of government' here (182), but in the light of common associations between bastardy and usurpation, Sir Richard's tentative use of the royal name 'Plantagenet' does raise suspicions about his intentions. News of the legitimate heir, Prince Henry, makes him realise that to come 'one way' of the Plantagenets does not justify an aspiration to the crown (Calderwood 1960: 355).

As a bastard, Sir Richard cannot inherit the kingdom without perpetuating the reign of illegitimacy begun by John. To convert the ordering of the present time into a *de facto* kingship would be to continue a corrupt form of rule based on strong possession rather than right. Sir Richard does not do this; he shows true heroism by sacrificing his self-interest and resigning the kingdom he has been preserving to the legitimate heir. Unlike King John with Arthur, the bastard recognises Prince Henry's 'right' as a relegitimation of the English hierarchy and can 'bequeath' him 'lineal state and glory' (5.7.102–5). It is the fundamental difference between John and Sir Richard – the illegitimacy of the latter – which makes this process possible. Because he cannot inherit, Sir Richard can be 'propertied' as the custodian of legitimate monarchy where the 'high-born' John or Lewis can not (5.2.79–82). M. M. Reese (1961) refers to Sir Richard as a 'vessel of royalty' (278). The term is peculiarly appropriate because it shows how bastardy makes him a temporary guardian of legitimate values, like the self-sacrificing mothers of the play. While he embodies and carries the principle of true royalty, as they have done, he is expected to make no claims on power himself because he is a mother's son.

The success of this process is dependent on Sir Richard's selflessness, his determination to remain a 'bastard to the time' (1.1.207) – outside the flow of history – rather than forcing himself into it. To argue that he cannot be a hero since he is not at the centre of the political action is unfair because he could only make history in this way by becoming a villain (a bastard usurper). Criticisms which argue that the end of the play is 'hardly a heroic climax' for Sir Richard and see him as 'somewhat confused and out of touch' with events (Beaurline 1990: 42) ignore his resignation of power and its consequences: a disintegration of the self in favour of service to society. This constitutes a very different kind of heroism, one which could be termed feminine. Unlike so many other bastard heroes, Sir Richard does not run away from his maternal legacy. He models himself on it, copying the mothers, and thus retains his uniqueness, his difference. In the final speech, he declares 'Nought shall make us rue, / If England to itself do rest but true' (5.7.117). This is a much broader incarnation of his personal principle of self-integrity 'I am I' (1.1.175). His individuality has been replaced by the community. The bastard steps outside the making of personal history and the speech elevates this kind of maternal self-sacrifice, the very opposite of 'commodity', as the highest form of heroism.

At the same time, the text questions an ideology which demands such sacrifices. The society which denies the mother's son (and the mother and daughter) any place in its power structure seems blatantly unfair. Sir Richard's role as a vessel of royalty links him to the subversive triad of mothers and 'embarrassing women' who are an energising force in the first part of the play (Dusinberre 1989). Far from losing interest in the official world once the mothers disappear, Shakespeare uses the bastard to continue their subversive questioning of patriarchal power. Sir Richard may appear to be 'annexed into the official discourse' (Dusinberre 1989: 52) but he reveals the exclusive nature of that discourse even as he uses it. His last speech celebrates the 'princes' who constitute the glory of 'this England' (5.7.112–15). At the same time, he reminds us of the unnamed queens, mothers and bastards whose contributions are unacknowleged by the historical record.

There was, of course, a notable exception to this rule – the reigning monarch. Queen Elizabeth's bastardy and her femininity both de-stabilised patriarchal ideas of national history. Philip of Spain was not the only person to suggest that it would be far better for the Queen to take a consort 'who might relieve her of those labours which are only fit for men' (Hibbert 1990: 67). Elizabeth showed that she was perfectly capable of wielding power, and Sir Richard's final speech, like the Queen, challenges the misogynist view. When he speaks to and for 'this England', he speaks for Queen Elizabeth, and draws attention to the problems her monarchy raised for patriarchal culture. The last line of the play is a plea for national integrity: 'Nought shall make us rue / If England to itself do rest but true' (5.7.117). By giving these words to a bastard, Shakespeare alerts the audience to a fissure at the centre of power. For England to rest true to itself would be to acknowledge that a woman and a bastard was ruling the country, something highly irregular, even unnatural when viewed from a patriarchal perspective. Sir Richard's patriotism threatens to undermine Elizabeth's government. Alternatively, and more importantly, it raises doubts about patriarchal history and the ideology which produces it. To legitimise Elizabeth's rule is to delegitimise a culture which grants positions of power only to men born in wedlock.

Sir Richard's bastardy thus works in two contradictory ways in the second part of the play. It is a virtuous condition which isolates him from ruinous self-interest and allows him, as the bastard of Coeur de Lion, to relegitimise the polity. As the bastard of Lady Falconbridge, his status as a mother's son has a more radical effect; it points up the injustice of a power structure which excludes so many, and criticises a culture which relies on female self-sacrifice rather than drawing on women's creative power. By working in both these ways, illegitimacy in *King John* simultaneously celebrates patriarchy and marks its exclusions.

The radical element of *King John* is pursued in Brome's *The Damoiselle*, written and performed in 1638. *The Damoiselle* is set in a London riddled with corruption and the alienated position of bastard offers detachment from this world. In addition, Brome uses illegitimacy to expose the relationship between money, sex and the exploitation or 'commodification' of women which the play satiries. In line with its proto-feminist critique, the bastard character is the exception to the rule in being female. She stands for those dispossessed by gender as well as by illegitimacy or poverty. Phillis is the daughter of Elynor Brookeall, a gentlewoman who was seduced by the knight Dryground and fled in shame to raise her child in obscurity amongst the beggar community in London. At the opening of the play the Brookeall family, headed by Elynor's brother, has been ruined by the aptly named Vermine, a usurer and 'Monster of our time, / For avarice and cruelty' (381). Vermine is an unsympathetic character who continues to oppress others and abuse the law but Dryground repents his former sin. The plot shows how he works out a scheme to repair the damage he has inflicted on the Brookeall family. The bastard figure is central to this scheme which, as well as righting wrongs, shows how lechery, usury and female sexuality are connected in a system of commodification controlled by men.

Unaware of Phillis's identity, her father uses the fact that he has a bastard daughter to help Brookeall's son, Frank, to a fortune. Frank dresses up as the bastard 'Frances' (also known as the Damoiselle) to take part in Dryground's plan to raise money for him. The scheme – the supposed raffling of the Damoiselle's virginity – exposes commodification in its crudest form. Dryground is apparently willing 'to sell [his] Childe / To Lust and Impudence' (422). Participation in this disgusting

system of exchange is governed by gender rather than by class.
Lords, justices and 'bustling Lawyers', 'Money-Masters',
'Merchant Venturers' and 'Muffled Citizens' all bid for the
'Forreine Commodity' (424–5). It is appropriate that Frank
should adopt the position of the bastard daughter since, like
the female characters in the play (who would also have been
played by boys), he has been dispossessed by the corrupt
economy of homosocial exchange.

In an environment where 'The World is turn'd / Quite upside
downe' (429), Phillis's 'unlawfull' birth (445) is virtuous rather
than vicious. She occupies a marginalised position as bastard,
beggar and woman. From here, she can anatomise the world of
commerce where a man can deal for another man's land, sell
another's right or match his own daughter for financial gain
(406–7). She offers a more detached commentary than the other
female characters who are bound up in this system. One scene,
where she begs money from Valentine and Bumpsey, is particularly interesting because it shows in miniature how the city
market place works. Bumpsey, Valentine's father-in-law, is
obliged to match any sum that Valentine spends as part of a
former agreement relating to the dowry of his daughter. When
Valentine gives Phillis money, Bumpsey copies him and Phillis
takes charge of the financial competition, inviting the other men
to join:

> *Phil.* Gentlemen, will you come in? will you vie it?
> *Amp.* No we deny it.
> *Phil.* You may revye it then, if you please. They come not to in
> binde it.
> *Val.* Will you come in againe Sir?
> *Bum.* Sir, after you, and't be to my last sixpence.
> I will keep Covenant w'ye,
> *Val.* A shilling more on that.
> *Bum* Done Sir: there tis.
> *Phil.* Why, these are Lads of bounty! Have you any minde yet
> Gentlemen?
>
> (444)

This sounds more like gaming at cards or dice than an expression
of charity, with Phillis apparently in control. It makes an obvious
parallel to the raffle for her counterpart's maidenhead. Her self-

assured command of the situation indicates the superficial power of female sexuality as a controlling force in the economy. Compulsive gambling is a metaphor for male sexual appetite and the men are unable to escape their desire for the foreign commodity. The raffle and the begging scene seem to reverse Marx's theory of commodity relations where 'commodities are things, and therefore lack the power to resist man', because they show that man lacks the power to resist commodities, no matter what their price (Marx 1976: 178). In the begging scene, the situation is more complicated, though, since Valentine and Bumpsey are playing their own bargaining game, related to the dowry of Bumpsey's daughter. Phillis's apparent control over the transfer of goods is only illusory, like the power of women as commodities. Brome shows how it is impossible for women to gain complete independence in a patriarchal market place. Since Phillis is begging to raise a dowry, she is still marginally attached to the economy anyway.

Phillis may be trying to raise her value as a bride, but she and her alter ego 'Frances' are ethically detached from the immoral financial transactions which govern the city. Bastardy is a redemptive force in the play. Oliver, a gallant, believes that he has found in 'Frances' 'a vertue, that / Might save a City' (426) and, on a personal level, Phillis helps to convert Wat (the son of Vermine) from a 'Riotous reprobate' (383) into a virtuous citizen. At the denouement of the play, the two bastard figures are brought together. Dryground assures everyone that he has not prostituted 'Frances' and introduces 'her' as personified Chastity who will 'beat Lust down to Hell, from whence it rose' (462). Phillis steps into 'Frances's' place a moment later and gives a physical reality to these words. The play concludes when the 'bastards' Frank and Phillis, are betrothed to the children of Vermine, Alice and Wat. The union between the Phillis and Wat, the heir of capitalist enterprise, symbolises a reform of economic exchange in the city. The play does not present Phillis as a radical who will re-fashion woman's position in society. Her active role in schooling Wat (434-5), and possibly contributing to future reform in the city, accords with the conventional maternal role of pious educator. Otherwise, her contribution to the action is small. It is Dryground rather than she who directs events and her part is a minor one in terms of lines. In spite of her subordinate position, she has considerable symbolic importance in the play. *The Damoiselle* depicts the mother's daughter as a figure of redemption. This treatment of virtuous bastardy is strikingly different from the one offered in texts like Heywood's *Ages* plays, where Hercules's identity as a mother's son is a cause of tragedy.

There are, then, many variants within the general category of virtuous bastard. The base sons of gods, kings or noblemen are romanticised as embodiments of superhuman strength or chivalric ideals. For some characters illegitimacy is an asset, a form of alienation which enables the individual to remain untainted by a corrupt society. Bastards who function as victims or figures of redemption in their plays are often compared to Christ. These characterisations reverse orthodox opinions about illegitimacy but they are not always as radical as they appear. Positive images of bastardy are usually qualified by presenting it as a fatal flaw (in the case of tragic heroes), or by emphasising paternity over maternity. What emerges from an overview of these plays is that virtuous bastards strive to model themselves on traditional ideas of what is good or right. They appear to reinforce rather than subverting patriarchal ideologies. In spite of this, their difference, as bastards, is an ever-present phenomenon. It means that within a conservative framework based on paternalistic values, bastard characters can destabilise dominant political and religious ideologies. Dramatists juxtapose alien 'other' and dominant authority to question just what society elevates and celebrates as heroic.

6

Bastards and theatre

In *The Bastard* (1652), the title character enters the stage with the words

> *The world so swarms with* Bastards *now, that I*
> *Need not despair for want of* Company;
> *I'me in among the Throng.*

(A4v)

His familiarity with his surroundings suggests a special relationship between bastard and theatre space. Of course attempts to discuss the nature of Renaissance playing spaces and types of audience are necessarily highly speculative so my examinations of audience–actor relationships are at best suppositions. In spite of these diffculties, numerous details in the play texts indicate the importance of the bastard's eccentric relationship to the performance arena and demand attention in a consideration of the type. Drawing on these textual details, on contemporary documents relating to theatres and playgoers, and on theories of performance, it is possible to suggest ways in which dramatists use bastard characters to activate the dynamics of the theatre with interesting effects. Reference to modern productions helps to illustrate some of the possibilities available to an actor playing these roles.

'An illegitimate product at best'

It is not surprising that bastards feel at home in the theatre because there was an immediate kinship between the two in Renaissance England. The theatre was an equivocal area, spatially and ideologically. In anti-theatrical writings it was demonised by the Church and only grudgingly tolerated by the City. Geographically, the public theatres (where many of the plays with bastard characters were performed) occupied a marginal position outside the city walls, like that of the bastard in the cultural landscape. Steven Mullaney (1988) has shown that this suburban space, known as the Liberties, represented a 'liminal area outside the law' (40) where lepers, deprived of their religious and legal identity, had been transported to die anonymously 'as a full sign of exteriority' (36). It was still occupied by figures who, like the bastard, were alienated from society – some by physical or mental ailments, others by legal anonymity, poverty or criminal activity. Playhouses were especially scandalous since their permanent, impressive structures made visible the subversive potential of the Liberties. Mullaney comments that public theatres became a 'bastard sort' of institution (47) and were perceived as 'an illegitimate product at best, an embarrassment if not a threat' (95). Before discussing bastards in performance, we must examine the equivocal nature of Renaissance theatres in general terms.

The playhouses were like the bastard: they demonstrated the full imposition of patriarchal authority and they marked the limits of that authority. The City Fathers showed their power by licensing theatres outside the walls but, by doing so, they sanctioned unconventional activities beyond their control. Playing and playgoing seemed to give social outcasts the chance to form new identities in defiance of the ruling culture's notion of a fixed social hierarchy. In 1597, the Lord Mayor and Aldermen complained that theatres attracted 'contrivers of treason and other idle and dangerous persons' and offered the opportunity 'for all maisterless men & vagabond persons that haunt the high waies, to meet together & to recreate themselves'. In addition, 'apprentices and other servants' were drawn away from their work to design 'mutinous attempts' (Dover Wilson 1968: 226–8). Dissenting groups formed part of the private theatre audiences as well. In the early days of Jacobean private theatre, the audience had 'an intellectual, even a radical bias' and included 'university men, Inns students, disenchanted seekers after court positions' (Sturgess 1987: 19). Martin Butler (1984) has shown that the audience of Caroline private theatres was

socially diverse and politically active. The fashionable society
which attended the indoor theatres 'was becoming a new and
dangerously permanent area in which political views could be
canvassed and interchanged' (118). Plays formed part of the
circulation of ideas. There was still a degree of interaction
between the elitist and popular modes which characterised
indoor and public theatres in the Caroline period. A backward-
looking element, including revivals of Elizabethan plays like
Edmund Ironside (1595), sustained a drama that was 'sceptical,
critical and levelling' (Butler 1984: 185).

Generalised condemnations of playing, found in anti-theatrical
writings, suggest that all theatre practice was perceived as socially
disruptive, no matter what the performance space. Even court
masques implicated the participating audience. In *The Anatomie
of Abuses* (1583), Stubbes claimed that plays encouraged unnatural behaviour: 'you will learn to rebel against princes, to
commit treasons . . . to play the whoremaster, the glutton,
drunkard, or incestuous person . . . to contemn God and all
his laws' (Dover Wilson 1968: 225). Bastard villains were guilty
of many of these crimes and, according to the Puritan view,
likely to teach such immoral behaviour to the spectators.
Theatres were themselves immoral because they promoted
'bargaines of incontinencie', or ungoverned sexual activity.
John Northbrooke claimed that players 'devoure the pure chastitie bothe of single and maried persons, men and women', and
Antony Munday argued that, by watching whoredom on stage,
'such as happilie came chaste unto showes, returne adulterers
from plaies' (Cook 1977: 272–4). Spectators' supposedly vor-
acious sexual appetites produced illegitimate thoughts and, in
some cases, children. Sir William Trumbull reported that the
Earl of Argyll 'was privy to the payment of 15 or 16 poundes
. . . for the nourseing of a childe which the world sayes is
daughter to my lady [Argyll] and N[at] Feild the Player'
(Cook 1977: 279). No doubt assignations between members of
the audience or between playgoers and professional prostitutes
also led to the birth of bastards.

Complaints against theatres as places of erotic exchange
reflected a wider insecurity about identity. Plays destabilised
clear distinctions between genders and classes, turning boy

actors into women and common players into kings, thus undermining a hierarchy which legitimated its power by presenting
dominant and subordinate roles as fixed and 'natural'. Insecurities about gender were emphasised by the practice of
cross-dressing, on-stage by boy actors and off-stage by transgressing women. This too is associated with illegitimacy. Bridewell
records of 1601 note that Margaret Wakeley 'had a bastard child
and went in man's apparell' (Howard 1988: 420). The pamphlet
Hic Mulier (1620) complains that 'deformite in apparell' is 'by
the rules of Heraldry basenesse, bastardie, and indignitie' (A3v–
A4). The cross-dressed woman is a bastard to her sex, her class
and her country, 'committing gross adultery' with foreign
fashions and bringing forth 'unnaturall conceptions' (C1). The
very practice of playgoing subverted gender roles because it
moved women outside the patriarchal household and transformed them into active participants in urban public life as
spectators, consumers and judges of what they saw in the
theatre (Howard 1989: 73).

The effect of playgoing on masculine identity was even more
disturbing because, according to anti-theatrical pamphlets,
watching plays turned men into beasts and simultaneously
effeminised them. In *Plays Confuted in Five Actions* (1582),
Gosson claims that the effeminate gestures of cross-dressed
boy actors transformed male spectators into sexually insatiate
women: 'these outward spectacles effeminate & soften the
hearts of men, vice is learned with beholding, sense is tickled,
desire pricked, & those impressions of mind are secretly con-
veyed to the gazers, which the plaiers do counterfeit on the
stage' (G4). Laura Levine (1986) argues that the fear of effemi-
nisation shown in such tracts disguised a profound conflict about
the nature of the self. By projecting this contradiction outwards,
on to the stage, Renaissance society could make manageable 'the
perception of something horrendously other at the core of the
"self"', a female identity locked away inside the male subject
which proved that there was no inherent gender, no essential self
(136). Levine suggests that accusations of sodomy put forward
by critics of the theatre were a scapegoat or metaphor for this
more disturbing idea. The hermaphroditic actor 'becomes the
embodiment of all that is frightening about the self' (130).

Bastard characters contribute to the theatrical display of gender insecurity because the bastard, like the hermaphrodite, embodies self-contradictons.

The male bastard is not often visually hermaphroditic, like the cross-dressed boy actor but, as a mother's son, he is an example of something horrendously 'other' at the core of the self. According to Lacan's Law of the Father, the bastard is a living contradiction: he is endowed with a positive signifier – the phallus – but is still defined in negative terms as 'other' because he is *filius nullius*, the son of no one. He is an unusually gendered subject, an 'uncertain' man. Sometimes his hermaphroditic nature is made explicit, as in *The Seven Champions of Christendom* (1635) where Suckabus looks more like his mother than his father. He asks the devil to 'make me a man like my mother' (B3) and Tarpax tells him he is 'effeminate in shape and favour / Just thy sweete mothers, sweete hu'd faire Effigies' (C4). In Heywood's *The Brazen Age* (1611) and Brome's *The Sparagus Garden* (1635) the bastards dress up as women. In the former play, the Princes think Hercules is 'some woman, some Hermaphrodite' (243). In *The Sparagus Garden* Tim Hoyden appears as a '*monstrum horendum*; a man in womens cloaths' (209), costumed like 'Master Maiors wife of *Taunton-Deane*' (221). The bastard's 'otherness', even when not represented visually, highlights the existence of a repressed feminine or maternal presence with the power to undermine legitimacy, fixed masculine identity, autonomy and supremacy.

If we use a Lacanian model to read the performance space, the male bastard appears as a hermaphrodite in terms of his relationship to the Symbolic order of the stage world and play text. His status as male gives him access to the language of public discourse (unlike most female characters) but his identity as a bastard excludes his speech from the most prestigious linguistic registers of the play. It denies his voice any final authority in that dramatic world. He is poised in a no man's land in between the 'masculine' authority of the speaking play text and the 'feminine' speech or silence of the audience, who, like the bastard, have no legitimacy of speech in the play's action but are vital to the theatre experience. As such, his speech is constructed and directed differently from that of the other *dramatis personae*.

It is with the audience rather than with other characters that bastards usually share their observations and feelings. In plays where they have a substantial role, they often speak a high proprotion of the soliloquies and asides. For example, in *King John*, *Edmund Ironside* and *Herod and Antipater*, the bastards have over eighty per cent of the soliloquies and extended asides in their plays. These include speeches when they are alone on stage and lines spoken in the presence of other characters which are purely introspective or choric in nature, giving the audience privileged access to the character's thoughts or providing a narrative on the play's action. Major bastard characters – such as Thersites in *Troilus and Cressida*, Edmund in *King Lear* or Fallacy in *The Sophister* – address a large number of their lines to the audience. My discussion will concentrate on bastard characters like these, although illustrations will be taken from other plays because even bastards with smaller roles seem to have a special closeness to the audience and tend to speak in soliloquy. In the anonymous play *Locrine* (1594), for instance, 52 of Sabren's 62 lines are soliloquy, appealing for company to mourn the death of her parents (5.6.65–93, 131–45). In *1 Henry VI* the bastard Bishop of Winchester has two confidential soliloquies (1.1.173–7, 5.1.56–62), the first of these being particularly appropriate to illustrate his isolation from the main characters and action.

The alienation caused by illegitimate status is dramatically realised in plays where characters labelled as bastards begin to speak in introspective soliloquy as they contemplate their new position. In Shirley's *The Politician* (1639), Haraldus overhears the courtiers discussing his suspected illegitimacy and breaks out into a series of questions and exclamations heard only by the audience:

> Oh my shame!
> What have my ears receiv'd? am I a bastard?
> 'Tis malice that doth wound my mother's honour:
> How many bleed at once! . . .
> . . . Ha! my fears
> Shoot an ice through me; I must know the truth
> Although it kill me.
>
> (113)

When he re-enters in the following scene, Haraldus continues to speak in detached aside for a full ten lines before addressing Gotharus (115). Similarly, in Middleton and Rowley's *A Fair Quarrel* (1617), Captain Ager's suspicions about his supposed illegitimacy are expressed in a long soliloquy (2.1.1–34) and an aside as he questions his mother (2.1.54–7). Arthur Wilson's play *The Swisser* (1631) includes a scene where Alcidonus is told that he is a bastard, and soliloquises on the horror of his incestuous love for Selina (4.3.87–95). The character becomes more detached from the world around him and the audience witness the development of his thoughts and feelings about his situation.

Such examples suggest that the label of bastardy forges a special connection between character and audience. The distribution of soliloquies between Edmund and Edgar in *King Lear* supports this view, as Michael Mooney (1988) demonstrates in his essay on *figurenposition* in the play. Edmund's first soliloquy establishes his privileged relationship with the audience but once Edgar loses his identity as a son of Gloucester, and is forced into the position of bastard outcast, he takes over Edmund's choric role (Mooney 1988: 156–7). Edmund begins to lose touch with the audience when he is legitimised as a 'Loyal and natural boy' (2.1.84). At the end of the play the brothers' roles are reversed again and Shakespeare returns 'the source of our privileged knowledge to Edmund', who has confided his intention to have Lear and Cordelia murdered (Mooney 1988: 165).

Unlike Hamlet or Richard of Gloucester, a bastard character is automatically detached from the world of the play by his birth. He needs no ghost come from the grave or decision to isolate himself in villainy to place him apart. The audience are not surprised by bastards who speak in isolation instead of to other characters so the type can deliver a variety of very different kinds of soliloquy in the same play. Direct address must have seemed natural for bastards; Gaspar's exclamation 'I'me in among the Throng' (*The Bastard* A4v) gives a sense of their identification with the audience. Illegitimate marginal status would probably have been reinforced spatially by placing the character downstage. This would be appropriate for the kinds of speech frequently given to bastards, such as self-introduction, pointing out another character, commenting on a scene without leaving it, or

revealing a secret. The bastard's downstage position would be
particularly apt if, as George Kernodle suggests, the back of the
Elizabethan stage represented a background of hierarchical
order in the universe while the open stage at the front was a
platform for Renaissance individualism. Kernodle argues that the
open stage was the domain of the mountebank player, who 'had
no place in medieval society. He was an outcast . . . Everyone
else had a place – a set place – and all the other stages of the time
had elaborate scenic symbols of the temporal order' (Kernodle
1959: 3). Like the mountebank, the bastard is displaced from the
hierarchy of temporal and cosmic order and so stands isolated at
the front of the stage.

A downstage position enables bastards to exploit the multi-
levelled nature of reality created by Renaissance theatre spaces
and performance conditions. More or less 'realistic' effects could
be used simultaneously and a bastard character is ideally placed
to activate the contradictory relationship between these. He
stands on the periphery of the play, not fully integrated into
the dramatic illusion of the stage world created by the authored
text, the actors and the audience's imaginary forces. Neither is
he part of the audience's reality and noise, in the theatre or
beyond it. He is a creature of both worlds, able to cross from
one level of reality to another with more ease than legitimate
characters, who occupy a fixed position in the fiction. This
endows him with a potentially subversive power. Robert
Weimann (1988) remarks that Renaissance theatre was composed of very disparate modes which co-existed and inter-
twined. It broke the 'fixed and determined correlations of
theatrical signs and ideological meanings' found in neoclassical
writing and sanctioned by the authorities. As he goes on to say,
'this "hodge-podge" form must have been one by which
cultural bastards and theatrical *factota* thrived' (406).

Bastard characters thrive by undercutting the authority of the
fictional world presented on stage. Their isolation identifies
them with what Weimann calls the *platea* function in his theory
of 'bi-fold authority' on stage. The *platea* function worked in
opposition to *locus*-centred authority which privileged 'what and
who was *represented*'. *Locus*-centred authority was characterised
by 'a certain verisimilitude, decorum, aloofness from the

audience, and representational closure'. It was powerfully conservative but it could be undercut by the *platea* mode which
privileged the actor and the 'neutral materiality of the platform
stage', who and what was representing the dramatic world
(Weimann 1988: 409).

Bastards' ideological, verbal and spatial detachment allow
them to use the *platea* function. Their power to deconstruct
the fictional world, or *locus*, was particularly important since
censorship endeavoured to control the disturbing energy of
the theatre by scrutinising and altering the texts of plays.
Dramatists could conform to the official condemnation of bastardy in their scripts and then use the bastard's eccentric position
in the theatre space to subvert the orthodox ideology presented.
Censorship of the written script ignored a huge part of the
performance – its non-verbal elements and the dynamics of
theatre spaces. Ultimately a script is only a grounding for an
ungovernable multi-faceted performance. Censorship took no
account of the bastard's intimacy with the audience and his
ability to use that position to undermine the authority of the
written text. Excluded from the play world's officially sanctioned
discourse of power, the bastard unites with the audience in a
subversive chemistry of the theatre which relocates authority
with them as readers of the performance rather than with the
written text and its male author(s).

Bastard characters undo the 'well-defined author function'
which was used to legitimate drama in the eyes of the *de jure*
authorities (Bristol 1985: 117). Thomas Docherty (1987) argues
that the author function is like a male genealogical line which
could be disrupted by the feminine power to produce bastards,
or illegitimate meanings. The illegitimate represents 'a genuinely
"rival" authority to that of the orthodox name of the father . . .
an element whose home is the genuinely historical, unamenable
to ritualisation'. Fatherless voices set out 'to oppose critically the
incipient tyranny of centralised civic and political authority
vested in "City Fathers"' (34–6). Bastard characters set up
such an opposition in the theatre, giving dramatists the opportunity to diffuse their own writerly authority and to develop anti-
authoritarian points of view. Personalised soliloquies, more
impersonal commentaries on the action, and explicit references

to the theatricality of events on stage, all undercut the ideas presented in the *locus* of the play. Many illegitimate characters perform more than one of these dramatic functions within their plays and probably used a mixture of acting styles for the different types of speech. These will be discussed in relation to each of the three main functions of the bastard as an intermediary between play and audience.

'Why bastard? Wherefore base?': personal Soliloquies

By giving bastards the chance to soliloquise on their position, the dramatist privileges the characters' often unconventional thoughts and feelings. In Renaissance theatres, either public or private, soliloquies would almost certainly have been addressed directly to the audience so it is wrong to define them as 'introspective' according to our standards of naturalistic performance. This is not to say that they were not psychologically convincing. Acting was thought at the time to be lifelike, even though it may not have been realistic in our terms, and many soliloquies invite the audience to follow the bastard's own thought patterns. The introspective nature of these speeches may be clearly indicated, as in the anonymous *Claudius Tiberius Nero* (1607), where Tiberius announces he will retire to his orchard 'to meditate alone' (2,029) and then shares his thoughts in a monologue of seventeen lines. In other cases, unfinished sentences or sudden jumps from one subject to another may indicate that the lines are supposed to be a spoken representation of the character's thoughts. In Hughes's *The Misfortunes of Arthur* (1588), for example, Mordred's anxious words on his first entrance (1.4.1–18) involve the audience in his desperate state, his fears for the future. Such speeches need not encourage moral approval but they do promote understanding of the bastard's unusual opinions.

A good example of their unsettling effect is found in *The Revenger's Tragedy* (1606). It is only in soliloquy that Spurio reveals his true bitterness about his bastardy. In a monologue of twenty-seven lines (1.2.176–202), he dwells on the scene of his conception with sado-masochistic pleasure. The speech mingles narrative with self-revelation: it explains to the audience why 'adultery' is his nature, and it shows dramatically the growth of his passion for revenge. Spurio imagines the scene vividly; his feelings about it literally 'mount up' in physical terms. The first part of the speech culminates with the grotesque line 'I feel it swell me' (1.2.189), suggesting an erection. The 's' alliteration carries the audience along on Spurio's tide of erotic energy, drawing them in to agree with his unorthodox conclusion that a bastard's revenge on his father is just (1.2.189–90). The second half of the speech follows a similar cumulative pattern which tricks the audience into accepting Spurio's morally 'perverted' logic once again. The rhythm of the lines encourages them to identify with his mounting feelings of hate for his family. His final throwaway couplet, with its nonchalant, witty proposition that 'a bastard by nature should make cuckolds / Because he is the son of a cuckold maker' (1.2.201) probably takes them by surprise. They unwittingly give their approval to Spurio's destructive and immoral impulses. Even if their association with the character is only temporary, it encourages them to reflect on their own judgemental values. It is far less easy to condemn a bastard as a villain having just been drawn in to feel his anger and resentment.

Dramatists can encourage spectators to question the ethics of a society which persecutes illegitimates by detailing a bastard's emotional motivation in soliloquy. In Richard Zouche's play *The Sophister* (1631), Fallacy has speeches which show his sense of inferiority and insecurity and so recruit sympathy. Questions are an important way of involving the audience in the bastard's situation. Fallacy tells them that he is neglected by his father in favour of his legitimate brothers and asks 'who can endure / Contempt and hatred to goe unreveng'd?' (B1). Their silence indicates complicity with his villainous plots. Later, when his corrupt regime is threatened, he has a long soliloquy which dramatises his feelings of panic (H3). The speech is a series of agonised questions about the cause of his imminent downfall; introspective, in that their attempts to attribute blame finally come to rest on the bastard himself, but extrovert because they actively engage the audience in his state of mind by appealing for information. The audience are included in Fallacy's thought-process and his distress. The insecurity they share with him becomes part of a broader uncertainty about the play's moral structure.

The bastard character need not occupy a low status position to unsettle the values prsented in the *locus* of the play. He can openly challenge these in soliloquy, as Gaspar does in *The Bastard* after Mariana has rejected his love because he is illegitimate (D1v). Gaspar's grievances about the injustice of his treatment do more than solicit sympathy for a personal cause; they direct critical attention towards the governing ideology. His opening line 'Is there no thunder left in heav'n?' recalls Vindice's questioning of providential power in *The Revenger's Tragedy* (4.2.196). It suggests either that heavenly justice doesn't exist or that the gods do not stand up for bastards and are unjustly partial when meting out divine retribution. By means of logical argument, Gaspar manipulates the audience into accepting his politically dangerous ideas. He argues that 'since all will be / Villains, why should I practise honesty?' (D1v). The question assumes that villainy is the natural rather than unnatural course. At the same time it suggests that Gaspar will become a villain by necessity rather than choice. It puts the onus on the spectators to come up with an alternative and implicitly makes them responsible, at least in part, for Gaspar's subsequent actions.

Although it is impossible to argue with certainty how a bastard's lines were originally delivered, reference to modern televised productions helps to suggest ways in which such soliloquies can win or regain audience support. Edmund's first soliloquy in *King Lear* demonstrates two possible types of entreaty typically found in the bastard's conversation with the audience. The speech can work on the level of the victim seeking sympathy because it shows Edmund unjustly disadvantaged by the 'plague of custom' (1.2.3). Its interrogation 'Why bastard? Wherefore base?' (1.2.6) is directed towards this system, but simultaneously reveals Edmund's own insecurity in trying to establish a sense of identity in the face of the label *filius nullius*. In the television production directed by Michael Elliot (1983), Robert Lindsay delivers the questions from an angry defensive viewpoint to emphasise Edmund's bitterness about his birth and rejection by Gloucester. Lindsay plays a menacing but nervous Edmund, a dangerous, pitiful victim who is dwarfed

by the huge megaliths which represent Lear's palace and the
power of the legitimate world.

An alternative approach to the first soliloquy, and to the
character as a whole, is offered in Michael Kitchen's performance in the BBC television production directed by Jonathan
Miller (1982). This Edmund asks 'Why bastard? Wherefore
base?' with beguiling surprise, which effectively leads the
audience to share his opinion that he is quite obviously the
better man and so will naturally 'to[p] th' legitimate' (1.2.21).
He is a high status character who speaks at a leisurely pace and
with great self-assurance. When he produces the trick letter with
the words 'Well, my legitimate' (1.2.19), his clever control of the
situation attracts admiration rather than pity. In the final line,
Kitchen looks up and makes an appeal to the gods in the suitably
pathetic voice of the victim, but an ironic half smile to the
camera afterwards tells viewers that this Edmund does not
need a god.

The rest of Edmund's lines to the audience continue the form
of conspiratorial confidence, characteristic of bastard villains who
follow in the tradition of the Vice character. They use direct
address to elide differences between player and spectator, thus
co-opting the audience on the side of villainy. Conventional
morality distances audiences from a full identification with the
Vice but a bastard character is more humanised and often
succeeds in allying audience sympathies in ways which obfuscate
clear moral positions. Speeches by Edricus in *Edmund Ironside*,
and *Antipater* in *Herod and Antipater* are some of the most
daring attempts among bastard soliloquisers to persuade the
audience to share their point of view. Their success invariably
depends on their skill in establishing a creative relationship with
the spectators. As with the morality Vice, the bastard's confidence that they are sympathetically disposed towards him is of
the utmost importance. In *Edmund Ironside* (1595), Edricus
treats them as fellow conspirators, using the pronouns 'we',
'us', 'our' when he is considering how useful it would be to
have the foolish Stitch as a servant:

We that by sly devices mean to mount
and creep into opinion by deceit . . .

> . . . we must favour fools
> and with promotions win their shallow pates.
> A ready wit would quickly wind us out
> and pry into our secret treacheries
> and wade as deep in policy as we.
> But such loose-brained windy-headed slaves
> such blockheads, dolts, fools, dunces, idiots
> such loggerheaded rogues are best for us
> for we may work their wills to what we will
> and win their hearts with gold to anything.
>
> (521)

Edricus appeals to the audience's pride, assuming they want to share his intellectual superiority (a technique employed by many other bastard villains). He subsequently involves them creatively in the plotting action when he writes a letter to King Edmund (1,159–1,215). In this very long soliloquy, the audience participate in his writer's block; he asks them 'With what exordion shall I win his heart? / How shall I tie his ears to my discourse?' (1163) and they have to wait patiently while the difficult letter is composed. They are frustrated, like Edricus, by errors and blots in the writing and relieved when it is finished and the action can move forward. The audience have considerable emotional investment in the letter by the time it is complete so they are keenly interested to see whether its deception will work when it is delivered to Edmund.

Markham and Sampson's play *Herod and Antipater* (1622) demonstrates more fully the subversive power which can be generated by the creative relationship between bastard villain and audience. In this text, Antipater is the only character with whom the spectators have any sustained emotional relationship. His soliloquies encourage them to identify, as fellow outsiders, with the inner life of the bastard. They are unable to escape his influence even though it is obvious that he is chillingly evil and has no redeeming features. The chorus remarks that Antipater's 'minde inchants him' (4.2.284); his speeches also bewitch the audience to become part of his demonic world. By a witty use of language, Antipater projects his villainous desires on to the audience's consciousness. In his first major soliloquy he repeats the word 'king' as a form of aural hypnosis:

When I complaine to Eccho but head-aking; it cries a king:
When I, in mirth, am musique making; it sounds, a king:
Each sight, when I am waking; presents a king:
When I my rest am taking; I see a king.

(1.3.342)

The word fills the audience's ears as well as Antipater's mind,
forcing them to share his obsessive ambitions. The subversive
power of the lines is disguised by the humour of Antipater's
verbal wit which entertains – perhaps even encouraging
applause. He gives a similar performance in his second soliloquy
where he repeats the word 'kill' as though relishing the sound
and idea of murder with the auditors (2.1.611–16). He also
makes use of colloquialisms and questions to establish direct
contact with them.

Antipater's evil imagination would certainly have been popular with the spectators at the Red Bull because his mind conjures
up dumb shows featuring devils, a much-loved part of this
theatre's performance repertoire (Leggatt 1992: 21). The dumb
shows are part of Antipater's soliloquies; when the devils appear
the audience are sufficiently 'drawn in' to experience the visions,
on one level, as part of Antipater's mind. By doing so, they give
his thoughts an external reality, demonstrated through the
different levels of realism in these interludes. The devils leave
scrolls of paper at Antipater's feet so the dumb shows are not just
representations of Antipater's thoughts. They are to be regarded
at surface value, as physical entities on the platform stage. They
are part of the shared consciousness of bastard and audience.
The demonic theatrical world finally has more immediate reality
for the audience than that of the saintly Marriam, the embodiment of transcendent good in the play. Antipater's visions suggest that supernatural reality is nothing more than a theatrical
fiction.

Much more so than the other characters, Antipater has a
strong sense of theatrical occasion. His second soliloquy comes
to a climax with a formal passage of grandiose exclamation which
'seems designed to get the performer an exit round' (Leggatt
1992: 90). His speeches display theatrical skill so openly that the
audience is encouraged to identify with him, against their better
judgement, because he shows an awareness of their presence and

their theatrical tastes. His scorn for Animis – 'Poxe of your purity, your ginger-bread' (5.2.79) – may have included a sly reference to the refreshments served in the playhouse since Overbury's character 'A Puny-Clarke' eats 'Ginger bread at a Play-house' (Gurr 1987: 37). Antipater's open acknowledgement of the theatre is dangerous; paradoxically, he appears more honest that the virtuous characters who do not admit the fictional nature of their moral world.

Watching Antipater, the audience are aware of the character, the role and the actor. Their interlinked consciousness forms the basis of what Martin Esslin calls the 'cubed semiosis' of the audience's response to character in performance. The character, Edmund or Gaspar or Antipater, also acts as an icon and stands for all bastards, symbols of isolation and villainy. At the same time, behind the icon, the audience see the original man – the actor – who is playing the part. As Esslin says, 'the man here stands for a sign that stands for a man who, in turn, is recognised and valued as the original man that he is' (Esslin 1987: 59). By establishing the performer's personal identity, the dramatist can use the bastard character as a commentator on other parts of the play and on the performance itself, as the following sections will go on to examine.

'Here's a large mouth indeed', bastard commentators

Detachment makes the bastard a useful figure to comment on the *locus* of the play. Because of the eclectic nature of popular Elizabethan and Jacobean theatre, a narrative structure was important in drawing the elements of a play together. Alexander Leggatt (1992) has shown how a freeze-frame effect, 'to hold a moment, an action, a character, a stage picture, and say to the audience 'Look at this', is one of the strongest tendencies in popular dramaturgy (114). The action is completed only by generalising the characters' experiences so that they embody principles which are operative outside the mimetic world, in the realm of the audience (115). To achieve this cross-over, locations and time periods are often blurred. Bastard characters are obviously suitable to effect this process since they stand on the borders of the play. The foot of the platform stage represents 'neutral ground that is even less localised than the acting area nearer the façade of the tiring house' (Styan 1959: 57) so, if placed here, the bastard has considerable power to deliver commentary of a didactic kind, perhaps reflecting the writer's own viewpoint.

Sometimes the bastard's choric voice clarifies the ideas dramatised in the *locus* of the play, thus consolidating the authority of that world. In *The Devil's Charter* (1606) by Barnabe Barnes, Alexander steps outside his role to moralise his experience and caution the audience about the evils of sin before he is dragged off to hell (3,239–47). Other bastard characters generalise the point of a scene in rhyming couplets, as in *The Troublesome Reign of John* (1591), where Philip's sentencing voice directs criticism towards the Catholic clergy. His rhyming couplets encourage the audience to read events as symbolic of widespread corruption in the Church. When he finds a nun inside the abbot's chest, he asks 'Is this the Nonries chastitie? Beshrewe me but I thinke / They goe as oft to Venery, as niggards to their drinke' (6.54). Philip's comments work as captions, showing how the tableaux of characters should be interpreted by loyal Protestant spectators. His role as sermonising chorus becomes obvious if we see the play as a dramatisation of the *Homilie Agaynst Disobedience and Wylful Rebellion* (1570). Even in later plays, written for private playhouses, the bastard continues to deliver *sententiae*. In Brome's *A Jovial Crew* (1641), Springlove concludes the first scene with the lines 'They dream of happiness that live in state / But they enjoy it that obey their fate' (1.1.494). His motto works on three levels: it applies to his own decision to abandon his position as steward, it prophesies Rachel and Meriel's plan to leave their father's estate and follow a beggar life, and it relates more generally to the play's message about the interrelated values of liberty and social responsibility.

More often than not, illegitimate commentary is used to subvert the authority of the play's *locus* rather than to crystallise the messages presented there. The bastard deconstructs the official text by reversing the normal functions of the moralising chorus. He can act as a safety valve for anti-official points of view which the dramatist wishes to express. At the simplest level, when a bastard uses *sententiae* to teach his own philosophy, his lines usually offer a controversial lesson. In *Ram Alley* (1608) by Lording Barry, Throat concludes a scene with words which challenge the traditional principle of a fixed social hierarchy: 'I now in pomp will ride, for 'tis most fit, / He should have state that riseth by his wit' (335). Similarly in *Edmund Ironside* (1595), Edricus tells the audience 'See what dissimulation brings to pass / how quickly I can make the king an ass' (1,426). He mocks the *locus* of the play by remarking on the skills used by himself and the actor playing the role of King.

Linguistic difference helps the bastard to comment on the language of the play and the value system inherent in it. Many bastard characters are set apart from their dramatic texts by a different register of speech – usually colloquial. Antipater's confidential phrases 'let me see' (1.3.396), or 'I have sent them packing' (5.2.51) and Edricus's exclamations 'Fie', 'Tut', 'Mass', in *Edmund Ironside* are typical. A bastard who appears to share the audience's vocabulary forms a verbal bridge between them and the play world. Soliloquies or asides with a marked speech difference, sometimes supplemented by the use of a rural accent, allow him to comment explicitly or implictly on the speech patterns used by other characters. Bastards follow the carnivalesque tradition of the Vice and the clown in the ways they deconstruct the dominant discourses of their plays. Michael Bristol (1985) argues that 'the extra-literary and even anti-literary interventions of clowns and their devilish accomplices reduce texts to schematic structures, partial scenarios' (150). The bastard commentator functions in the same way.

Bastard villains commonly use a deliberately direct form of speech to explain their plots. Their plain diction separates them, like the audience, from the elevated rhetoric of the dramatic world. In 1575 Goerge Gascoigne commented that 'the most ancient English words are or one syllable, so that the more monosyllables you use, the truer Englishman you shall seem' (Gascoigne 1982: 140). Jeremy Rowe (1986) shows that usurpers appear more attractive to the audience by employing 'units of a single phoneme, colloquial repetitions of a monosyllabic word' in soliloquy or direct address (33). Bastard usurpers follow this pattern, outlining their plots in simple language so as to appeal to the audience as honest men. Edricus in *Edmund Ironside* is a typical example. His first soliloquy (278–331) uses 338 monosyllables, 60 words of two syllables, 24 words of three syllables (six of which are proper names) and only three words of four syllables (one of which is the name Ambodexter).

Even when the bastard character does not appear to occupy a geographically marginal position on stage, his colloquial diction can set him apart, as in *The Revenger's Tragedy*. Like many bastards, Spurio uses the informal term 'dad' to refer to his father, thus undercutting the importance of paternal authority in the play. His interventions 'Pox on't, / What makes my dad speak now?' (1.2.81) and 'Old dad dead?' (5.1.109) make a striking contrast to the sham reverence of other characters at the trial and their hypocritical grief for the Duke's death. Spurio's exposé of the court's rottenness is related to Vindice's satirical purpose but, unlike Vindice, he speaks from a marginal position *within* the luxurious circle of the court, and so precipitates an internal collapse of its rhetoric.

Incongruous interventions by the bastard villain are humorous and demonstrate his joint inheritance from the Vice and the clown. The clown is a vital part of the theatre's carnival atmosphere who 'traverses the boundary between a represented world and the here-and-now world he shares with the audience' (Bristol 1985: 141). He is able to do this because his vernacular speech gives him a fluid social identity. Bastard commentators use a similar style; they frequently change the play's register from verse to prose and throw the verse into relief as the stiff, formal language of dramatic text rather than real life. A good example is the servant Scrub in Tatham's *Love Crowns the End* (1632), probably written for private performance. He stands out from the romantic narrative because he uses such homely turns of phrase as 'that time my mother's cat miscarried in the horse pond' (15). The heroes and heroines speak in verse and frequently in rhyme, while Scrub's prose reduces the concept of courtly love to an earthy physicality. However much the audience may have wished to isolate themselves from the popular voice, Scrub makes it impossible to ignore.

The characters who develop the disruptive possibilities of commentary most fully are Suckabus in *The Seven Champions of Christendom*, Thersites in *Troilus and Cressida* and Sir Richard in *King John*. By examining these figures in some detail it is possible to outline the subversive strategies found in less concentrated form in the choric speech of other bastards. *The Seven Champions of Christendom* (1635) is a skilful combination of popular ingredients designed to please the audience of the Red Bull. Suckabus – the only character not found in the source – seems to have been created specifically to provide a link between the audience and the make-believe world presented in the play. He is part of the fiction (the son of Tarpax and Calib and the hero's servant), but linguistically he occupies the same space as the audience. Suckabus's colloquial prose detaches him from the heroic bombast used by the champions of the epic narrative and makes them sound ridiculous. His speeches are cluttered with domestic detail; by focusing in on vulgar shared experience – food and sex – they make direct social contact with the London audience.

In a long soliloquy which opens the fifth act, Suckabus describes his search for food, beginning with an address to a particular individual: 'Ah sirrah, the world is pretty well amended with me now' (I3). His surprise at the romantic world of the play is made all the more amusing by his attempts to compare it to the audience's environment. He tells them that the giant's 'Pottage-pot will hold more water than the Thames' (I3) and tries to explain the size of a giant to an incredulous shepherd by comparing it to Tuttle-field 'neare *London* in *England*, where men goe a Trayning to get 'em good stomacks' (F4). Suckabus refers to the contemporary figures Cottingham (C4) and Tarre Box (F3). When he asks the devil 'Is Hobson there, or Dawson, or Tom Long?' (H1v), his familiarity with these well-known carriers locates him firmly in London (Freehafer 1969: 88–91). He identifies himself with a particular group of spectators, telling Tarpax 'Ile set all the prentices in the house about your eares if you strike me' (C3). He also shares the popular tastes of the Red Bull audience, asking Tarpax about the special effects he can expect in hell: 'Oh I doe love those things a life i'faith. Have you any squibs in you Country? any Green-men in your shows, and Whizers upon lines, Jacke Pudding upon Rope, or Sis in fire-workes?' (H1v–H2). Suckabus's interest in theatrical effects destroys the epic distance between audience and the heroic

material presented, undermining the play's glorification of
military valour in the defence of Christendom.

In *Troilus and Cressida* (1602), Thersites has nine out of the
play's fourteen soliloquies and addresses over half his lines to the
audience, indicating his importance as a commentator. As W. W.
Lawrence notes, 'the question is not of the effect of Thersites
upon the persons of the play, but upon the spectators in the
theatre' (Lawrence 1942: 433). It is easy to see what kind of
commentary Thersites gives by glancing at any of his soliloquies, all of which are in prose. They offer a very different
perspective on events from that put forward through the elevated and formal verse of the council scenes and the romanticised elements of the love plot. Thersites's speeches have an
extra-literary quality unique in the play. His observations on
the heroic figures of the epic narrative elaborate the project of
the bastard in Heywood's *Love's Mistress*, who reduces the story
of the Trojan war to that of 'a village of some twenty houses; and
Priam, as silly a fellow as I am, onely loving to play the good
fellow, hee had a great many bowsing lads; whom he called
sonnes' (113). Thersites satirises the Homeric myth by bringing
in the context of everyday life to familiarise the military leaders.
It is not easy to take these characters seriously having been told
that Ulysses and Nestor's wit 'was mouldy ere your grandsires
had nails on their toes' (2.1.105), and that the 'policy of those
crafty swearing rascals, that stale old mouse-eaten dry cheese,
Nestor, and that same dog-fox, Ulysses, is not proved worth a
blackberry' (5.4.9). The 1985 Royal Shakespeare Company production, directed by Howard Davies, placed Agamemnon, 'one
that . . . has not so much brain as ear wax' (5.1.51), and
Menelaus, 'a thrifty shoeing-horn in a chain' (5.1.55), on stage
while Thersites described them. Alun Armstrong's Thersites had
a Geordie accent, which helped to bring out the wry wit in such
comments and successfully set the character apart from both
Greeks and Trojans. In Act 3 Scene 3, he entered with bags of
groceries, performing the pageant of Ajax with the help of a
French bread stick and a pan for a helmet. The comic element of
the everyday again formed a bridge between the heroic material
and audience.

Thersites, whose comments emphasise a common human

physicality, mocks the social and intellectual hierarchies set up in the *locus* of the play and in the audience's world. It is impossible to identify *Troilus and Cressida* with a theatre space, although theories of a private performance at the Inns of Court are persuasive, especially since the epistle added to the 1609 quarto claims that the play was 'never clapper-clawd with the palmes of the vulger' or 'sullied, with the smoaky breath of the multitude' (Palmer 1982: 95). If this is true, then the comments of Theristes would be well suited to make fun of the intellectual snobbery of the audience. The epistle may include mockery of their elitism; it claims that spectators of the comedies 'have found that witte there, that they never found in themselves, and have parted better wittied then they came: feeling an edge of witte set upon them' (Palmer 1982: 95). Perhaps the 'edge of witte set upon them' is the voice of Thersites whose satire includes numerous references to the mouldy wit or lack of wit shown by figures of authority.

Thersites gives an interpretation of events which is obviously biased. It has a powerful influence on the audience because his irreverent humour is entertaining and uses a language familiar to them. For this reason, its effect is particularly dangerous. Thersites exposes the futility of the any endeavour to construct a fixed sense of self and to immortalise that self, either through the pursuit of honour or through reproduction. As a bastard, he is a constant reminder of the gap at the centre of patriarchal control. His presence on stage, in close proximity to the audience, makes conspicuous the uncertainty of paternal origin which undermines masculine identity. Janet Adelman rightly points out that Thersites is an emblematic bastard son of Helen, the whore/mother of the play whose infidelity undoes the whole masculine historical project, making everyone bastards (Adelman 1992: 45).

Thersites gives voice to the current of disruptive female sexuality and the fragmentations it creates in the play. Interposed between the action and the spectators, he forces the audience to hear that subversive voice, especially in the fifth act where he emerges as a guide to events. His line 'Now are they clapper-clawing one another; I'll go look on' (5.4.1) introduces the audience to the battle scenes through his eyes. He points out Diomedes and Troilus: 'Soft, here comes sleeve and t'other' (5.4.18), and Paris and Menelaus: 'The cuckold and the cuckold-maker are at it' (5.7.9), like a sports commentator. In the Howard Davies production (1985), Alun Armstrong spoke the introductory lines to the audience, pointing and gesturing to the characters before sitting on a suitcase – a personal prop – to watch each fight and comment. Thersites is isolated from the action. He reacts to the threats of Hector (5.4.26–32) and Margarelon (5.7.13–22) with the surprise of an audience member being asked to enter the play world. He appeals to his fellow spectators for information – 'What's become of the wenching rogues?' (5.4.32) – after the smooth progress of his narrative is interrupted. The text persistently encourages them to identify with the bastard's sceptical viewpoint.

The bastard in Shakespeare's *King John* seems further removed from the clownish commentator but he does have an important choric role. From the very beginning of the play his voice is notably different from that of the other *dramatis personae*. He is a 'good blunt fellow' (1.1.71) who has come 'from the country' (1.1.45), a detail emphasised by giving him a West Yorkshire accent in the BBC television production directed by David Giles (1986). Sir Richard speaks with a colloquial turn of phrase, referring to his brother's arms as 'eel-skins stuff'd' (1.1.141) and alluding to popular figures like 'Colbrand the Giant' (1.1.225). His vocabulary distances him from the rhetoric of the court and the battlefield. As Hillman (1992) remarks, 'the constant thrust of his commentary is to say the unsayable, to expose rotten façades and hypocritical accommodations masquerading as statecraft' (44). In this, he is like the female characters: Elinor begins the play by undercutting John's flamboyant line 'Our strong possession and our right for us' by reminding him that there is no right behind his fine words. Later Constance mocks King Philip's romantic description of the marriage of Lewes and Blanch as a 'blessed day' (3.1.75–82), pointing out that his betrayal has made 'faith itself to hollow falsehood change' (3.1.83–112). The bastard elaborates this deconstructive strategy more fully in soliloquies and asides.

In the second act, Sir Richard is a mediator of the audience's response. David Giles sees him as the 'touchstone and voice of

the audience's feelings' who diffuses their reaction by giving
expression to their impatience and disgust at the political
wrangling of the protagonists. To reinforce this idea, all Sir
Richard's comments are delivered directly to the camera in
close-up, which Giles sees as a substitute for the the actor's
movement 'right down to the front of the forestage' (Giles
1986: 30). The actor stands between the viewers and the
action, obliging them to interpret events from his ironic perspective. He satirises the use of elaborate rhetoric in his
comment on Citizen Hubert's words:

> Here's a large mouth indeed,
> That spits forth death and mountains, rocks and seas,
> Talks as familiarly of roaring lions
> As maids of thirteen do of puppy dogs!
> What cannoneer begot this lusty blood?
> He speaks plain cannon-fire, and smoke, and bounce,
> He gives the bastinado with his tongue;
> Our ears are cudgell'd – not a word of his
> But buffets better that a fist of France.
> 'Zounds, I was never so bethump'd with words
> Since I first call'd my brother's father dad.
>
> (2.1.457)

Behind his delight in the explosive alliterated consonants and the
rhythm of the verse, Sir Richard's sarcasm reminds spectators
that many words have been spoken but little has happened on
the battlefield. It also reminds them that they are watching a
series of artificially arranged speeches, a play. His earlier comment, comparing the citizens of Angiers to spectators in a
theatre (2.1.375–6), establishes the idea of metatheatre in pre-
paration for these lines on Hubert's role. The sarcasm works so
effectively because the heightened style contrasts with Sir
Richard's usually colloquial idiom to which he returns in the
last two lines with humorous effect. His reference to the lie of
calling his brother's father dad implies that all these grand
speeches are illegitimate – untrue in the world of the play and
parts of a fiction, a dramatic lie. Sir Richard then goes on to
criticise the style and content of Lewis's hypocritical declaration
of love to Blanch. In an aside, he sarcastically repeats Lewis's
words 'Drawn in the flattering table of her eye', and deliberately

mistakes the metaphorical meaning by elaborating an image of execution, which is probably what most of the audience would like to imagine happening to Lewis (2.1.504–9). In Shakespeare's play (unlike *The Troublesome Reign*), the bastard has no personal interest in Blanch as a marriage partner so his view seems more objective. His soliloquies compel the spectators to see behind the rhetoric used to celebrate the marriage and to recognise it for the hypocritical and shabby compromise which it is.

Sir Richard dramatises the discourse of power as well as analysing it. In his very first soliloquy he stages a dialogue between himself, the new-made knight, and a traveller, whose responses he also performs (1.1.189–204). His self-conscious role play mocks the 'dialogue of compliment' (1.1.201), and shows how easy it is to shift between the parts of bastard, knight and traveller. He demonstrates that social position, including the high status of princes or kings, is a construct of performance not the result of natural authority. Since his lines are directed outwards to the audience, his performance implicity argues that power in the 'worshipful society' beyond the theatre is no less theatrical.

Sir Richard's soliloquies and asides teach the audience to regard the political and rhetorical manoeuvrings of all the characters on stage with suspicion. It is difficult to believe that, with this sophisticated awareness, either he or the audience can become totally immersed in his patriotic bombast of the last act, and particularly the last speech:

> This England never did, nor never shall,
> Lie at the proud foot of a conqueror,
> But when it first did help to wound itself.
> Now these her princes are come home again,
> Come the three corners of the world in arms,
> And we shall shock them. Nought shall make us rue,
> If England to itself do rest but true.
>
>   (5.7.112)

As David Scott Kastan (1983) has noted, this speech has a self-conscious fictionality about it. Sir Richard deliberately fictionalises history as part of his project to theatricalise power and so emphasise its exclusions and its paradoxes (as discussed in the previous chapter). The Renaissance regarded the truth-status of the chronicles as an important element of their political effectiveness (Braunmuller 1988: 321). Sir Richard therefore behaves radically by bringing into a public arena – the theatre – the barely articulated awareness that the chronicles were themselves moulded for specific political purposes. His final speech is spoken out to the English audience as much as to the other characters. It fictionalises not only the drama but the whole historical record as different but related types of political 'play'.

'*O this is* serio joco' *bastards and metatheatre*

In the last act of *Herod and Antipater*, Antipater is imprisoned by Herod and steps back to contemplate his situation in soliloquy:

> Never till now hadst thou Antipater,
> True cause t' account with wisedome; all thy life
> Has beene but sport and tennis-play: but this,
> O this is *serio joco* such a game,
> As cals thy life in question; nay, thy fame;
> Thy vertue, praise, and reputation:
> What art thou now? a prisoner; that's a slave:
> Nay, slave to slaves; slavish extremity!
> But now a king; but now a cast-away;
> Crown'd and uncrown'd.
>
> > (5.2.7)

His lines work on several levels of dramatic reality: they show an emotional detachment as though describing Antipater's eventful career from the outside. They are also about the actor's changing roles through the play and in his career. The irony of the words is, of course, that the actor's job is 'sport and tennis-play' rather than reality. It involves imitating the roles of bastard, king, or slave. It is *serio joco* or serious play, in that it is the actor's livelihood and, because of the equivocal nature of performance, it is a 'game' which calls his life in question in the minds of the authorities.

Antipater's soliloquies in this scene demonstrate the disruptive potential of the *platea* function which priviliges the act of representing over what is represented. By drawing attention to his own playing, the actor makes the role of king and slave seem equally artificial and interchangeable, a point that is reinforced by the subsequent action which involves a daring split-scene effect rather like the one at the end of Shakespeare's *Richard III*. When Antipater has finished his soliloquy, Herod appears in his palace on a different part of the stage. Awareness of the actor exposes his high status position as a theatrical role. Antipater goes on to extend the boundaries of his radical exposé beyond the dramatic world by generalising the point. He explains to the audience

> O, what a thing is man! how quickly made
> And mar'd, and yet againe reedified,
> All with a breath; to make us know, in kings,
> Consists the great worke of creation

(5.2.83)

Antipater implies that the 'great worke of Creation' which makes and unmakes people in the real world outside the Red Bull theatre is nothing more substantial than the stuff of drama, the 'breath' of a governing discourse of power. Having shown that stage kings are no more than the text they live in, Antipater proposes that this is also true of rulers who perform on the stage of the world. Their words may have the power to raise or ruin others, but they are utterly dependent on language to sustain their own authority.

As we can see from this example, the bastard is adept at using metatheatre to undermine powerful figures on stage and beyond. Obviously, he does not have a monopoly on such effects, but he is naturally located on the periphery of the drama and so is well placed to give this kind of commentary. His liminal nature allows him to exploit a schizophrenic identity as character and actor, part of the audience and part of the play, and to confuse the boundaries between 'playing' and 'being' with disturbing consequences for the spectators.

Villainous bastards take up a theatrical stance in relation to their plots, once again showing their inheritance from the Vice tradition. They name themselves, or other characters, as actors in their schemes and behave like stage managers of the action, displaying the props or costumes they will use. In Barnes's *The*

Devil's Charter, Lucretia plans to perform 'a cunning parte' (679) by killing her husband. She brings in her own scenery – a chair on which she will tie Gismond in order to stab him – and introduces him with the words 'Heere comes the subject of my Tragedy' (581). She makes him sign a suicide note declaring her innocence and remarks 'So now that part is playd, what followes now?' (658), echoing the audience's own curiosity and drawing attention to the structured order of events in the play as a whole. Her confident direction of the action creates a critical distance between the audience and the horrific murder, encouraging them to see it as an ingenious work of art rather than be moved by it as tragedy.

This is an important element of the villain's metatheatrical function. In *Claudius Tiberius Nero*, Tiberius treats the murders of his family as pieces of theatre and so diffuses the heightened tension which could easily produce laughter at an inopportune moment. When the number of deaths escalates at an alarming rate, he becomes self-consciously theatrical. He hears that Nerva is dead, and says 'Well, vertue go with him, vice stay with me' (3,123). After the death of Celsus, he comments 'His part is past, part of my part's to come' (3,195). The humour generated by this remark is necessary as the swift succession of violent deaths is reaching the point of ridiculousness. Tiberius's metatheatrical references draw attention to a theatre of power because of his high status position. When Sejanus begins to report Tiberius's villainy, the Emperor says 'The man begins to play the Orator / Get him a Throne to grace his eloquence' (2,688). Behind the reference to Sejanus, and the actor who plays him, the audience perceive the theatrical nature of Tiberius's own position as an eloquent emperor with a throne. Rhetorical skill rather than divine right is the essence of authority.

Tiberius's lines on the actor as orator give support to B. L. Joseph's theory of a formal style of acting which relied on a series of conventional gestures (Joseph 1951). If the gestures of oratory from Bulwer's *Chirologia* and *Chironomia* were used in the theatre, then several of them seem peculiarly appropriate to a 'conventional' presentation of a bastard villain. Joseph points out that the use of the left hand to accompany speech indicated the slyness and evil intentions of the speaker, and quotes Bulwer on the subject of 'the fellonious procacity and craft of this guilefull *Hand*, which is prone by a slie insinuation with more subtile secrecie to present it selfe to any sinister intention' (Joseph 1951: 103). Use of the left hand would be very apt for the bastard character because of his strong associations with the 'bar sinister', and his birth 'Something about, a little from the right' (*King John* 1.1.170). In fact Sir Richard's speech about his birth could make use of such gestures to emphasise the darker side of his nature in the early part of *King John*. A folding of the arms, indicating a refusal to communicate or participate, would also be appropriate for the bastard figure excluded from the legitimate world's business. At the beginning of Armin's *The Valiant Welshman* (1612), for instance, Codigune's silence throughout the betrothal of Guiniver and Caradoc in Act 1 Scene 4 would have been strengthened by this pose. His soliloquy of anger at the end of the scene, delivered with accompanying gestures from his left hand to signify 'the captivity of unlawfull desire and rapacity' (Joseph 1951: 103), would have quickly established his identity as a villainous bastard malcontent.

If the actor playing a bastard villain assumed a conventional set of gestures to suggest his role, then the character's adoption of another role – to deceive – must have entailed the use of another set of gestures. In *The Devil's Charter*, Alexander counsels Caesar to act 'With Arte, looke sullaine and demure, / Hold downe thy head, like one swolne up with sorrow' (1,985). In such cases, the audience would have been able to judge the skill of the character in producing these gestures 'naturally', and the skill of the actor in illustrating the practice of his own art. This would have added an extra dimension to the 'contemplation of regression' effect achieved when the actor played a character who was playing a part within the action of the play. By admiring the bastard character's acting ability, the audience become aware of the actor's own skill in playing the bastard. The art of the player is brought to the fore.

This happens in deceptions like Gaspar's pretences to be the 'honest' and humble servant of Alonzo in *The Bastard*, and in Edricus's adopted roles as Stitch (1,226–41), and as a wounded follower of Edmund in *Edmund Ironside* (5.1.1,653–736). The spectators' enjoyment of the play is due, at least partly, to their appreciation of the actor's skill in rendering the part(s) he plays. The metatheatrical dimension could have produced much humour to be shared by bastard and audience – if the bastard's 'acting' was overdone, or he found it difficult to maintain his new set of gestures and reverted to using his left hand when setting out to persuade another character of his good intentions towards them. A consummate performance of honesty could have had a much more unsettling effect, making it impossible to distinguish between the insincere performance by the bastard and that of the really 'honest' characters. Seeing this, the audience would be encouraged to doubt the sincerity of any social role – outside the theatre as well as inside it – and to suspect the piety, virtue or intelligence of those society held up for admiration.

Bastard villains who act in their own plots blur divisions between sincere and insincere performance, highlighting the theatrical nature of all social interaction on and off stage. Edmund's performance in *King Lear* is a particularly strong example. In the manner of the Vice, Edmund creates a play within the play, setting up the moral structure of the *Lear* world as fiction by describing his plot in extra-dramatic terms. He introduces Edgar as 'the catastrophe of the old comedy' (1.2.134), alludes to his own 'cue', and adopts his part as 'villainous melancholy' (1.2.135). In Act 2 Scene 1 he becomes an actor-director, forcing Edgar to play the roles of villain and fugitive, then drawing his own sword to stage-manage an artificial fight. Edmund's metatheatre has a useful distancing effect in that it helps to concentrate tragic energy onto the Lear plot. His acting skills with Edgar and Gloucester have a more sinister resonance as well. His superb impersonations of the loyal son and brother obscure differences between his villainous role play and the genuine performance of social roles dictated by natural law. He shows that this law may be a fictional construct adopted by fathers and legitimate sons to promote self-advancement.

Role play can delegitimise particular authoritarian figures, as we can see from Throat's part in *Ram Alley* by Lording Barry (1608). Throat uses two contrasting languages to focus critical attention on the legal profession. When he puts on his gown to 'seem a lawyer, which am indeed / But merely dregs and off-scum of the law' (288), he embellishes his speech with Latin quotations and allusions. In confidential address to the audience, he reverts to informal English to criticise his own role and that of other lawyers who use language to deceive:

> these are tricks of the long fifteens
> To give counsels, and to take fees on both sides;
> To make 'em friends, and then to laugh at them!
> Well, this thrives well, this is a common trick
> . . . I have a trick
> To go beyond all these. If Small-shankes come,
> And bring rich Sommerfield's heir – I say no more
> But 'tis within this sconce to go beyond them.
>
> (300)

His confidential phrase 'I say no more' gives the audience a conspiratorial 'wink' and encourages them to follow his subversive argument about the nature of legal discourse. According to Throat, this language has no higher claim to authority than dramatic scripts. Its performative nature is obvious when Throat meets another representative of the legal profession, Justice Tutchin. Tutchin is a genuine lawyer in the urban world of the play but, as far as the audience is concerned, both characters are roles presented by actors. *Ram Alley* uses Throat to show that real lawyers are the same as the scandalous actors who mimic the powerful on stage. Since the play was performed at the White-friars, in close proximity to the Inns of Court, the actions of a juvenile player aping the lawyers would have been all the more resonant.

Perhaps the finest example of lines which reflect the dual consciousness of bastard character and actor is found in the anonymous *Wily Beguiled* (1602). The Prologue establishes the identity of the actor behind the role of Robin Goodfellow when he says 'tell their fiery poet that, before I have done with him, I'll make him do penance upon the stage in a calf's skin' (222). As the 'fiery poet', the actor playing Robin has another identity as author of himself. He seems to be constructed outside the official text and the Prologue's later comments elaborate his independent existence by making it clear that he is part of a self-fashioned play. This may have been *Wylie Beguilye*, performed in 1566 at Merton College, Oxford, and probably

revised as *Wily Beguiled* (Maxwell 1922). Robin's calf-skin suit,
the costume which was worn by the festival fool, links his text to
folk ritual and points up the incongruity of his appearance in the
revised play. The Prologue says:

> Go to that barm-froth poet, and to him say,
> He hath quite lost the title of his play;
> His calf-skin jests from hence are clean exil'd.
> Thus once you see, that Wily is beguil'd.
>
> (223)

It seems to be a superfluous part where the actor will have to
force his way into the drama, which is what happens when Robin
appears. Other characters fear him as an alien and he seems to
exist on a different level of reality from them, telling the audience 'I play the bugbear whersoe'er I come and make them all
afraid' (246). It is only with directions from Churms that Robin
finds a place to perform his part. His preparations to frighten
Sophos in the woods emphasise his metatheatrical identity. It
seems to be the actor rather than the character who promises the
audience 'you shall see, I'll make fine sport with him' (268), and
tells them 'I'll put me on my great carnation-nose, and wrap me
in a rowsing calf-skin suit, and come like some hobgoblin . . . I'll
play the devil, I warrant ye' (268).

The audience have been anticipating the arrival of this fiend-
like character since the prologue. To their disappointment, no
doubt, its eventual appearance is but brief. Robin returns
dejected and without calf-skin costume (316), to reinforce the
identity of the performer, rejected from this particular play as the
Prologue had warned. Like the satanic Antipater in *Herod and
Antipater*, Robin theatricalises the supernatural, thereby undercutting society's belief in a spiritual world. His mockery of the
costume and verse used by the actor playing Sophos, a love-
stricken student (268), would probably have had an extra-
dramatic effect, satirising members of the student audience of
Wylie Beguile at Merton College and perhaps spectators of the
later performance, supposedly by the children of St Paul's.

Metatheatrical effects are not confined to the bastard descen-
dants of the Vice. Sometimes a virtuous character can employ an
extended use of theatrical metaphor. A good example is seen in

Brome's *A Jovial Crew*, performed at the Cockpit Theatre in 1641. Springlove, the bastard, is used to fuse the worlds of the action, the plays within the play, and the world of the spectators. This would have won approval at the Cockpit because, as Michael Neill (1978) points out, Caroline audiences had a very sophisticated theatrical awareness. Their preoccupation with dramatic wit meant that a playwright could exploit a mannerist style which encouraged both emotional engagement and a detached intellectual analysis of how that engagement had been achieved. An audience could be drawn into the action only to be forced, a moment later, to step back and contemplate the witty artifice which was used to do this. The danger was that cultivation of a social aesthetic was often at the expense of larger moral and political issues. *A Jovial Crew* is a play deeply engaged with contemporary politics. It makes Springlove responsible for manipulating the audience's theatrical sophisitication for directly political ends.

From the beginning, Springlove is both actor and spectator. He supervises events with an omniscience which other characters do not have. When Rachel and Meriel reveal their plan to turn beggars, he tells them that he already knows their decision, using imagery of performance to describe their proposed roles:

> I have seen you, too, kind gentlemen and ladies, and overheard you in your quaint design to new create yourselves out of the worldly blessings and spiritual graces Heaven has bestow'd upon you, to be partakers and coactors, too, in those vile courses, which you call delights
>
> (2.1.218)

This, and his revelation that he has overheard the conversation between Hearty and Oldrents (2.1.254–5), suggests that he does not leave the stage unless, perhaps, to be concealed amongst the audience during scenes where his character does not appear. Springlove is also established as a performer. He tells Rachel and Meriel how he had to act the part of a beggar (2.1.294–308) and shows his skill in this role in later scenes (3.1.53–67, 3.1.141–74, 3.1.455–506). Once he has begged from Amie and Martin, Springlove reverts to his omniscient viewpoint again, telling the lovers that he knows who they are and did so throughout the exchange that preceded (3.1.510–14). A strange duality of playing and living echoes through Springlove's words. After the beggars' Utopia masque, Vincent says 'If, Springlove, thou could'st post now to thy tiring-house, and fetch all our clothes, we might get off most neatly' (4.2.267). Springlove's world is that of the Cockpit Theatre as well as the world of the action. Kaufmann (1961) and Butler (1984) both feel that he is Brome's spokesman, demonstrating the value of theatre at a time when the playhouses were threatened with closure. Springlove shows on-stage and off-stage audiences that the theatre is a place with a social and political function. In the rural environment of *A Jovial Crew* he regenerates the intransigent social order by means of role-playing games which reveal the theatrical nature of social hierarchy. He impresses this lesson on the patriarchal figures of authority – Oldrents, Justice Clack and Hearty – by re-presenting the events he has directed 'in little' in 'The Merry Beggars', a play within the play. Springlove's on-stage use of theatre for an educational purpose alerts the off-stage audience to the fact that *A Jovial Crew* will have the same immediate relevance for them. A bridge is forged between 'The Merry Beggars' and the 'real' world of *A Jovial Crew* when Springlove claims Amie, the heiress, as his wife. It is unclear to Justice Clack whether the marriage contract is part of the play or part of 'reality':

> *Sent.* See, sir, your niece presented to you.
>   Springlove takes Amie
> *Cla.* What, with a speech from one of the players?
>   Speak, sir, and be not daunted. I am favorable.
> *Spr.* Then, by your favor, sir, this maiden is my wife.
> *Cla.* Sure you are out o' your part. That is to say,
>   You must begin again.
> *Spr.* She's mine by solemn contract sir.
>
>   (5.1.454)

Springlove's challenge to bring the play world into the 'real' world remarkably reveals the performative nature of all vows, and all speech acts. In the light of his bastardy it is highly appropriate that the vow in question is a marriage vow. The tense confrontation between fact and fiction capitulates Oldrents's revelation 'Here are no beggars . . ., no rogues, nor players: but a select company' (5.1.469). Social identity is very unstable, a point that is reinforced when the 'real' beggar, the Patrico, also turns out to be a gentleman by birth. Springlove, who is transformed from beggar to steward and then to gentleman (as the son of Oldrents), reconciles differences between these socially diverse roles by representing them all as an actor. His rise in status argues the value of actors to an elitist audience but at the same time it mocks their snobbery, revealing that all social positions are theatrical, that their speech is performative or context-dependent, and that the people who embody them are actors – whether self-consciously or not.

In the epilogue, Springlove makes explicit the relationship between the political lessons of the plays and the off-stage audience. (To form a framework around events he should have the prologue as well. This would establish his link with the audience and set up the idea of levels of 'play', since he could then remain at the side of the stage with his books and watch the exchange between Oldrents and Hearty, before making his first entrance as Springlove the character.) Even in the epilogue he continues to play with the audience's sense of dramatic wit. He superimposes the identities of actors, characters, and characters as beggars in the text; then strips away the levels of 'play' to show the actors begging for the acceptance of their performance:

> Tho' we are, now, no beggars of the crew,
> We count it not a shame to beg of you.
> The justice, here, has given his pass free
> To all the rest unpunish'd; only we
> Are under censure, till we do obtain
> Your suffrages, that we may beg again;
> And often, in the course we took today,
> Which was intended for your mirth, a play;
> Not without action, and a little wit.
> Therefore we beg your pass for us and it.

$$(5.1.503)$$

Springlove, the omniscient engineer of the piece, is an appropriate spokesperson for the theatre. He has conducted the audience through the events of the play, appealing to their sense of theatrical wit by crossing boundaries from actor to character. Having won their trust, in the final act he collapses the division between aesthetic appreciation and political purpose and stands as an eloquent spokesman for the socially transformative power of theatrical art.

Springlove's use of metatheatre to win the audience's 'suffrages' and so free actors from 'under censure' (5.1.507–8) is a much more elaborate version of the strategy employed by all bastard characters who speak outside the official discourse of their plays. All draw more or less explicitly on the subversive power provided by the theatre itself. They activate a shared awareness of the theatrical occasion to defy the authorities' attempts to control drama (and illegitimate energy) by censorship. In a few plays their rebellions against the 'well-defined author-function' are made quite explicit, as in *Wily Beguiled* where the bastard brings in an unauthorised performance against the wishes of the Prologue (who presumably speaks for the controlling author-function). Another way of expressing open defiance was to make the text itself illegitimate, without an authorising paternal signature, anonymous.

'Not so wise to know's own father': bastard texts

Illegitimacy is a metaphor for loss of authorial control, as in the preface to Heywood's *The English Traveller* (1625). Heywood relates how, hearing that his play had come 'accidentally to the Presse', he did not wish 'that it should passe as *filius populi*, a Bastard without a father to acknowledge it', and so published it under his own name (1964, 2: 5). Bastardy is identified with anonymity. The preface to the anonymous play *Claudius Tiberius Nero* also defines the text as illegitimate. It is 'a yong Scholler' whose verbal construction seems to indicate 'that his Father was an Academian'. The publisher points out 'eyther hee hath lost his Father or his Father hath lost him' and asks Sir Arthur Mannering to adopt the play as a guardian 'in regard he is fatherles' (A3). Tiberius not only dominates the text and gives it his name; by means of the preface, he becomes the play. A similar set of associations surrounds *The Sophister*. Like *Claudius Tiberius Nero*, it is published anonymously and is linked to an academic context. The name 'The Sophister' relates to the bastard usurper, the fatherless play, and the persuasive skill of the actor who will perform the part. It is a focus for the multi-levelled realities designed specifically to appeal to the 'Academi-call Auditors' who make up 'the Vatican of Wit', in the University (A3). Mercury, who acts as a prologue, addresses the auditors with the words

> But here the Sophister, *how to* commence,
> *Or* take's Degree, *as yet is in* suspence:
> *By* keeping of his Acts, *he now will try*
> *To get your* Placet *by his* Fallacy.

(A3v)

The Sophister, held in suspense by the prologue, constructed in 'Acts', and employing the character of Fallacy, is the play. As its name makes clear, it is a fictional construct. At the same time, the Sophister who uses the quality of dishonesty (fallacy) to engineer several 'Acts' or actions, in order to take on the 'Degree' of ruler, and the title 'The Sophister', is the bastard character. Also held 'in suspense' is the actor, who will try to 'get your Placet', or approval, by his good performance of the character Fallacy.

Loss of authorial control is dramatised in the madness of Discourse who has been poisoned by illegitimate Fallacy:

> *Fal.* How lik'st thou this Ambiguity? is not his Style chang'd since?
> *Am.* Yes me thinks; before he spake in Verse, now hee scannes not his words.
> *Fal.* Oh thou shalt heare him talke out of all measure.

(B3v)

When Fallacy usurps the chair of State, he renames himself The Sophister, linking his own illegitimate rule and the un-authorised printed text. The play concludes by cementing this link and commenting on the sophistication of the audience's response. The Epilogue refers to the actor, the character and the work in the lines '*The* SOPHISTER *doth on your suffrage stand,* / *That for* his grace, *you would put to your Hand*' (I4). The important words here are 'his grace', the title of authority which Fallacy had usurped. By accepting THE SOPHISTER (play, character and actor) as 'his grace', and applauding, the academic auditors show their agreement that all authority is an illegitimate verbal

construction rather than a god-given right. They give their
placet, or approval, to the play's radical suggestion.

The process of bastardising the text is taken further in *The
Bastard*. The prologue and epilogue form a strong framework
round Gaspar's metatheatrical remarks by presenting the play
and the character as synonymous. The Prologue tells the audience 'by your hand / Our Brat must dye or live, must fall or
stand', and asks them to act as a guardian to the drama and 'take
him to his feet' (A4). The text's illegitimacy, as 'not so Wise to
know's own Father', draws attention to its anonymous authorship, and could refer to the dangers of writing, printing or
performing plays at a time when the theatres were closed
(1652). The Prologue suggests that the audience may have
participated in the production of such works themselves: 'My
Faith assures me, many of you have known / To make some
Bastards which you durst not own / For shame or fear' (A4). As
well as referring to illegitimate people, these lines indicate literary texts and performances. The fact that their authors dare not
own them 'for shame of fear' implies their radical nature. In the
light of *The Bastard*'s own controversial elements, the absence of
Cosmo Manuche's name on the title page is perhaps not as 'hard
to explain' as Harbage suggests (1936: 227).

Illegitimate identity is especially appropriate for this play
because it is constructed out of fragments from other Renaissance texts. It is described by the Prologue as 'A Spanish Bastard
in an English dresse' (A4) indicating its debt to Leonard
Digges's *Gerado, the Unfortunate Spaniard* (1622) a translation
of a Spanish poem by Cespedes y Meneses. This forms the basis
of the play but it also borrows heavily from Shakespeare, including a whole scene from *Romeo and Juliet* and part of 1.3 from
Richard III (Hayton 1988). The epilogue makes a wry allusion
to these unacknowledged borrowings by describing the bastard's
grave in lines that resemble the inscription on Shakespeare's
tombstone:

Let not your hasty Censures *raise those stones*
Which doe Inurn him or disturb his Bones,
And throw his Ashes *in the air, be wise,*

Lest his proud Dust *rise, and put out your eyes.*
. . . 'twere sin, your breath
Should sting his Name, *and blast him after* Death

(M1)

The speech elides the dead Shakespeare with the dead character and the illegitimate text. It is an appropriate monument to the subversive activities of bastard characters across the period, whose interventions between official text and audience bring about the death of the author and open up the text as a piece of theatre which disrupts accepted notions of authority. Even though it is impossible to know for certain how these characters' soliloquies worked in the theatres for which they were originally written, it is clear that the bastard is a powerful means to manipulate the audience's response.

Ideas of illegitimate literary and theatrical production make a fitting conclusion to my consideration of bastardy as a subversive force in Renaissance drama. It presented a very basic threat to order in England because it exposed the fragility of masculine verbal law around which society was structured. As something deviant, it could be constructed as a useful 'other', persecuted as an object lesson which demonstrated the full power of patriarchal authority. At the same time it existed beyond the limits of that authority in a world of 'otherness' whose presence forced the ruling ideology into a state of play. A politics of illegitimacy encoded and threatened to deconstruct some of the most basic tenets of patriarchy. By treating bastardy in their plays, dramatists were engaging with a contemporary economic and practical problem and dealing with a politically sensitive issue. Throughout the period, the majority of plays appear to follow orthodox public opinion by characterising bastards as villains. These characters can be read as projections of social and spiritual insecurity in the period. In a secular context they are linked to malcontented groups in Renaissance England produced by contemporary social and economic problems. Dramatists found ways of constructing their bastard villains so as to vindicate the letter of the orthodox view while subverting its spirit. The dynamics of the performance space were especially important for this. The popular belief that bastards conceived in the 'lusty stealth of nature' were of a more 'fierce quality' led to the creation of very dynamic and dramatically attractive characters whose energy makes them eloquent spokesmen for suppressed or disadvantaged groups and revolutionary ideas. Prejudices notwithstanding, the bastard is a theatrically versatile character. Some plays challenge the view of bastardy as evil and depict virtuous illegitimates or 'naturals' who are foolish but can still make a searching critique of legitimate hegemony. The popularity of the type suggests the importance of illegitimacy as an indicator, and perhaps instigator, of crisis in Renaissance England. It is testament to the dangers of illegitimate power that in a play published in 1652, the bastard turns to the audience and says

> *The world so swarms with* Bastards *now, that I*
> *Need not despair for want of* Company;
> *I'me in among the Throng.*

> (*The Bastard*: A4v)

The Parliamentary forces had triumphed, the paternal governor, Charles I, had been tried and executed. The world had been turned upside down and was, at least from some perspectives, in everything illegitimate.

Appendix

Plays with bastard characters, 1588–1652

The Appendix lists plays with bastard characters, or characters threatened with bastardy, but excludes plays dealing with bastard baby situations. The editions cited are those from which quotations and references are taken.

1588   *The Misfortunes of Arthur*, Thomas Hughes (with Bacon, Trotte, Fulbeck, Lancaster, Yelverton, Penroodock and Flower), in John W. Cunliffe (ed.), *Early English Classical Tragedies*, Oxford, Clarendon Press, 1912, 217–96.

1590   *Henry VI Part One*, William Shakespeare, in G. Blakemore Evans (ed.), *The Riverside Shakespeare*, Boston, Houghton Mifflin, 1974, 596–629.

1590   *Henry VI Part Two*, William Shakespeare, in *The Riverside Shakespeare*, 630–70.

1590   *The Cobbler's Prophecy*, Robert Wilson, ed. A. C. Wood, Malone Society Reprints, Oxford, Oxford University Press, 1914.

1591   *Edward I*, George Peele, in C. T. Prouty (ed.), *Life and Works*, New Haven, Yale University Press, 1952–70, 2, 1–212.

1591   *The Life and Death of Jack Straw*, Anon., ed. Kenneth Muir and F. P. Wilson, Malone Society Reprints, Oxford, Oxford University Press, 1957.

1591   *The Troublesome Raigne of John, King of England*, Anon., ed. J. W. Sider, Garland Renaissance Drama, New York, Garland Publishing, 1979.

1592   *A Knack to Know a Knave*, Anon., in W. Carew Hazlitt (ed.), *Dodsley's Old English Plays*, fourth edition, London, Reeves & Turner, 1874–6, 6, 503–91.

1594   *The Lamentable Tragedy of Locrine*, Anon., ed. Jane Lytton Gooch, Garland English Texts, London, Garland Publishing, 1981.

1595   *Shakespeare's Lost Play Edmund Ironside*, Anon., ed. Eric Sams, London, Wildwood House, 1986.

1596   *King John*, William Shakespeare, in *The Riverside Shakespeare*, 765–99 (may have been written in 1591 before *The Troublesome Raigne*).

1596 *The Famous History of Captain Thomas Stukeley*, Anon., ed. Judith
      C. Levinson, Malone Society Reprints, Oxford, Oxford University
      Press, 1975.

1598 *Much Ado About Nothing*, William Shakespeare, in *The Riverside
      Shakespeare*, 327–64.

1599 *Edward IV Part One*, Thomas Heywood, in R. H. Shepherd (ed.),
      The Dramatic Works of Thomas Heywood, New York, Russell &
      Russell, 1964, 1, 1–90.

1599 *The Thracian Wonder*, Anon., printed by Thomas Johnson, sold by
      Francis Kirkham, London, 1661.

1600 *The Blind Beggar of Bednal Green*, Henry Chettle, John Day and
      William Haughton, in *The Works of John Day*, ed. A. H. Bullen
      (1881), reprinted with an introduction by Robin Jeffs, London,
      Holland Press, 1963, 1–116.

1600 *Lust's Dominion*, Thomas Dekker, John Day and William Haugh-
      ton, in Fredson Bowers (ed.), *The Dramatic Works of Thomas
      Dekker*, Cambridge, Cambridge University Press, 1961, 4, 115–230.

1601 *All Fools*, George Chapman, ed. Frank Manley, Regents Renaissance
      Drama, London, Arnold, 1968.

1602 *Troilus and Cressida*, William Shakespeare, in *The Riverside Shake-
      speare*, 443–98.

1602 *Wily Beguiled*, Anon., in *Dodsley's Old English Plays*, 9, 219–330.

1604 *The Birth of Hercules*, Anon., ed. R. Warwick Bond, Malone Society
      Reprints, Oxford, Oxford University Press, 1911.

1605 *King Lear*, William Shakespeare, in *The Riverside Shakespeare*,
      1, 255–305.

1606 *The Devil's Charter*, Barnabe Barnes, ed. R. B. McKerrow, Louvain,
      A. Uystpruyst (1904), Kraust Reprint, Nendeln, Liechtenstein, 1970.

1606 *Volpone, or, The Fox.* Ben Jonson, ed. R. B. Parker, Revels Plays,
      Manchester, Manchester University Press, 1983.

1606 *The Revenger's Tragedy* (Middleton?) Tourneur, ed. Brian Gibbons,
      New Mermaids, London, Benn, 1971.

1606 *The Miseries of Enforced Marriage*, George Wilkins, ed. Glenn H.
      Blayney, Malone Society Reprints, Oxford, Oxford University Press,
      1964.

1606 *A Yorkshire Tragedy*, Anon., ed. A. C. Cawley and Barry Gaines,
      Revels Plays, Manchester, Manchester University Press, 1986.

1607 *The Tragedy of Claudius Tiberius Nero*, Anon., ed. W. W. Greg,
      Malone Society Reprints, Oxford, Oxford University Press, 1914.

1608 *Ram-Alley; or, Merry Tricks*, Lording Barry, in *Dodsley's Old English
      Plays*, 10, 265–380.

1608   *The Birth of Merlin*, William Rowley and ?, Worcester, Element
       Books, 1989.

1610   *The Golden Age*, Thomas Heywood, in *Dramatic Works*, 3, 1–79.

1610   *The Winter's Tale*, William Shakespeare, in *The Riverside Shake-
       speare*, 1,564–605.

1611   *A King and No King*, Francis Beaumont and John Fletcher, in
       Fredson Bowers (ed.), *Dramatic Works*, Cambridge, Cambridge
       University Press, 1966–92, 2, 167–314.

1611   *The Silver Age*, Thomas Heywood, in *Dramatic Works*, 3, 81–164.

1611   *The Brazen Age*, Thomas Heywood, in *Dramatic Works*, 3, 165–256.

1611   *The Tempest*, William Shakespeare, in *The Riverside Shakespeare*,
       1,606–38.

1611   *Tom a Lincoln*, Anon., ed. John Pitcher, Malone Society Reprints,
       Oxford, Oxford University Press, 1992.

1612   *The Valiant Welshman*, R[obert] A[rmin], ed. John S. Farmer, Old
       English Drama, Students Facsimile edition, London, 1913.

1612   *The Iron Age Parts 1 and 2*, Thomas Heywood, *Dramatic Works*, 3,
       257–431.

1612   *Every Man in his Humour*, Ben Jonson, ed. Martin Seymour Smith,
       New Mermaids, London, Benn, 1966 (1612 = approximate date of
       revision of Q1).

1613   *A Chaste Maid in Cheapside*, Thomas Middleton, ed. Alan Brissen-
       den, New Mermaids, London, Benn, 1968.

1613   *The Witch*, Thomas Middleton, in Peter Corbin and Douglas Sedge
       (eds), *Three Jacobean Witchcraft Plays*, Revels Plays Companion
       Library, Manchester, Manchester University Press, 1986, 85–142.

1613   *The Hector of Germanie; or, the Palsgrave Prime Elector*, Wentworth
       Smith, ed. Leonidas Warren Payne, Jr, Publications of the University
       of Pennsylvania Series in Philology and Literature, 11, Philadelphia,
       1906 (I have followed the editor's dating).

1617   *A Fair Quarrel*, Thomas Middleton and William Rowley, ed. R. V.
       Holdsworth, New Mermaids, London, Benn, 1974.

1617   *The Devil's Law-Case*, John Webster, ed. Elizabeth M. Brennan,
       New Mermaids, London, Benn, 1975.

1621   *The Maid of Honour*, Philip Massinger, in Philip Edwards and Colin
       Gibson (eds), *Plays and Poems*, Oxford, Clarendon Press, 1976, 1,
       105–97.

1621   *Women Beware Women*, Thomas Middleton, ed. J. R. Mulryne,
       Revels Plays, Manchester, Manchester University Press, 1975.

1622   *The Noble Spanish Soldier*, Thomas Dekker, in Fredson Bowers (ed.),
       Dramatic Works, Cambridge, Cambridge University Press, 1953–61,
       4, 231–300.

1622 *Herod and Antipater*, Gervase Markham and William Sampson, ed. Gordon Nicholas Ross, Garland Renaissance Drama, New York, Garland Publishing, 1979.

1623 *The Welsh Ambassador*, Thomas Dekker (and John Ford), in *Dramatic Works*, 4, 301–404 (a reworking of *The Noble Spanish Soldier*).

1623 *The Spanish Gipsie*, Thomas Dekker and John Ford, in Edgar C. Morris (ed.), *'The Spanish Gipsie', and 'All's Lost by Lust'*, Belles-Lettres Series, The English Drama, Boston, Heath & Co., 1908, 1–135.

1629 *The Just Italian*, William Davenant, in James Maidment and W. H. Logan (eds), *Dramatic Works*, Edinburgh, Paterson, 1872–4, 1, 207–80.

1630 *The Inconstant Lady*, Arthur Wilson, ed. Linda V. Itzoe, Garland Renaissance Drama, New York, Garland Publishing, 1980.

1631 *The Swisser*, Arthur Wilson, ed. Linda V. Itzoe, Renaissance Imagination, New York, Garland Publishing, 1984.

1631 *The Sophister: a Comedy*, R[ichard] Z[ouche], London, 1639 (the play may have been written earlier (1614–20) but the British Library Ms Harleian 6869 is dated 1631. This may record the date of a performance at Oxford.)

1632 *The Ball*, James Shirley, in William Gifford and Alexander Dyce (eds), *Dramatic Works and Poems*, London, Murray, 1833, 3, 1–91.

1632 *Love Crowns the End*, John Tatham, in James Maidment and W. H. Logan (eds), *Dramatic Works*, Edinburgh, Paterson, 1879, 1–32.

1634 *The Late Lancashire Witches*, Richard Brome and Thomas Heywood, ed. Laird H. Barber, Garland Renaissance Drama, New York, Garland Publishing, 1979.

1634 *Love's Mistress; or, The Queen's Masque*, Thomas Heywood, in *Dramatic Works*, 5, 81–160.

1634 *A Mask Performed at Ludlow Castle*, John Milton, in John T. Shawcross (ed.), *The Complete Poetry of John Milton*, Anchor Books, New York, Doubleday, 1957, 124–52.

1635 *The Sparagus Garden*, Richard Brome, in *Dramatic Works*, London, John Pearson, 1873, 3, 109–223.

1635 *The Seven Champions of Christendom*, John Kirke, London, 1638.

1637 *The English Moore; or The Mock Marriage*, Richard Brome, ed. Sara Jayne Steen, Columbia, University of Missouri Press, 1983.

1637 *The Fool Would Be a Favourit; or, The Discreet Lover*, Lodowick Carlell, printed from the 1657 edition with an introduction by Allardyce Nicoll, Berkshire Series, III, Waltham St Lawrence, Golden Cockerel Press, 1926.

1637 *Microcosmus*, Thomas Nabbes, in A. H. Bullen (ed.), *The Works of Thomas Nabbes*, A Collection of Old English Plays, 1882–9, reprinted New York, Benjamin Blom Inc., 1964, 2, 158–218.

1638 *The Damoiselle or The New Ordinary*, Richard Brome, in *Dramatic Works*, 1, 375–468.

1639 *The Unfortunate Mother*, Thomas Nabbes, in A. H. Bullen (ed.), *The Works of Thomas Nabbes*, A Collection of Old English Plays, 1882–9, reprinted New York, Benjamin Blom Inc., 1964, 2, 83–158.

1639 *The Politician*, James Shirley, in *Dramatic Works and Poems*, 5, 89–176.

1640 *The Court Beggar*, Richard Brome, in *Dramatic Works*, 1, 180–271.

1641 *A Jovial Crew*, Richard Brome, ed. Ann Haaker, Regents Renaissance Drama, London, Arnold, 1968.

1652 *The Bastard: a Tragedy*, Anon. (Cosmo Manuche?), London.

References

Acheson, A. (1920), *Shakespeare's Lost Years in London 1586–1592*, London, Quaritch.

Adelman, Janet (1992), *Suffocating Mothers: Fantasies of Maternal Origin in Shakespeare's Plays, 'Hamlet' to 'The Tempest'*, New York and London, Routledge.

Agrippa, Henry Cornelius (1545), *The Commendation of Matrimony*, trans. David Clapham, London.

Alciatus, Andreas (1985), *Emblems in Translation*, ed. Peter M. Daly, Toronto, University of Toronto Press.

Allen, William [Cardinal] (1588), *An Admonition to the Nobility and People of England and Ireland*, London.

Ames, William (1659), *The Substance of Christian Religion: or, a plain and easie Draught of the Christian Catechisme in LII lectures*, London.

Amussen, Susan Dwyer (1988), *An Ordered Society: Gender and Class in Early Modern England*, Oxford, Basil Blackwell.

Andromana; or, The Merchant's Wife, in W. Carew Hazlitt (ed.) *Dodsley's Old English Plays*, fourth edition, London, Reeves & Turner, 1874–6, 14, 193–271.

Here begynneth the byrthe and lyfe of Antechryst (1525), London, Wynkyn de Worde.

A[rmin], R[obert] (1612), *The Valiant Welshman*, ed. John S. Farmer, Old English Drama, Students Facsimile edition, London, 1913.

Armstrong, William A. (1956), Elizabethan themes in *The Misfortunes of Arthur*, *Review of English Studies*, new series, 7: 27, 238–49.

Armstrong-Davison, M. H. (1965), *The Casket Letters: a Solution to the Mystery of Mary Queen of Scots and the Murder of Lord Darnley*, London, Vision Press.

The Assembly of the Gods; or The Accord of Reason and Sensuality in the Fear of Death, attributed to John Lydgate, ed. Oscar Lovell Triggs, Early English Text Society, London, Kegan Paul Trench Trubner & Company, 1896.

Augustine, St (1620), *The Citie of God with the Learned Comments of Jo. Lodovicus Vives, Englished first by J. H. And now in the Second Edition compared with the Latine Originall and in very many places corrected and amended*, London.

Axton, Marie (1977), *The Queen's Two Bodies: Drama and the Elizabethan Succession*, London, Royal Historical Society.

Bacon, Francis (1857–61), *Works*, ed. James Spedding, R. L. Ellis and D. D. Heath, London.

Bacon, Francis (1974), *The Advancement of Learning and New Atlantis*, ed. Arthur Johnston, Oxford, Clarendon Press.

Bacon, Francis (1985), *The Essays*, ed. John Pitcher, Penguin, Harmondsworth.

Bakhtin, Mikhail (1967), From the prehistory of novelistic discourse, in David Lodge (ed.), *Modern Criticism and Theory: a Reader*, London, Longman, 1988.

Bakhtin, Mikhail (1968), *Rabelais and His World*, trans. Hélène Iswolsky, Cambridge: Mass., M.I.T. Press.

Bale, John (1538), *King Johan*, ed. Barry B. Adams, San Marino, Huntington Library Publications, 1969.

Bale, John (1547), *The Three Lawes*, ed. M. M. Arnold Schroeer, Halle, Niemeyer, 1882.

Barish, Jonas A. (1976), The true and false families of *The Revenger's Tragedy*, in S. Henning, R. Kimbrough and R. Knowles (eds), *English Renaissance Essays in Honor of Madeleine Doran and Mark Eccles*, Carbondale, Southern Illinois University Press, 142–54.

Barnes, Barnabe (1875), *The Poems*, ed. A. Grosart, Manchester, Charles Simms.

Barnes, Barnabe (1606), *The Devil's Charter*, ed. R. B. McKerrow, Louvain A. Ustpruyst (1904), Kraust Reprint, Nendeln, Liechtenstein, 1970.

Barnes, Robert (1573), *The Whole Workes of W. Tyndall, John Frith and Doctour Barnes, three worthy martyrs, and principall teachers of this church of England*, London.

Barry, Lording (1608), *Ram-Alley; or, Merry Tricks*, in W. Carew Hazlitt (ed.), *Dodsley's Old English Plays*, London, Reeves & Turner, 1874–6, 10, 265–380.

Bataille, Georges (1988), *The Accursed Share: an Essay on General Economy*, trans. Robert Hurley, New York, Zone Books.

Bates, E. H., ed. (1907), *Quarter Session Records for the County of Somerset* 1, James I, Somerset County Record Society, 23, London.

Bawcutt, N. W. (1982), Barnabe Barnes' ownership of Machiavelli's *Discoursi, Notes and Queries*, 29, 411.

Beaumont, Francis and Fletcher, John (1966–92), *The Dramatic Works in the Beaumont and Fletcher Canon*, ed. Fredson Bowers, Cambridge, Cambridge University Press.

Beaurline, L. A., ed. (1990), *King John* by William Shakespeare, Cambridge University Press, Cambridge.

Becon, Thomas (1563), *The Acts of Christ and Antichrist*, London.

Becon, Thomas (1564), *The Worckes of Thomas Becon, whiche he hath hyther to made and published, with diverse other newe bookes added*, London.

Beetham, David (1991), *The Legitimation of Power*, London, Macmillan.

Beier, A. L. (1985), *Masterless Men: the vagrancy Problem in England 1560–1640*, London, Methuen.

Belsey, Catherine (1985), *The Subject of Tragedy: Identity and Difference in Renaissance Drama*, London, Methuen.

Bentley, Gerald Eades (1956), *The Jacobean and Caroline Stage*, Oxford, Clarendon Press (1941–68), 4.

Berry, Ralph (1972), *The Art of John Webster*, Oxford, Clarendon Press.

Bevington, David (1968), *Tudor Drama and Politics: a Critical Approach to Topical Meaning*, Cambridge, Mass., Harvard University Press.

The Birth of Hercules, ed. R. Warwick Bond, Malone Society Reprints, Oxford, Oxford University Press, 1911.

Boccaccio, Giovanni (1956), *Genealogy of the Pagan Gods*, trans. Charles G. Osgood as *Boccaccio on Poetry*, Library of Liberal Arts, Indianapolis, Bobbs.

Boyd, William K., ed. (1903), *Calendar of State Papers Relating to Scotland and Mary, Queen of Scots, 1569–1571*, H. M. General Register House, Edinburgh.

Bramly, Serge (1992), *Leonardo, the Artist and the Man*, trans. Sian Reynolds, London, Michael Joseph.

Braunmuller, A. R. (1988), *King John* and historiography, *English Literary History*, 55, 309–32.

Braunmuller, A. R., ed. (1989), *King John* by William Shakespeare, The Oxford Shakespeare, Oxford, Oxford University Press.

Brigden, Susan (1982), Youth and the English Reformation, *Past and Present*, 95, 47–51.

Bristol, Michael D. (1985), *Carnival and Theater: Plebian Culture and the Structure of Authority in Renaissance England*, New York and London, Methuen.

Brome, Richard (1638), *The English Moore; or The Mock Marriage*, ed. Sara Jayne Steen, Columbia, University of Missouri Press, 1983.

Brome, Richard (1641), *A Jovial Crew*, ed. Ann Haaker, Regents Renaissance Drama, London, Arnold, 1968.

Brome, Richard (1873), *The Dramatic Works of Richard Brome Containing Fifteen Comedies*, London, John Pearson.

Brome, Richard and Heywood, Thomas (1634), *The Late Lancashire Witches*, ed. Laird H. Barber, Garland Renaissance Drama, New York, Garland Publishing, 1979.

Brown, Paul (1985), 'This thing of darkness I acknowledge mine': *The Tempest* and the discourse of colonialism, in Jonathan Dollimore and Alan Sinfield (eds), *Political Shakespeare: New Essays in Cultural Materialism*, Manchester, Manchester University Press, 48–71.

Buck, Sir George (1614), *A Commentary on the Book of Domus Dei*, Bodleian MS Eng. Misc. b.106.

Buck, Sir George (1982), *The History of King Richard the Third*, ed. Arthur Noel Kincaid, Gloucester, Sutton.

Bullinger, Henry (1575), *The Christian State of Matrimony*, trans. Miles Coverdale, London.

Bullough, Geoffrey, ed (1962), *Narrative and Dramatic Sources of Shakespeare*, London, Routledge & Kegan Paul, 4.

Burton, Robert (1964), *The Anatomy of Melancholy*, ed. Holbrook Jackson, Everyman's Library, London, Dent, 2.

Butler, Martin (1984), *Theatre and Crisis 1632–1642*, Cambridge, Cambridge University Press.

Calderwood, James L. (1960), Commodity and honour in *King John*, *University of Toronto Quarterly*, 29, 341–56.

Cameron, G. M. (1982), *Robert Wilson and the Plays of Shakespeare*, Riverton, New Zealand, G. M. Cameron.

Candido, Joseph (1989), Blots, stains and adulteries: the impurities in *King John*, in Deborah T. Curren-Aquino (ed.), *King John: New Perspectives*, London and Toronto, Associated University Presses, 114–25.

The Famous History of Captain Thomas Stukeley (1596), ed. Judith C. Levinson, Malone Society Reprints, Oxford, Oxford University Press, 1975.

Cardan, Jerome (1580), *De Subtiltate*, London.

Carew, Thomas (1969), *Poems*, Menston, Scolar Press Facsimile.

Carlell, Lodowick (1637), *The Fool Would Be a Favourit; or, The Discreet Lover*, printed from the 1657 edition with an introduction by Allardyce Nicoll, Berkshire Series, 3, Waltham St Lawrence, Golden Cockerel Press, London, 1926.

Carroll, William C. (1987), 'The base shall top th' legitimate': the bedlam beggar and the role of Edgar in *King Lear*, *Shakespeare Quarterly*, 38, 426–41.

Cavendish, William, First duke of Newcastle (1649), *The Country Captaine, and The Varietie, two comedies, written by a person of honor*, London.

Cespedes y Menses, Gonsalo de (1622), *Gerardo, the Unfortunate Spaniard*, trans. Leonard Digges, London.

Chapman, George (1601), *All Fools*, ed. Frank Manley, London, Arnold, 1968.

Cixous, Hélène (1976), The laugh of the medusa, trans. Keith Cohen and Paula Cohen, in Elaine Marks and Isabelle de Courtivron (eds), *New French Feminisms*, Brighton, Harvester, 245–64.

Cixous, Hélène (1988), Extreme fidelity, trans. Ann Liddle and Susan Sellers, in Susan Sellers (ed.), *Writing Differences: Readings from the Seminar of Hélène Cixous*, Milton Keynes, Open University Press, 10–38.

Cixous, Hélène and Clément, Catherine (1986), *The Newly Born Woman*, trans. Betsy Wing with an introduction by Sandra M. Gilbert, Theory and History of Literature, 24, Manchester, Manchester University Press.

Clark, Arthur Melville (1931), *Thomas Heywood, Playwright and Miscellanist*, Oxford, Blackwell.

The Tragedy of Claudius Tiberius Nero (1607), ed. W. W. Greg, Malone Society Reprints, Oxford, Oxford University Press, 1914.

Clavell, John (1629), *The Soddered Citizen*, ed. John Henry Pyle Pafford, Malone Society Reprints, Oxford, Oxford University Press, 1936.

Clerke, William (1594), *The Triall of Bastardie*, London.

Coke, Sir Edward (1629), *The First Part of the Institutes of the Lawes of England*, second edition, London.

Cook, Anne Jennalie (1977), 'Bargaines of Incontinencie': bawdy behaviour in the playhouses, *Shakespeare Studies*, 10 (1977), 271–90.

Cooper, Thomas (1589), *An Admonition to the People of England: wherein are answered, not onely the slaunderous untruethes, uttered by Martin but also other crimes*, London.

Cope, Jackson I. (1973), *The Theater and the Dream: From Metaphor to Form in Renaissance Drama*, Baltimore and London, Johns Hopkins University Press.

Curtis, M. (1962), The alienated intellectuals of early Stuart England, *Past and Present*, 23, 25–43.

Danby, John F. (1948), *Shakespeare's Doctrine of Nature: a Study of King Lear*, London, Faber & Faber.

Davenant, William (1872–4), *The Dramatic Works of Sir William Davenant*, ed. James Maidment and William Hugh Logan, Edinburgh, William Paterson.

Davies, Sir John (1612), *A Discoverie of the True Causes why Ireland was never entirely Subdued*, London.

Davies, Stevie (1986), *The Idea of Woman in Renaissance Literature*, Brighton, Harvester.

Day, John (1963), *The Works of John Day*, ed. A. H. Bullen (1881) reprinted 1963, ed. Robin Jeffs, London, Holland Press.

Dekker, Thomas (1953–61), *The Dramatic Works of Thomas Dekker*, ed. Fredson Bowers, Cambridge, Cambridge University Press.

Dekker, Thomas and Ford, John (1623), *The Spanish Gipsie*, in Edgar C. Morris (ed.), *'The Spanish Gipsie' and 'All's Lost by Lust'*, Belles-Lettres Series, The English Drama, Boston, Heath & Co., 1908.

Derrida, Jacques (1966), Structure, sign and play in the discourse of the human sciences, trans. Alan Bass, in Rick Rylance (ed.), *Debating Texts: a Reader in Twentieth-Century Literary Theory and Method*, Milton Keynes, Open University Press, 1987, 123–36.

Dessen, Alan (1965), The 'estates' morality play, *Studies in Philology*, 62, 121–36.

Docherty, Thomas (1987), *On Modern Authority: the Theory and Condition of Writing 1500 to the Present Day*, Brighton, Harvester.

Dollimore, Jonathan (1986), Subjectivity, sexuality and transgression, *Renaissance Drama*, 17, 55–81.

Dollimore, Jonathan (1991), *Sexual Dissidence – Augustine to Wilde, Freud to Foucault*, Oxford, Oxford University Press.

Donne, John (1980), *Problems and Paradoxes*, ed. Helen Peters, Oxford, Clarendon Press.

Dover Wilson, John (1968), *Life in Shakespeare's England*, Harmondsworth, Penguin.

Draper, John W. (1938), Bastardy in Shakespeare's plays, *Shakespeare Jahrbuch*, 74, 123–36.

Drayton, Michael (1931–41), *Works*, ed. William Habel, Oxford, Blackwell.

Dusinberre, Juliet (1989), *King John* and embarrassing women, *Shakespeare Survey*, 42, 37–52.

Earle, John (1628), *Microcosmography*, ed. Alfred S. West, Cambridge, Cambridge University Press, 1897.

Eccles, Mark (1933), Barnabe Barnes, in Charles J. Sisson (ed.), *Thomas Lodge and Other Elizabethans*, Cambridge, Mass., Harvard University Press, 165–241.

Edmund Ironside (1595), ed. Eric Sams, London, Wildwood House, 1986.

Eliza's Babes: or The Virgins-Offering. Being Divine Poems and Meditations. Written by a Lady, who desires onely to advaunce the glory of God and not her own, London, 1652.

Elliot, Michael, dir. (1983), *King Lear*, by William Shakespeare, Granada Television.

Emmison, F. G. (1970), *Elizabethan Life: Disorder*, Essex Record Office Publications, 56, Chelmsford, Essex County Council.

Emmison, F. G. (1973), *Elizabethan Life: Morals and the Church Courts*, Essex Record Office Publications, 63, Chelmsford, Essex County Council.

Emmison, F. G. (1976), *Elizabethan Life: Home, Work and Land*, Essex Record Office Publications, 69, Chelmsford, Essex County Council.

Erasmus, Desiderius (1549), *The Praise of Folie*, trans. Sir Thomas Chaloner, London.

Erasmus, Desiderius (1971), *The Praise of the Folly*, trans. Betty Radice with an introduction and notes by A. H. T. Levi, Harmondsworth, Penguin.

Esslin, Martin (1987), *The Field of Drama*, London, Methuen.

Farmer, John S. (1906), *Anonymous Plays*, Third Series 1550–1565, Early English Drama Society, London.

Field, Nathan (1609), *A Woman is a Weathercock*, in W. Carew Hazlitt (ed.), *Dodsley's Old English Plays*, fourth edition, London, Reeves & Turner, 1874–6, 11, 1–86.

Fletcher, Anthony and Stevenson, John, eds (1985), *Order and Disorder in Early Modern England*, Cambridge, Cambridge University Press.

Forbes, Thomas Rogers (1971), *Chronicle From Aldgate: Life and Death in Shakespeare's London*, New Haven, Yale University Press.

Ford, John (1632), *Love's Sacrifice*, in *The Works of John Ford*, ed. William Gifford and Alexander Dyce, New York, Russell & Russell, 1965, 2, 1–108.

Ford, John (1632), *'Tis Pity She's a Whore*, ed. Brian Morris, New Mermaids, London, Benn, 1968.

Fortescue, Sir John (1573), *A Learned Condemnation of the Politique Laws of England*, trans. Robert Mulcaster, London.

Freehafer, John (1969), Shakespeare's *Tempest* and *The Seven Champions*, *Studies in Philology*, 56: 1, 87–103.

French, Marilyn (1982), *Shakespeare's Division of Experience*, London, Cape.

Gardiner, Harold C. (1967), *Mysteries' End: an Investigation of the Last Days of the Medieval Religious Stage*, New Haven, Yale University Press.

Gascoigne, George (1982), *The Green Knight: selected poetry and prose of George Gascoigne*, ed. Roger Pooley, Manchester, Carcanet New Press.

Gauthier, Xavière (1976), Why witches?, in Elaine Marks and Isabelle de Courtivron, *New French Feminisms*, Brighton, Harvester, 199–203.

Geoffrey of Monmouth (1982), *The History of the Kings of Britain*, trans. Lewis Thorpe, London, Guild Publishing.

Giles, David, dir. (1986), *King John*, by William Shakespeare, British

Broadcasting Corporation (accompanying text published by the British Broadcasting Corporation at The Bath Press, Avon).

Given-Wilson, Chris and Curteis, Alice (1984), *The Royal Bastards of Medieval England*, London, Routledge & Kegan Paul.

Goldberg, Jonathan (1984), Sodomy and society: the case of Christopher Marlowe, in David Scott Kastan and Peter Stallybrass (eds) (1991), *Staging the Renaissance*, New York and London, Routledge, 75–82.

Gouge, William (1622), *Of domesticall Dueties Eight Treatises*, London.

Greenaway, Peter (1991), *Prospero's Books*, London, Chatto & Windus.

Greenblatt, Stephen (1980), *Renaissance Self-Fashioning from More to Shakespeare*, Chicago, University of Chicago Press.

Greenblatt, Stephen (1988), *Shakespearean Negotiations: the Circulation of Social Energy in Renaissance England*, Oxford, Clarendon Press.

Griffith, Matthew (1633), *Bethel; or a Forme for Families: [showing how] all sorts, may best serve in their severall places, for useful pieces in God's building*, London.

Grivelet, Michel (1954), 'Th' untun'd kennel': note sur Thomas Heywood et le théâtre sous Charles I, Études Anglaises, 7, 101–6.

Gurr, Andrew (1987), *Playgoing in Shakespeare's London*, Cambridge, Cambridge University Press.

Halpern, Richard (1986), Puritanism and Maenadism in 'A Mask', in Margaret W. Ferguson, Maureen Quilligan and Nancy J. Vickers (eds), *Rewriting the Renaissance*, Chicago, University of Chicago Press, 88–105.

Hamilton, Donna B. (1992), *Shakespeare and the Politics of Protestant England*, Lexington, University Press of Kentucky.

Harbage, Alfred (1936), *Cavalier Drama*, London, Oxford University Press.

Harsnett, Samuel (1603), *A Declaration of Egregious Popish Impostures. Practised by Edmunds, alias Weston a jesuit*, London.

Harvey, Gabriel (1578), *Gratulationes Valdinenses*, London.

Hayton, Alison G. (1988), Richard woos again and Romeo remarries, *Notes and Queries*, 35, 67.

Heywood, Thomas trans. Sallust (1609), *The two most worthy and notable histories The Conspiracie of Cateline, and the Warre which Jugurth Maintained*, London.

Heywood, Thomas (1635), *The Hierarchie of the Blessed Angels*, London.

Heywood, Thomas (1812), *The Life of Merlin, Surnamed Ambrosius, And His Predictions Interpreted and Their Truth Made Good by Our English Annals*, Camarthen, J. Evans.

Heywood, Thomas (1964), *The Dramatic Works of Thomas Heywood*, New York, Russell & Russell.

Hibbert, Christopher (1990), *The Virgin Queen: the Personal History of Elizabeth I*, London, Viking.

Hic Mulier or the Man Woman, London, 1620.

Hill, Christopher (1971), *Antichrist in Seventeenth Century England*, London, Oxford University Press.

Hill, Christopher (1986), *The Collected Essays of Christopher Hill: Religion and Politics in Seventeenth Century England*, Brighton, Harvester.

Hill, Christopher (1993), *The English Bible and the Seventeenth Century Revolution*, London, Penguin.

Hillman, Richard (1992), *Shakespearean Subversions: the Trickster and the Play Text*, London, Routledge.

An Homilie Agaynst Disobedience and Wylful Rebellion, London, 1570.

Howard, Jean (1988), Crossdressing, the theatre and gender struggle in early modern England, *Shakespeare Quarterly*, 39, 418–40.

Howard, Jean (1989), Scripts and/versus playhouses: ideological production and the Renaissance public stage, *Renaissance Drama*, 20, 31–41.

Hudson, W. and Tingey, J. C. (1910), *Records of the City of Norwich*, Norwich, Jarrold.

Huggarde, Miles (1555), *The Displaying of Protestants*, London.

Hughes, Thomas et al. (1588), *The Misfortunes of Arthur*, in John W. Cunliffe (ed.), *Early English Classical Tragedies*, Oxford, Clarendon Press, 1912, 217–96.

Hume, Martin S. ed. (1899), *Calendar of Letters and State Papers relating to English Affairs preserved principally in the Archives of Simancas*, 4, Elizabeth 1587–1603, Her Majesty's Stationery Office, London, Eyre & Spottiswoode.

Hyde, Thomas (1985), Boccaccio: the genealogies of myth, *Publications of the Modern Language Association of America*, 100, 737–45.

Ingram, Martin (1985), Ridings, rough music and mocking rhymes in early modern England, in Barry Reay (ed.), *Popular Culture in Seventeenth Century England*, London, Routledge, 1988, 166–97.

Ingram, Martin (1987), *Church Courts, Sex and Marriage in England 1570–1640*, Past and Present Publications, Cambridge, Cambridge University Press.

The Life and Death of Jack Straw, ed. Kenneth Muir and F. P. Wilson, Malone Society Reprints, Oxford, Oxford University Press, 1957.

James I (1597), *Daemonologie*, The English Experience, 94, Amsterdam, Theatrum Orbis Terrarum; New York, Da Capo Press, 1969.

James I (1918), *Political Works*, ed. Charles Howard McIlwain, Cambridge, Mass., Harvard University Press.

Jardine, Lisa (1983), *Still Harping on Daughters: Women and Drama in the Age of Shakespeare*, Brighton, Harvester.

Johnson, Richard (1599) and (1607), *The Most Pleasant History of Tom a Lincoln*, in William J. Thoms (ed.), *Early English Prose Romances*, London, Nattali & Bond, 1858, 2, 217–61.

Jones, Emrys (1977), *The Origins of Shakespeare*, Oxford, Clarendon Press.

Jonson, Ben (1606), *Volpone, or, The Fox*, ed. R. B. Parker, Revels Plays, Manchester, Manchester University Press, 1983.

Jonson, Ben (1612?), *Every Man in his Humour*, ed. Martin Seymour-Smith, New Mermaids, London, Benn, 1966.

Jonson, Ben (1633), *A Tale of a Tub*, in *The Selected Plays of Ben Jonson*, ed. Martin Butler, Cambridge, Cambridge University Press, 1989, 2, 417–518.

Joseph, B. L. (1951), *Elizabethan Acting*, London, Oxford University Press.

Kastan, David Scott (1983), 'To set a form upon that indigest': Shakespeare's fictions of history, *Comparative Drama*, 17, 1–16.

Kaplan, Cora (1986), Language and gender, in Deborah Cameron (ed.), *The Feminist Critique of Language*, London, Routledge, 1990, 57–69.

Kaufmann, R. J. (1961), *Richard Brome: Caroline Dramatist*, New York, Columbia University Press.

Kernodle, George (1959), Open stage: Elizabethan or existentialist? *Shakespeare Survey*, 12, 1–7.

King Darius (1565), in J. S. Farmer (ed.), *Anonymous Plays, Third Series 1550–1565*, Early English Drama Society, London, 1906, 41–92.

Kirke, John (1638), *The Seven Champions of Christendom*, London.

A Knack to Know a Knave (1592), in W. Carew Hazlitt (ed.), *Dodsley's Old English Plays*, fourth edition, London, Reeves & Turner, 1874–6, 6, 503–91.

Kocher, Paul H. (1962), *Christopher Marlowe: a Study of his Thought, Learning and Character*, New York, Russell & Russell.

Kramer, Heinrich and Sprenger, James (*c.* 1486), *Malleus Maleficarum*, trans. Montague Summers, London, Pushkin Press, 1951.

Kristeva, Julia (1974), La femme, ce n'est jamais ça, trans. Marilyn M. August, in Elaine Marks and Isabelle de Courtivron (eds), *New French Feminisms*, Brighton, Harvester, 137–41.

La Calprenède, Gautier de Coste de (1639), *La Mort des enfants d'Hérodes, ou Suite de Mariane, tragedie*, Paris, A. Courbé.

Lake, Peter (1980), The significance of the Elizabethan identification of the Pope as Antichrist, *Journal of English History*, 31, 161–78.

Lanyer, Aemilia (1978), *The Poems of Shakespeare's Dark Lady*, ed. A. L. Rowse, London, Jonathan Cape.

Laslett, Peter, Oosterveen, Karla, and Smith, Richard M. (1980), *Bastardy and Its Comparative History*, London, Arnold.

Lawrence, W. W. (1942), Troilus, Cressida and Thersites, *Modern Language Review*, 37, 422–37.

Leggatt, Alexander (1992), *Jacobean Public Theatre*, London and New York, Routledge.

Levin, Richard A. (1985), *Love and Society in Shakespearean Comedy: a Study of Dramatic Form and Content*, Newark, University of Delaware Press.

Levine, David and Wrightson, Keith (1980), The social context of illegitimacy in early modern England, in Peter Laslett, Karla Oosterveen and Richard M. Smith (eds), *Bastardy and Its Comparative History*, London, Arnold, 158–75.

Levine, Laura (1986), Men in women's clothing: anti-theatricality and effeminization from 1579 to 1642, *Criticism*, 28, 123–28.

The Lamentable Tragegy of Locrine (1594), ed. Jane Lytton Gooch, Garland English Texts, London, Garland Publishing, 1981.

Luther, Martin (1960), *Lectures on Deuteronomy*, ed. Jaroslav Pelikan, St Louis, Concordia Publishing House.

Macfarlane, Alan (1980), Illegitimacy and illegitimates in English history, in Peter Laslett, Karla Oosterveen and Richard M. Smith (eds), *Bastardy and its Comparative History*, London, Arnold, 70–85.

Lytel Treatyse of ye Byrth and P[ro]phecye of Marlyn, London, 1510.

Manheim, Michael (1989), The four voices of the bastard, in Deborah T. Curren-Aquino (ed.), *King John: New Perspectives*, London and Toronto, Associated University Presses, 126–35.

Mannoni, O. (1964), *Prospero and Caliban: the Psychology of Colonization*, trans. Pamela Powesland, second edition, New York, Praeger.

Manuche, Cosmo(?), (1652), *The Bastard: a Tragedy*, London.

Markham, Gervase and Sampson, William (1621), *The True Tragedy of Herod and Antipater*, ed. Gordon Nicholas Ross, Garland Renaissance Drama, New York, Garland Publishing, 1979.

Marks, Elaine and Courtivron, Isabelle de, eds. (1981), *New French Feminisms*, Brighton, Harvester.

Marlowe, Christopher (1589), *The Jew of Malta*, ed. T. W. Craik, New Mermaids, London, Benn, 1966.

Marprelate, Martin (pseud.) (1588), *Oh read over D. John Bridges for it is a worthy worke*, East Molesey.

Martin, K. S. (ed.) (1926), *Records of Maidstone: being selections from the documents in possession of the corporation*, Maidstone.

Marx, Karl (1976), *Capital: a Critique of Political Economy, Volume One*, trans. Ben Fowles, Harmondsworth, Penguin Books in association with New Left Review.

Massinger, Philip (1976), *The Plays and Poems of Philip Massinger*, ed. Philip Edwards and Colin Gibson, Oxford, Clarendon Press.

Maxwell, Baldwin (1922), *Wily Beguiled, Studies in Philology*, 19, 206–37.

Merchant, Paul (1978). Thomas Heywood's hand in *The Seven Champions, Library*, 33: 3, 226–30.

Meyer, Edward (1897), *Machiavelli and the Elizabethan Drama*, Litterarhistorische Forschungen, 1, Weimar, Felber.

Michelet, Jules (1952), *La Sorcière*, ed. Lucien Rochefort, Société des Textes Français Modernes, Paris, Didier.

Middleton, Thomas (1603), *The Family of Love*, in A. H. Bullen (ed.), *The Works of Thomas Middleton*, London, Nimmo (1885–6), 3, 1–120.

Middleton, Thomas (1606), *The Revenger's Tragedy*. See under Tourneur.

Middleton, Thomas (1613), *The Witch*, in Peter Corbin and Douclas Sedge (eds), *Three Jacobean Witchcraft Plays*, Revels Plays Companion Library, Manchester, Manchester University Press, 1986, 85–142.

Middleton, Thomas (1613), *A Chaste Maid in Cheapside*, ed. Alan Brissenden, New Mermaids, London, Benn, 1968.

Middleton, Thomas (1621), *Women Beware Women*, ed. J. R. Mulryne, Revels Plays, Manchester, Manchester University Press, 1975.

Middleton, Thomas and Rowley, William (1617), *A Fair Quarrel*, ed. R. V. Holdsworth, New Mermaids, London, Ernest Benn, 1974.

Miller, Jonathan, dir. (1982), *King Lear*, British Broadcasting Company Television Shakespeare.

Milles, Thomas (1613), *The Treasurie of Auncient and Moderne Times*, London.

Milton, John (1957), *The Complete Poetry of John Milton*, ed. John T. Shawcross, Anchor Books, New York, Doubleday.

Mooney, Michael E. (1985), 'Edgar I nothing am': *figurenposition* in *King Lear, Shakespeare Survey*, 38, 153–66.

Mullaney, Steven (1988), *The Place of the Stage: Licence, Play and Power in Renaissance England*, Chicago, University of Chicago Press.

Nabbes, Thomas (1964), *The Works of Thomas Nabbes*, ed. A. H. Bullen, A Collection of Old English Plays, 1882–9, reprinted New York, Benjamin Blom Inc.

Nashe, Thomas (1966), *The Works of Thomas Nashe*, ed. Ronald B.

McKerrow, revised with supplementary notes by F. P. Wilson, Oxford, Basil Blackwell.

Neill, Michael (1978), 'Wit's most accomplished senate': the audiences of the Caroline private theatres, *Studies in English Literature*, 18, 341–60.

Neill, Michael (1993), 'In everything illegitimate': imagining the bastard in Renaissance drama, *Yearbook of English Studies*, 23, 270–92.

Oosterveen, Karla and Smith, Richard M. (1980), Bastardy and the family: reconstitution studies of Colyton, Aldenham, Alcester and Hawkeshead, in Peter Laslett, Karla Oosterveen and Richard M. Smith (eds), *Bastardy and Its Comparative History*, London, Arnold, 94–110.

Orgel, Stephen (1984), Prospero's Wife, in Stephen Greenblatt (ed.), *Representing the English Renaissance*, Berkeley, University of California Press, 1988, 217–29.

Palmer, Kenneth, ed. (1982), *Troilus and Cressida*, by William Shakespeare, The Arden Shakespeare, London, Methuen.

Paré, Ambroise (1982), *On Monsters and Marvels*, trans. Janis L. Pallister, Chicago, University of Chicago Press.

Peacham, Henry (1634), *Peacham's Compleat Gentleman 1634*, with an introduction by G. S. Gordon, Oxford, Clarendon Press, 1906.

Peele, George (1952–70), *The Life and Works of George Peele*, ed. C. T. Prouty, New Haven, Yale University Press.

Phelps, Wayne (1979), Cosmo Manuche, Royalist Playwright of the Commonwealth, *English Language Notes*, 16, 207–11.

Pinchbeck, Ivy and Hewitt, Margaret (1969), *Children in English Society, Volume 1: From Tudor Times to the Eighteenth Century*, London, Routledge & Kegan Paul.

Pittock, Malcolm (1984), 'Top the legitimate', *Notes and Queries*, 31, 208–10.

Potter, Robert (1975), *The English Morality Play: origins, history and influence of a dramatic tradition*, London, Routledge & Kegan Paul.

Praz, Mario (1966), *The Flaming Heart: Essays on Crashaw, Machiavelli and other Studies in the Relations between Italian and English Literature from Chaucer to T. S. Eliot*, Gloucester, Mass., Smith.

The Problemes of Aristotle, with Other Philosophers and Phisitions (1597), London.

Prothero, G. W. (1913), *Select Statutes and other Constitutional Documents Illustrative of the Reigns of Elizabeth and James I*, fourth edition, Oxford, Clarendon Press.

Quaife, G. R. (1987), *Godly Zeal and Furious Rage: the witch in early modern Europe*, London, Croom Helm.

Raab, Felix (1964), *The English Face of Machiavelli; A Changing Interpretation 1500–1700*, London, Routledge & Kegan Paul.

Rackin, Phillis (1990), *Stages of History: Shakespeare's English Chronicles*, London, Routledge.

Reay, Barry (1985), Popular religion, in Barry Reay (ed.), *Popular Culture in Seventeenth Century England*, London, Routledge, 1988.

Reese, Gertrude (1945), Political Import of *The Misfortunes of Arthur*, *Review of English Studies*, 21, 81–91.

Reese, M. M. (1961), *The Cease of Majesty: a study of Shakespeare's history plays*, London, Arnold.

Reibetanz, John (1977), *The Lear World: a study of King Lear in its dramatic context*, London, Heinemann.

Rickert, Edith, ed. (1910), *Ancient English Christmas Carols 1400–1700*, London, Chatto & Windus.

Ridley, Jasper (1987), *Elizabeth I*, London, Constable.

Rivers, Isabel (1979), *Classical and Christian Ideas in Renaissance Poetry*, London, Unwin Hyman.

Robert, John ap (1624), *An Apology for a Younger Brother*, Oxford.

Robert the Devyl, in William J. Thoms, ed. (1858), *Early English Prose Romances*, London, Nattali & Bond, 1, 1–56.

Roberts, Alexander, ed. (1869), *The Writings of Origen*, trans. Frederick Crombie, Ante-Nicene Christian Library, Edinburgh, Clark.

Romer, John (1988), *Testament: the Bible and History*, London, Michael O'Mara Books.

Ronsard, Pierre de (1555), *Hercule Chrestien* in *Hymnes* avec un introduction et des notes par Alfred Py, Textes Littéraires Français, Genève, Librairie Droz, 1978, 263–74.

Rosen, Barbara (1991), *Witchcraft in England 1558–1618*, Amherst, University of Massachusetts Press.

Rowe, Jeremy (1986), Usurpation and soliloquy in Elizabethan drama, unpublished M. Phil. thesis, University of Birmingham.

Rowley, William and ? (1608), *The Birth of Merlin*, Worcester, Element Books, 1989.

Russell, Bertrand (1961), *The History of Western Philosophy*, London, Allen & Unwin.

Saltonstall, Wye (1946), *Picturae Loquentes*, reprinted from the editions of 1631 and 1635 with an introduction by C. H. Wilkinson, Oxford, Basil Blackwell.

Sams, Eric, ed. (1986), *Shakespeare's Lost Play Edmund Ironside*, London, Wildwood House.

Schoeck, R. J. (1990), *Erasmus of Europe: the Making of a Humanist*, Edinburgh, Edinburgh University Press.

Scot, Reginald (1964), *The Discoverie of Witchcraft*, ed. Hugh Ross Williamson, London, Centaur Press.

Schaberg, Jane (1987), *The Illegitimacy of Jesus*, San Francisco, Harper & Row.

Scragg, Leah (1964), The bastard in Elizabethan and Jacobean drama, unpublished M. A. thesis, University of Liverpool.

Segal, Naomi (1990), Patrilinear and matrilinear, in Helen Wilcox, Keith McWatters, Ann Thompson and Linda R. Williams (eds), *The Body and the Text; Hélène Cixous, Reading and Teaching*, Brighton, Harvester.

Seneca, L. Annaeus (1581), *His Tenne Tragedies (1581)*, The English Experience, 131, Amsterdam, Theatrum Orbis Terrarum; New York, Da Capo Press, 1969.

Shadey, Raymond C. (1975), A critical edition of Thomas Heywood's play *Love's Mistress or the Queen's Masque*, unpublished Ph. D. dissertation, University of Toronto.

Shakespeare, William (1974), *The Riverside Shakespeare*, ed. G. Blakemore Evans, Boston, Houghton Mifflin.

Sharp, Buchanan (1985), Popular protest in seventeenth century England, in Barry Reay (ed.), *Popular Culture in Seventeenth Century England*, London, Routledge, 1988.

Sharpe, J. A. (1987), *Early Modern England: a Social History 1550–1760*, London, Edward Arnold.

Shirley, James (1833), *The Dramatic Works and Poems of James Shirley*, ed. William Gifford and Alexander Dyce, London, Murray.

Shulman, Jeff (1983), At the crossroads of myth: the hermeneutics of Hercules from Ovid to Shakespeare, *English Literary History*, 50, 83–106.

Sidney, Philip (1977), *The Countess of Pembroke's Arcadia*, ed. Maurice Evans, Harmondsworth, Penguin.

Slack, Paul (1988), *Poverty and Policy in Tudor and Stuart England*, Themes in British Social History, London and New York, Longman.

Smith, S. R. (1973), The London apprentices as seventeenth century adolescents, *Past and Present*, 61, 149–61.

Smith, Wentworth (1613), *The Hector of Germanie; or, The Palsgrave Prime Elector*, ed. Leonidas Warren Payne Jr, Publications of the University of Pennsylvania Series in Philology and Literature, 11, Philadelphia, 1906.

Spender, Dale (1980), *Man Made Language*, London, Routledge.

Spong, John Selby (1992), *Born of a Woman: a Bishop Rethinks the Birth of Jesus*, San Francisco, Harper.

Spriet, Pierre (1984), *King Lear* ou la vérité du fils, *Caliban*, 21, 175–90.

Spufford, Margaret (1985), Puritanism and social control?, in Anthony Fletcher and John Stevenson (eds), *Order and Disorder in Early Modern England*, Cambridge, Cambridge University Press, 41–57.

Stallybrass, Peter (1986), Patriarchal territories: the body enclosed, in Margaret Ferguson, Maureen Quilligan and Nancy J. Vickers (eds), *Rewriting the Renaissance: the Discourses of Sexual Difference in Early Modern Europe*, Chicago, University of Chicago Press, 123–44.

Stallybrass, Peter and White, Allon (1986), *The Politics and Poetics of Transgression*, London, Methuen.

Starkey, Thomas (1989), *A Dialogue between Pole and Lupset*, ed. T. F. Mayer, Camden Fourth Series, London, Offices of the Royal Historical Society.

Stow, John (1611), *The Abridgement or Summarie of the English Chronicle, continued unto* 1610 by E. H[owes], London.

Stow, John (1956), *The Survey of London (1603)*, ed. H. B. Wheatley, Everyman's Library, London, Dent.

Sturgess, Keith (1987), *Jacobean Private Theatre*, London, Routledge.

Styan, J. L. (1959), The actor at the foot of Shakespeare's platform, *Shakespeare Survey*, 12, Cambridge, Cambridge University Press, 56–63.

Swinburne, Henry (1590), *A Brief Treatise of Testaments and Last Willes*, London.

Tatham, John (1879), *Dramatic Works*, ed. James Maidment and W. H. Logan, Edinburgh, Paterson.

Taylor, Michael (1973), *Much Ado About Nothing*, the individual in society, *Essays in Criticism*, 23: 2, 146–53.

Teichman, Jenny (1982), *Illegitimacy: a Philosophical Examination*, Oxford, Basil Blackwell.

Thirsk, Joan (1969), Younger sons in the seventeenth century, *History*, 54, 358–77.

Thoms, William J., ed. (1858), *Early English Prose Romances*, London, Nattali & Bond.

Tom a Lincoln (1611), ed. John Pitcher, Malone Society Reprints, Oxford, Oxford University Press, 1992.

The Thracian Wonder (1661), printed by Thomas Johnson, sold by Francis Kirkham, London.

Tourneur, Cyril (1606), *The Revenger's Tragedy*, ed. Brian Gibbons, New Mermaids, London, Benn, 1971.

Trace, Jacqueline (1980), Shakespeare's bastard Faulconbridge: an early Tudor hero, *Shakespeare Studies*, 13, 59–69.

The Troublesome Raigne of John, King of England (1591), ed. J. W. Sider, Garland Renaissance Drama, New York, Garland Publishing, 1979.

Varchi, Benedetto (1615), *The Blazon of Jealousie*, trans. R. Toste, London.

Veevers, Erica (1989), *Images of Love and Religion: Queen Henrietta Maria and Court Entertainments*, Cambridge, Cambridge University Press.

Vives, J. L. (1550), *The Office and Duetie of an Husband*, trans. Thomas Paynell, London.

Waith, Eugene M. (1962), *The Herculean Hero in Marlowe, Chapman, Shakespeare and Dryden*, London, Chatto & Windus.

Waller, Evangelia (1925), A possible interpretation of *The Misfortunes of Arthur*, *Journal of English and Germanic Philology*, 24, 219–45.

Webster, John (1617), *The Devil's Law Case*, ed. Elizabeth M. Brennan, New Mermaids, London, Ernest Benn, 1975.

West Suffolk Record Office, Sudbury Town Book D, 1618–1634.

Weimann, Robert (1988), Bi-fold authority in Shakespeare's theatre, *Shakespeare Quarterly*, 39, 401–17.

Willis, Clair (1989), Upsetting the public: carnival, hysteria and women's texts, in Ken Hirschkop and David Shephard (eds), *Bakhtin and Cultural Theory*, Manchester, Manchester University Press.

Wilkins, George (1606), *The Miseries of Enforced Marriage*, ed. Glenn H. Blayney, Malone Society Reprints, Oxford, Oxford University Press, 1964.

Willson, David Harris (1959), *King James VI and I*, Bedford Historical Series, London, Jonathan Cape.

Wilson, Arthur (1630), *The Inconstant Lady*, ed. Linda V. Itzoe, Renaissance Imagination, New York, Garland Publishing, 1980.

Wilson, Arthur (1631), *The Swisser*, ed. Linda V. Itzoe, Renaissance Imagination, New York, Garland Publishing, 1984.

Wilson, F. P. (1969), *The English Drama 1485–1585*, Oxford History of Literature, 4, Oxford, Clarendon Press.

Wilson, Robert (1589), *The Cobler's Prophecy*, ed. A. C. Wood, Malone Society Reprints, Oxford, Oxford University Press, 1914.

Wily Beguiled, in *Dodsley's Old English Plays* ed. W. Carew Hazlitt, fourth edition, London, Reeves & Turner, 1874–6, 9, 219–330.

Wiseman, Susan J. (1990), *'Tis Pity She's A Whore*: representing the incestuous body, in Lucy Gent and Nigel Llewellyn (eds), *Renaissance Bodies: the Human Figure in English Culture c. 1540–1660*, London, Reaktion Books, 180–97.

Woodbridge, Linda (1984), *Women and the English Renaissance: Literature and the Nature of Womankind 1520–1620*, Brighton, Harvester.

Wright, N. T. (1992), *Who Was Jesus?*, Society for Promoting Christian Knowledge, London, Triangle.

Wrightson, Keith (1975), Infanticide in earlier seventeenth century England, *Local Population Studies*, 15, 10–22.

Wrightson, Keith (1982), *English Society 1580–1680*, London, Unwin Hyman.

A Yorkshire Tragedy (1606), ed. A. C. Cawley and Barry Gaines, Revels Plays, Manchester, Manchester University Press, 1986.

Z[ouche], R[ichard] (1639), *The Sophister: A Comedy*, London.

Index

Printed in the United Kingdom by
Lightning Source UK Ltd., Milton Keynes
140387UK00001BA/2/P

9 780719 080852